Series: Strategic Information Systems Management

Volume I

TOWARDS STRATEGIC INFORMATION SYSTEMS

STRATEGIC INFORMATION SYSTEMS MANAGEMENT

General Editors

Elizabeth K. Somogyi
PA Computers and Telecommunications and London School of Economics

Dr. Robert D. Galliers
Western Australian Institute (Curtin University) of Technology

Vol. 1
Towards Strategic Information Systems
Elizabeth K. Somogyi & Dr. R. D. Galliers
ISBN 0 85626 460 1

Vol. 2
User Systems Analysis: a guide to computer users conceptual models and attitudes for systems analysis and design
Dr. A. P. Jagodzinski & Dr. D. D. Clarke
ISBN 0 85626 430 X

Vol. 3
Case Studies in Strategic IS Analysis
Dr. John M. Ward & Elizabeth K. Somogyi

FURTHER TITLES IN PREPARATION

SOME OTHER BOOKS IN RELATED SUBJECTS FROM ABACUS PRESS

Practical Business Forecasting with your micro: The Box-Jenkins Approach
C. Beaumont
ISBN 0 85626 459 8

Data Processing: Current Theories and Practices
C. P. Clare & P. Loucopoulos
ISBN 0 85626 449 0

Computational Techniques in Operations Research
A. M. Andrew
ISBN 0 85626 425 3

Cybernetics: A New Management Tool
Dr. Barry Clemson
ISBN 0 85626 166 1

General System Theory: Essential Concepts and Applications
A. Rapoport
ISBN 0 85626 172 6

Artificial Intelligence
A. M. Andrew
ISBN 0 85626 165 3

TOWARDS STRATEGIC INFORMATION SYSTEMS

Elizabeth K. Somogyi

PA Computers & Telecommunications and London School of Economics

and

Robert D. Galliers

Western Australian Institute (Curtin University) of Technology

Tunbridge Wells, Kent

&

Cambridge, Mass

First published in 1987

ABACUS PRESS
Abacus House,
Tunbridge Wells,
Kent, TN4 0HU, UK

and

ABACUS PRESS
PBS, PO Box 643,
Cambridge,
Mass 02139, USA

Typeset by Best Set Typesetters, Hong Kong and printed by
Robert Hartnoll, Bodmin, Cornwall, U.K.

British Library Cataloguing in Publication Data

Somogyi, Elizabeth K.
Towards strategic information systems.

(Strategic information systems management)
1. Electronic data processing
2. Technological innovations
I. Title. II. Galliers, Robert D. III. Series.
001.5 QA87
ISBN 0-85626-460-1

FOREWORD TO THE SERIES

It is widely held that Information and Communication Technology provides the mechanism by which organisations will become more effective. Enterprises in the private sector can gain competitive advantage through the employment of the technology, whilst organisations in the public sector can be more effectively managed and at the same time can provide a higher quality of public service. Conversely, failure to invest in the technology spells industrial decline and administrative backwardness. So goes the theory.

In practice, both users and professionals dealing with the technology have accumulated useful experience. The technology is constantly improving and it provides facilities that yesterday's users could only dream about. Yet, recent reports suggest that, for many organisations – both private and public – employment of the technology has proved a disappointment. Expected benefits have not been realised and unexpected difficulties have been encountered in implementing new systems. Despite nearly thirty years of experience with the deployment of the technology and its wide-spread use, there is little evidence of the technology having made a major contribution to the profitability or administrative efficiency of its users.

Although, in a surprisingly large number of cases, the expectations attached to the technology have not been fully realised, there are some notable exceptions. These show clearly, that the successful application of the technology requires qualities and skills beyond technical competence. The series, published by ABACUS PRESS, of which this is the first volume, addresses itself to these issues. Its aims are, to highlight the key aspects of managing information systems for the successful deployment of information technology, to analyse the critical areas of applications, to dispel the myth around the technology and to offer clear guidelines for exploiting the technology successfully.

In selecting the volumes of the series, the editors have mostly those people in mind, who do not need to be, or do not wish to become, experts in handling the technology itself, but rather wish to gain an understanding of the key issues associated with the planning and management of information technology. Thus, the series offers equally valuable information to the manager of information technology, to the businessman wishing to deploy technology to the benefit of his organisation and to students of information technology and business management.

The first volume is a compilation of classic papers which have been selected to provide an understanding of the evolutionary process leading to the expectations we have of the technology now. It goes on to examine some of the problems of managing information, finishing with an examination of the way information and information systems provide an opportunity for radically rethinking the future role and structure of an enterprise. A clear message coming from the book is that some of the most significant information systems were designed to improve quite mundane operational problems. Their – often strategic – impact has less to do with technological sophistication than with business impact. These systems were successful because the business implications had been thought through. A technology 'fix' is not a sufficient recipe for successful information systems. All designers must anticipate that a system will produce completely unexpected consequences. Anticipating these, taking advantage of them and managing the changed scenario is the key to gaining strategic advantage through the technology.

I am delighted to welcome the series, which is concerned with the use of information technology in industry, commerce and administration; which focusses on the use of information in the context of business needs; which stresses the role of management as the user of information and the implementer of strategic information systems; and which examines the obstacles to, and provides guidelines for, the successful deployment of the technology.

Prof. F. F. LAND
London Business School
February, 1987

PREFACE

Books on computers, applications, information technology are plentiful. Furthermore, there are large numbers of serious technical magazines reporting theory, practice, products and other interesting topics associated with IT. Even daily newspapers and non-technical magazines regularly carry articles that deal with various aspects of the technology. Yet, it is difficult to find a single volume that gives a reasonably clear and up-to-date picture of the non-technical aspects of using information technology successfully.

Our aim in compiling the current volume of seventeen selected readings is to provide a non-technical overview to the subject which shows how the use and impact of information technology has changed during its brief history. In particular, we wish to draw attention to the planning and management tasks without which technology cannot be deployed successfully. We aim to demonstrate how these tasks have moved from technical management to the boardroom, while the technology itself has moved from back-room, administrative support to become a competitive weapon in the marketplace.

The book can be read with profit by the manager responsible for information systems (or for the information centre). It will indicate to him that his problems are shared problems, but that newer methods and guidelines are available which can help him in his task. It can be read with equal profit by the user manager who wants to improve his understanding of how information technology can be relevant to him, and what his role should be in relation to the design and implementation of information systems. To the businessman, the book provides an insight into the impact of technology on the business and the applications which have fundamental effects on the enterprise. Finally, the book is designed to be read by students – both students intending to be specialists in information systems, and students taking more general business studies degrees and MBAs, but with an interest in the management issues of information, information systems and information technology.

Information Technology, which at the start meant only computers, crept upon mankind quite unexpectedly, originating really in the 1950s. This 'stupid intelligent machine' had great potential, everyone agreed. But at the beginning very few knew how to use it, let alone imagined what problems it might cause, or how important it might become.

Technological innovation during the second part of this century has made it possible to make the computer progressively smaller and faster. New application areas have opened up as the technology has become more and more reliable and progressively cheaper. Through these new applications, other, hitherto independent technologies – telecommunications, office equipment, to name a few – have become enmeshed with computers. It has been slowly realised that all these various technologies have one thing in common: they are all technologies for information. The convergence of these various types of technologies into a complex new form – Information Technology – also meant that conscious effort was now made to interlink and integrate the various forms of technology into a common base.

There is a danger, when the rate of change is so great, that we take it for granted and fail to recognise its effects and implications. Indeed, there were regularly recurring themes in the news media in the late 1950s and early 1960s about the computer revolution. Further predictions were made in 1978 about the impact of the microprocessor (although the latter had been manufactured and marketed since 1971). However, very few of the popular predictions that foreshadowed a new industrial revolution have given a realistic picture about the nature of the likely problems and the impact the technology has made and will continue to make well into the future.

Looking, as it were, through the 'retrospectroscope', it is easy to see patterns emerging that governed the progress of information technology, from large, expensive computers for administrative processing to interconnected world-wide networks which have the potential to change trading patterns and the basis for competition.

In this volume, we trace this progress up to the mid-1980s, when information technology surfaced as a new competitive weapon for businesses. We do this through a selection of papers, magazine articles and documents which aim to illustrate key progress points and impact areas.

The first step towards developing a new technology successfully is to master the manipulation of the technology itself, so that it can be used for some purpose. In the case of information technology, it meant that we had to learn first how to develop information systems which are useful in their areas of application. In the first chapter of the book (An Easy Start to a Difficult Problem), we trace this progress and indicate the major problems that occupied the minds of the computing community in the early stages.

It took a considerable length of time (almost 30 years), before the realisation dawned, that a much larger problem was lurking in the background. It was not the technology itself that caused much of the early problems. It was the fact that we had not yet mastered the discipline of how this technology should be deployed. Understandng information, rather than information technology, was the key to further progress and the need for information management emerged. The second chapter (Managing Information) examines the ideas and practices that emerged as a result of this realisation.

At the beginning, most companies saw the computer solely as a means of reducing the cost of internal administrative operations. Some of the actual side-effects, which occurred when introducing computers in the organisation, were both unexpected and wide-ranging. It was slowly realised that businesses and whole industries would need to take the impact of information technology into account when planning for their future. The third chapter (Learning to Live with the Technology) shows a few characteristic examples of what it means to live with, and suffer from, the unexpected side-effects of, technology, and indicates how the need for wide, business-based planning arose.

Since the early 1980s, more and more cases have emerged from the United States where information systems were playing an increasingly indispensable role in formulating the destiny of companies. At the same time, as competition became more intense and the stakes higher, companies started looking for new instruments when positioning themselves for survival and growth. We see the emergence of strategic business planning which focuses on competitive position rather than on the hitherto fashionable narrow lines of investment and diversification. A situation is developing where, on the one hand, companies are searching for new ways of differentiating and competitive positioning and, on the other hand, the new technology is proving itself capable of underpinning moves which result in changed industry structures and practices. The realisation that information technology can be used as a major instrument in competition is expressed in the term 'strategic weapon'. The last chapter (The Information System as a Strategic Weapon) examines both the strategic impact of information technology and the methods which have emerged to take IT into consideration when planning for the company's future.

It is normally reckoned to be the job of the editors to summarise the lessons to be drawn from the readings and, indeed, also the large body of relevant literature, which has been included following each paper. In the introduction to each chapter, we therefore, provide both a summary of the points made there and also the context in which those points should be interpreted.

We are indebted to all those who gave permission to include their papers in this volume. The selection was not easy and, for the sake of making the volume reasonably compact, we had to leave out many valuable articles. Indeed, some of these may appear in future volumes. We believe that this opening volume offers not only an interesting insight, but also a fair summary of the key issues associated with the application of information technology.

E. K. Somogyi
R. D. Galliers
London, February 1987

CONTENTS

CHAPTER I

AN EASY START TO A DIFFICULT PROBLEM

INTRODUCTION

An Easy Start to a Difficult Problem

Elisabeth K. Somogyi

Computers were originally used for data processing. Data processing, in turn, was employed largely to ease the large-scale, back-room administrative operations of companies. The job of developing these data processing systems was reckoned to be technical and the effect of using computers this way was regarded as an operational issue, having little impact on the firm itself, except in two areas: capital expenditure for the hardware, which was considered to be important, and cost of administration, which it was hoped would soon diminish.

Problems, if any, were regarded as being technical, belonging solely to the DP department. The impact on organisations or jobs, as a result of introducing data processing systems, were regarded as necessary side-effects that had to be suffered in the name of progress. It wasn't long before the shortcomings of this original approach became visible. As soon as computers became cheaper, more available and robust, and the usual administrative operations had been largely computerised, three different, but inter-related problem areas emerged:

- Centralised data processing had to give way to a more distributed form of operation. After all, the relevant technologies were available. Processing, therefore, could be moved to be conveniently near to where data was needed, ie. where the administrative work was done. But beyond the technical hitches, unexpected organisational problems occurred. These were issues which technical DP departments were ill-equipped to deal with, and which even surprised company management.
- System users, who were originally carefully left out of the process of developing data processing systems, got less and less service and the – by then – Management Services departments' credibility had begun to diminish. The emergence of micro-computers gave users a new choice: to purchase their own equipment and develop and operate their own systems. End-user-computing, as this practice had become known, had created problems of its own: fragmented data, duplication of effort, proliferation of incompatible equipment to name a few. These issues were again new to the Management Services department.
- Large-scale administrative processing uses and stores large quantities of data, important, not only for the operations, but also in the management of a business. As most of the operational data was already stored, it was reasonable that various levels of management requested (and got promised) timely and accurate reports based on the collection of operational data. These new types of systems, called Management Information Systems, backed by large integrated databases, were hailed as the most important areas of computer-related

development in many companies. However, many of these systems did not live up to the expectations attached to them.

Although it is hard to blame a technical computer department for not dealing with many of these issues, in practice, it was the computer specialist who often had to carry the blame for not perceiving and solving these problems. Those in the profession and associated closely with it, realised that the management of information throughout the company, rather than the technical aspects of computing, needs to be tackled if computers are to be exploited to their full potential.

The first paper of this chapter gives a general overview of the way computing moved out of the technical areas and toward information management. The following three papers illustrate one by one the three separate problem areas mentioned above. The final paper describes the need for information management and proposes measures that Management Services departments can take to rectify the situation.

1. FROM DATA PROCESSING TO STRATEGIC INFORMATION SYSTEMS–A HISTORICAL PERSPECTIVE*

Elisabeth K. Somogyi and Robert D. Galliers

ABSTRACT: This paper presents a brief historical overview of the application of information technology. An extensive reading list is included.

Computers have now been in use commercially for over three decades in business administration and for providing information. The original intentions, the focus of attention in – what was originally called – data processing, and the nature of the data processing effort itself have changed considerably over this period. The actual expression describing the activity has changed from the original 'data processing', through 'management information' to the more appropriate 'information processing'.

A great deal of effort has gone into the development of computer-based information systems since computers were first put to work automating clerical functions in commercial organisations. Although it is well-known now that supporting businesses with formalised systems is not a task to be taken lightly, the realisation of how best to achieve this aim was gradual. The change in views and approaches and the shift in the focus of attention have been partly caused by the rapid advancement in the relevant technology. But the changed attitudes that we experience today have also been caused by the good and bad experiences associated with using the technology of the day. In recent years, two other factors have contributed to the general change in attitudes. As more coherent information was made available through the use of computers, the general level of awareness of information needs grew. At the same time, the general economic trends, especially the rise in labour cost, combined with the favourable price trends of computer-related technology, appeared to have offered definite advantages in using computers and automated systems. Nevertheless, this assumed potential of the technology has not always been realised.

This paper attempts to put the various developments (how the technology itself changed, how we have gone about developing information systems, how we have organised information systems support services, how the role of systems has changed, etc) into perspective, and to identify trends and key turning points in the brief history of computing. But most importantly, it aims to clarify what has really happened, so that one is in a better position to understand this seemingly complex world of information technology, the developments in its application, and to see how it relates to our working lives. One word of warning, though. In trying to interpret events, it is

* *A version of this paper has been published by the Journal of Information Technology in March-1987.*

possible that we might give the misleading impression that things developed smoothly. They most often did not. The trends we now perceive were most likely to be imperceptible to those involved at the time. To them, the various developments might have appeared mostly as unconnected events which merely added to the complexity of information systems.

In this paper, we trace the history of this period, provide an overview of developments in computing and attempt to place these developments in a framework. Within this framework we might then gain perspective into the future, perhaps having more reason to believe that the large investments of effort, time and money in information systems will produce fruitful results and that the potential of information technology will be tapped even more effectively.

THE EARLY DAYS OF DATA PROCESSING

Little, if any, commercial applications of computers existed in the early 1950s when computers first became available. The computer was hailed as a mammoth calculating machine, relevant to scientists and code-breakers. It was not until the second and third generation of computers appeared on the market that commercial computing and data processing emerged on a large scale.

Early commercial computers were used mainly to automate the routine clerical work of large administrative departments. It was the economies of large-scale administrative processing that first attracted the attention of the system developers. The cost of early computers, and later the high cost of systems development, made any other type of application economically impossible, or very difficult to justify.

These first systems were batch systems using fairly limited input and output media, such as punched cards, paper tape and printers. Using computers this way was in itself a major achievement. The transfer of processing from unit record equipment such as cards allowed continuous batch-production runs on these expensive machines. This was sufficient economic justification and made the proposition of having a computer in the first place very viable indeed. Typical of the systems developed in this era were payroll and general ledger systems, which were essentially integrated versions of well-defined clerical processes.

Selecting applications on such economical principles had side effects on the systems and the resulting application portfolio. Systems were developed with little regard to other, possibly related, systems and the systems portfolio of most companies became fragmented. There was usually a fair amount of duplication present in the various systems, mainly caused by the duplication of interrelated data. Conventional methods that evolved on the basis of practical experience with developing computing systems, did not ease this situation. These early methods concentrated on making the computer work, rather than on rationalising the processes they automated.

A parallel but separate development was the increasing use of operational research (OR) and management science (MS) techniques in industry and commerce. Although the theoretical work on techniques such as linear and non-linear programming, queueing theory, statistical inventory control, PERT-CPM, statistical decision theory, and so forth, was well established prior to 1960, surveys indicated a burgeoning of OR and MS activity in industry in the United States and Europe during the 1960s. The surge in industrial and academic work in OR and MS was not unrelated to the presence and availability of ever-more powerful and reliable computers.

In general terms, the OR and MS academics and practitioners of the 1960s were technically competent, enthusiastic and confident that their discipline would transform management from an art to a science. Another general remark that can fairly be made about this group, with the wisdom of hindsight, is that they were naive with respect to the behavioural and organisational aspects of their work. This fact unfortunately saw many enthusiastic and well-intentioned endeavours fail quite spectacularly, setting OR and MS into unfortunate disrepute which in many cases prohibited necessary reflection and reform of the discipline. (Galliers and Marshall, 1985)

Data processing people, at the same time, started developing their own theoretical base for the work they were doing, which showed signs that a new profession was in the making. The different activities that made up the process of system development gained recognition and – as a result – systems analysis emerged as a key activity, different from O & M and separate from programming. Up to this point, data processing people possessed essentially two kinds of specialist knowledge, that of computer hardware and programming. From this point onwards, a separate professional – the systems analyst – appeared, bringing together some of the OR, MS and O & M activities hitherto performed in isolation from system development.

However, the main focus of interest lay in making those operations, which were closely associated with the computer, as efficient as possible. Two important developments resulted. First, programming (ie communicating with the machine the instructions that it needed to perform) had to be made less cumbersome. A new generation of programming languages emerged, with outstanding examples such as COBOL and FORTRAN. Second, as jobs for the machine became plentiful, development of special operating software became necessary, which made it possible to utilise computing power better. Concepts such as multi-programming, time-sharing, time-slicing, started to emerge and the idea of a complex large operating system, such as the IBM 360 OS was born.

New facilities made the use of computers easier, attracting further applications, which in turn required more and more processing power. The vicious circle in which excess processing power attracts more applications, which – in turn – require more processing power, became visible for the first time. The pattern was documented – in a light-hearted manner – by Grosch's law (1953). In simple terms it states that the power of a computer installation is proportional to the square of its cost. While this was offered as a not-too-serious explanation for the rising cost of computerisation, it was quickly accepted as a general rule, representing fairly the realities of the time.

THE FIRST SIGN OF MATURITY

Computers quickly became pervasive. As a result of improvements in system software and hardware, commercial systems became efficient and reliable, which in turn made them more widespread. By the late 1960s most large corporations had acquired big mainframe computers – the era was characterised by the idea that 'large was beautiful'. Most of these companies had large centralised installations operating remotely from their users and business.

Three separate areas of concern emerged. First, businesses started examining seriously the merits of introducing computerised systems. Systems developed in this period were effective, given the objectives of automating clerical labour. But the reduction in the number of moderately paid clerks was more than offset by the new, highly-paid class of data processing (DP) professionals and the high cost of the necessary hardware. In addition, a previously unexpected cost factor, that of maintenance, started eating away larger and larger portions of the DP budget. The remote 'ivory-tower' approach of the large DP departments made it increasingly difficult for them to develop systems that appealed to the various users. User dissatisfaction increased to frustration point as a result of inflexible systems, too formal arrangements, the very long time required for processing changes and new requests and the apparent inability of large DP departments to satisfy user needs.

Second, some unexpected side-effects occurred when these computer systems took over from the previous manual operations: substantial organisational and job changes became necessary. It was becoming clear that data processing systems had the potential of changing organisations (Seligman, 1964). Yet, the hit and miss methods of system development concentrated solely on making the computer work. This laborious process was performed on the basis of ill-defined specifications, often the result of a well-meaning technologist interpreting the unproven ideas of a remote user manager. No wonder, that most systems turned out to be not the best! But even when the specification was reasonable, the resulting system was often technically too cumbersome, full of errors and difficult to work with.

Third, it became clear that the majority of systems, by now classed as 'transaction processing' systems, had major limitations. Partly, the centralised, remote, batch processing systems did not fit many real-life business situations. These systems processed and presented historical rather than actual information. Partly, data was fragmented across these systems, and appeared often in duplicated, yet incompatible format.

It was therefore necessary to re-think the fundamentals of providing computer support. New theoretical foundations were laid for system development. The early trial and error methods of developing systems were replaced by more formalised and analytical methodologies, which emphasised the need of engineering the technology to pre-defined requirements. 'Software Engineering' emerged as a new discipline (Hall, 1972; Manchester, 1981). The search for requirement specification methods started.

Technological development also helped a great deal clarifying both the theoretical and practical way forward. From the mid 1960s a new class of computer – the mini – was being developed and by the early 1970s it emerged, rivalling the mainframe. The mini was equipped for 'real' work, having arrived at the office from the process control environment of the shop-floor. These small versatile machines quickly gained acceptance, not least for their ability to provide an 'on-line' service. By this time, the commercial transaction processing systems became wide-spread, efficient and reliable. It was therefore a natural next step to make them more readily available to users, and often the mini was an effective way of achieving this aim.

Beyond their flexibility, minis also represented much cheaper and more convenient computing power: machine costs were a magnitude under the mainframe's; the physical size was much smaller; the environmental requirements (air conditioning, dust control, etc) less stringent and operations required less professional staff. The mini opened up the possibility of using computing power in smaller companies. This, in turn, meant that the demand grew for more and better systems, and through these, for better methods and a more systematic approach to system development.

PRACTICAL SOLUTIONS TO PRACTICAL PROBLEMS

A parallel but separate area of development was that of project management. Those who followed the philosophy that 'large is beautiful' did not stop at thinking in terms of large machines. They aspired to large systems which meant large software and very large software development projects. Retrospectively, it seems that those who commissioned such projects had little understanding of the work involved (Lehman, 1979). These large projects suffered from two problems: false assumptions about development and inadequate organisation of the manpower. Development was based on the idea that the initial technical specification, developed in isolation from the users, was infallible. In addition, 'large is beautiful' had an effect on the structure of early data processing departments. The highly functional approach of the centralised DP departments meant that the various disciplines were compartmentalised. Armies of programmers existed in isolation from systems analysts and operators, with – very often physical – brick walls dividing them from each other and their users. Managing the various steps of development in virtual isolation from each other, as one would manage a factory or production line (without of course the appropriate tools!) proved to be unsatisfactory. The initial idea of managing large computer projects using mass-production principles missed the very point that no two systems are the same and no two analysts or programmers do exactly the same work. Production-line management methods in the systems field back-fired and the large projects grew many fold during development, eating up budgets and time-scales at an alarming rate.

The idea that the control of system development could and should be based on principles different from those of mass-production and of continuous process management, dawned on the profession relatively late. By the late 1960s the problem of large computing projects reached epidemic proportions. Books, such as Brooks's, 'The Mythical Man Month' (1972), likening system development to the pre-historic fight of dinosaurs in the tar-pit, appeared on the book-shelves. Massive computer projects, costing several times the original budget and taking far longer than the original estimates indicated, hit the headlines in the popular press.

Salvation was seen in the introduction of management methods that would allow reasoned control over system development activities in terms of controlling the intermediate and final products of the activity, rather than the activity itself. Methods of project management and principles of project control were transplanted to data processing from complex engineering environments and from the discipline developed by the American space programme (Canning, 1973).

Dealing with things that are large and complex produced some interesting and far-reaching side-effects. Solution to the problems associated with the – then fashionable – large computer programs were discovered through finding the reasons for their apparent unmaintainability. Program maintenance was difficult because it was difficult to understand that the code was supposed to do in the first place. This, in turn, was largely caused by three problems. First, most large programs had no apparent control structure, they were genuine monoliths. The code appeared to be carved from one piece. Second, the logic that was being executed by the program was often jumping in an unpredictable way across different parts of the monolithic code. This 'spaghetti logic' was the result of the liberal use of the 'GO TO' statement (Dijkstra, 1968). Third, if documentation existed at all for the program, it was likely to be out of date, not representing acurately what the program was doing. So, it was difficult to know where to start with any modification, and any interference with the code created unforeseen side-effects. All this presented a level of complexity that made program maintenance quite difficult.

As a result of realising the causes of the maintenance problem, theoreticians started work on concepts and methods that would help reducing program complexity. They argued that the human mind is very limited when dealing with highly complex things, be they computer systems or anything else. Humans can deal with complexity only when complexity is broken down into 'manageable' chunks or modules, which – in turn – can be inter-related through some structure (Weinberg, 1971; Myers, 1975). Researchers suggested that programs, similarly to the electronic equipment on which they run, should be built using limited logic constructs (Boehm and Jacopini, 1967; Parnas, 1972; Stevens, Myers and Constantine, 1974). The uncontrolled use of the GO TO statement was also attacked (Dahl, Dijkstra and Hoar, 1972), and the concept of 'GOTO-less' programming emerged. Later on, specific languages were developed on the basis of this concept. PASCAL is the best known example of such a language.

Modularity and structure in programming became important. From the 1970s onwards the process by which program modules and structures could be designed to simplify complexity attracted increased interest. The rules which govern the program design process, the structures, the parts and their documentation became a major preoccupation of both practitioners and academics. The concept of structuring was born and structured methods started emerging to take the place of traditional methods of development (Jackson, 1975; Yourdon and Constantine, 1975; Warnier, 1976). Structuring and modularity have remained a major intellectual drive ever since in both the theoretical and practical work associated with computer systems.

It was also realised that the principles of structuring were applicable outside the field of programming. One such effect of structuring was the realisation that not only systems but projects and project teams can be structured to bring together – rather than to divide – complex, distinct disciplines associated with the development of systems (Daly, 1979). IBM, from the early 1970s, pioneered the idea of structured project teams with integrated administrative support using structured methods for programming (Baker, 1972), which proved to be one of the first successful ploys for developing large systems.

FROM PROCESSES TO DATA

Most early development methods concentrated on perfecting the processes that were performed by the machine, putting less emphasis on data and giving little, if any, thought to the users of the system. But, as more and more routine company operations became supported by computer systems, need for a more coherent and flexible approach arose. Management's need for cross-relating and cross referencing data which arises from basic operational processes, in order to produce coherent information and exercise better control, meant that the cumbersome, stand-alone and largely centralised systems operating in remote batch mode were no longer acceptable. By the end of the 1960s the focus of attention shifted from collecting and processing the 'raw material' of management information, to the raw material itself: data. It was discovered that inter-related operations cannot be effectively controlled without maintaining a clear set of basic data, preferably in a way that would allow data to be independent of its applications. It was therefore important to de-couple data from the basic processes. The basic data could then be used for information and control purposes in new kinds of systems (Zani, 1970; Nolan, 1973). The drive for data independence brought about major advances in thinking about systems and in the practical methods of describing, analysing and storing data. Independent data management systems became available at about this time.

The need for accurate information also highlighted a new requirement. Accurate information needs to be precise, timely and available. During the 1970s most companies changed to 'on-line' processing to provide better access to data. Many companies also distributed a large proportion of their central computer operations in order to collect, process and provide access to data at the most appropriate points and locations. As a result, both the nature of the systems and that of the systems effort changed considerably. By the end of the 1970s the relevance of data clearly emerged (Kent, 1978). It became viewed as *the* fundamental resource of information, deserving treatment that is similar to any other major resource of a business.

There were some, by now seemingly natural, side effects of this new direction. Several approaches and methods were developed to deal with the specific and intrinsic characteristics of data (Date, 1980). The first of these was the – not so amazing – discovery that complex data can be understood better by discovering its apparent structure. It became also obvious, that separate 'systems' were needed for organising and storing data. As a result, databases and database management systems (DBMS) started appearing. The intellectual drive was associated with the problem of how best to represent data structures in a practically useable way (Chen, 1976; Davenport, 1979). A hierarchical representation was the first practical solution. IBM's IMS was one of the first DBMSs adopting this approach. Suggestions for a network-type representation of data structures, using the idea of entity-attribute relationships, were also adopted, resulting in the CODASYL standard (1974). At the same time, Codd started his theoretical work on representing complex data relationships and simplifying the resulting structure through a method called normalisation.

Codd's fundamental theory (1970) was quickly adopted by academics. Later it also became the basis of practical methods for simplifying data structures. Normalisation became the norm (no pun intended) in better data processing departments and whole methodologies grew up advocating data as the main analytical starting point for developing computerised information systems. The drawbacks of hierarchical and network-type databases (such as the inevitable duplication of data, complexity, rigidity, difficulty in modifications, large overheads in operations, dependence on the application, etc) were by then obvious. Codd's research finally opened up the possibility of separating the storage and retrieval of data from its use. This effort culminated in the development of a new kind of database: the relational database.

Design was also emerging as a new discipline. First, it was realised that programs, their modules and structure should be designed before being coded. Later, when data emerged as an important subject on its own right, it also became obvious that system and data design were activities separate from requirement analysis and program design. The choice of alternative orientation towards data or porcesses in development became visible, resulting in separate data-driven (Palmer and Rock-Evans, 1980), and process-driven (De Marco, 1978; Gane and Sarson, 1979) approaches.

These new concepts had crystallised towards the end of the 1970s. Sophisticated, new types of software started appearing on the market giving a helping hand with organising the mass of complex data on which information systems were feeding. Databases, data dictionaries and database management systems became plentiful, all promising salvation to the overburdened systems professional. New specialisations split the DP discipline: the database designer, data analyst, data administrator joined the ranks of the systems analyst and systems designer. At the other end of the scale the programming profession split by language specialisation as well as by the programmer's conceptual 'distance' from the machine. As operating software became more and more complex, a new breed – the systems programmer – appeared, emphasising the difference between dealing with the workings of the machine and writing code for 'applications.'

TOWARDS MANAGEMENT INFORMATION SYSTEMS

The advent of databases and more sophisticated and powerful mainframe computers gave rise to the idea of developing corporate databases (containing all pertinent data a company possessed), in order to supply management with information about the business. These database related developments also required DP professionals who specialised in organising and managing data (Martin, 1976). The logical and almost clinical analysis these specialists performed, highlighted not only the structures of data but also the many inconsistencies which often exist in organisations. Data structures reflect the interpretation and association of data in a company, which in turn reflect interrelationships in the organisation. Some DP professionals engaged in data analysis work began to develop their own view of how organisations and the management of organisations could be transformed on the basis of the analysis. They also developed some visionary notions about themselves. They thought that they would decide (or help to decide) what data an organisation should have in order to function efficiently, and who would need access to which piece of data in what form.

The idea of a corporate database that is accurate and up-to-date with all the pertinent data from the production systems, is attractive. All we need to do – so the argument goes – is aggregate the data, transform it in certan ways and provide it to management (Siegel, 1975). This way, a powerful information resource is on tap for senior management. Well, what is wrong with this idea?

Several practical matters presented difficulties to the naive DP visionary who believed in a totally integrated Management Information System (MIS) resting on a corporate database. One problem is the sheer technical difficulty of deciding what should be stored in the corporate database and then building it satisfactorily before an organisational change, brought about by internal politics or external market forces, or both, makes the database design and the accompanying reports inappropriate. In large organisations it may take tens of man-years and several elapsed years to arrive at a partially integrated MIS. It is almost certain that the requirements of the management reports would change over that period. It is also very likely that changes would be necessary in some of the transaction processing systems and also in the database design. Furthermore, assuming an efficient and well integrated set of transaction processing systems, the only reports that these systems can generate without a significant quantum of effort, are historical reports containing aggregated data, showing variances – 'exception reports' (eg purchase orders for items over a certain value outstanding for more than a pre-defined number of days) and the like. Reports that would assist management in non-routine decision making and control would, by their nature, require particular views of the data internal to the organisation, that could not be specified in advance. Management would also require market data, ie data external to the organisation's transaction processing systems. Thus, if we are to approach the notion that seems to lie behind the term MIS and supply managers with information that is useful in business control, problem solving and decision making, we need to think carefully about the nature of the information systems we provide (Galliers and Marshall, 1985).

It is worth nothing that well-organised and well-managed businesses always had 'systems' for business control, albeit these systems might have been wholly or partly manual. In this sense, 'management information systems' always existed and the notion of having such systems in an automated form was quite natural, given the advances of computing technology that was taking place at the time. However, the unrealistic expectations attached to the computer, fuelled by the over-enthusiastic approaches displayed by the DP profession, made several, not-so-well-run companies believe that shortcomings in management, planning, organisation and control could be overcome by the installation of a computerised MIS (Mancinelli, 1972). Much of the later disappointment could have been prevented, had these companies realised that technology can only solve technical and not management problems.

Nevertheless, the notion that information provision to management, with or without databases, was an important part of the computing activity, was reflected by the fact that deliberate attempts were made to develop MISs in greater and greater numbers. Indicative of this drive towards supporting management rather than clerical operations is the name change that occurred around this time: most DP Departments became Management Services Departments. The notion was that they would provide, via corporate databases, not only automated clerical processing, but also – by aggregating and transforming such data – the information that management needed for running the business.

Undoubtedly the DP profession, during the 1970s, developed useful and powerful data analysis and data management techniques and learned a great deal about data management. But the notion that they could provide Management, through their data management, data aggregation and reporting activities, with information to assist managerial decision making, had clearly not been thought through. As Keen and Scott Morton (1978) point out, the MIS activity was not really a focus on management information but on information management. We could go further: the MIS activity of the era was concerned with *data* management, with little real thought being given to meeting management information needs.

In the late 1970s Keen and Scott Morton were able to write without fear of severe criticism that the

> . . . management information system is a prime example of a 'content-free' expression. It means different things to different people, and there is no generally accepted definition by those working in the field. As a practical matter MIS implies computers, and the phrase 'computer-based information systems' has been used by some researchers as being more precise.

Sprague and Carlson (1982) attempted to give meaning to the term MIS by noting that when it is used in practice, one can assume that what is being referred to is a computer system with the following characteristics:

- an information focus, aimed at middle managers
- structured information flows
- integration of DP jobs by business function (Production MIS, Personnel MIS, etc)
- inquiry and report generation (usually with a database).

They go on to note that

> . . . the MIS era contributed a new level of information to serve management needs, but was still very much oriented towards, and built upon, information flows and data files.

The idea of integrated MISs seem to have presented an unrealistic goal. The dynamic nature of organisations and the market environment in which they exist forces more realistic and modest goals on the DP professional. Keeping the transaction processing systems maintained, sensibly integrated and in line with organisational realities is a more worthwhile job than freezing the company's data in an overwhelming database.

The era also saw DP professionals, the management science and business modelling fraternities move away from each other into their own specialities, to the detriment of a balanced progress in developing effective and useful systems.

THE EMERGENCE OF INFORMATION TECHNOLOGY

Back in the 1950s Jack Kilby and Robert Noyce noticed the semi-conducting characteristics of silicon. This discovery and the resulting developments in integrated circuitry led to large-scale miniaturisation in electronics. By 1971 microprocessors using 'silicon chips' were available on the market (Williams and Welch, 1985). In 1978 they hit the headlines, commentators predicting unprecedented changes to business and personal life as a result. A new, post-industrial revolution was promised to be in the making (Tofler, 1980).

The impact of the very small and very cheap, reliable computers – micros – which resulted by building computers with chips, became quickly visible. By the early 1980s computing power and facilities suddenly became available and possible in areas hitherto untouched by computers. The market was flooded with 'small business systems', 'personal computers', 'intelligent work stations' and the like, promising the naive and the uninitiated instant computer power and instant solution to problems.

As a result, three separate changes occurred. First, users, especially those who had suffered unworkable systems and waited for years to receive systems to their requirements, started bypassing DP departments. They started buying their own computers. They might not have achieved the best results but the increased familiarity with the small machines started to change attitudes of both users and management.

Second, the economics of systems changed. The low cost of the small machines highlighted the enormous cost of human effort required to develop and maintain large computer systems. Reduction – at any cost – of the professional system development and maintenance effort was now a prime target in the profession, as, for the first time, hardware costs could be shown to be well below that of professional manpower.

Third, it became obvious that small dispersed machines were unlikely to be useful without interconnecting them – bringing telecommunications into the limelight. And many office activities, hitherto supported by 'office machinery' were seen for the first time as part of the process started by large computers – that is, automating the office. Office automation emerged, not least as a result of the realisation by office machine manufacturers, who now entered the computing arena, that the 'chip' could be used in their machines. As a consequence, hitherto separate technologies – that of telephony, telecommunication, office equipment and computing – started converging. This development pointed to the reality that voice, images and data are simply different representations of information and that the technologies that deal with these different representations are all part of a new complex technology: information technology.

The resulting developments became diverse and complex: systems developers had to give way to the pressure exercised by the, now not so naive, user for more involvement in the development of systems. *End user computing* emerged as a result, promoting the idea that systems are the property of users and not the technical department. In parallel, the realisation occurred that useful systems can only be produced if those who will use them take an active part in their development (Mumford and Henshall, 1979). Integrating the user became a very useful obsession, helping the development of new kinds of systems.

It also became clear that a substantial reduction in the specialist manual activity of system development is necessary if the new family of computers and the newly-discovered information technology are to be genuinely useful. Suddenly, there were several alternatives available. Ready-made application systems emerged in large numbers for small and large machines, and *packages* became a fashionable business to be in. *Tools for system development*, targetting directly the end-user and supporting end-user computing, were developed in the form of special, high-level facilities for interrogating databases and formatting reports. Ultra-high-level languages emerged carrying the name 'fourth generation languages' (4GLs) to support both professional and amateur efforts at system development.

For the first time in the history of computing, serious effort was made to support with automation the manifold and often cumbersome activities of system development (Lehman, 1981). Automated programming support environments, systems for building systems, analysis and programming workbenches appeared on the market, many backing the specialist methodologies which, by now, became well-formulated, each with their own cult following.

NEW APPROACHES TO SYSTEM DEVELOPMENT

In addition, new discoveries were made about the nature of systems and system development. From the late 1960s, it was realised that the development of a system and its operations can be viewed as a cycle of defined stages. The 'life-cycle' view of systems emerged and this formed the basis of many methods and methodologies for system development. It became clear only later that – while the view of a life-cycle was the correct one – a *linear* view of the life cycle was counter-productive. The linear view was developed at the time when demand for large-scale systems first erupted and most practitioners were engaged mainly in development. The first saturation point brought about the shock that these systems needed far more attention during their operational life than was originally envisaged. As the maintenance load on DP departments increased from a modest 20% to 60%, 70% and 80% during the 1970s, many academics and practitioners started looking for the reasons behind this – for many, undersirable and unexplained – phenomenon.

It was discovered that perhaps three different causes can explain the large increase in maintenance. First, the linear life-cycle concept can cause problems. Systems developed in a linear fashion were built on the premise that successive deductions would be made during the development process, each such deductive step supplying a more detailed specification to the next one. As no recursive action was allowed, the misconceptions, errors and omissions left in by an earlier step would result in an ever-increasing number of errors and faults being built into the final system. This, and the chronic lack of quality control over the development process, delivered final systems which were far from perfect. As a result, faults were being discovered and needed to be dealt with during the operational part of the life-cycle, thereby increasing unnecessarily the maintenance load. It was discovered that early faults, left in a system, increase the number of successive faults in an exponential way, resulting in hundred-fold increases in effort when dealing with these faults in the final system.

Second, specifications are not as easy to derive as it was thought. The linear life-cycle view also assumed that, once a specification had been correctly developed, a system could be safely built for a long life, as adjustments would probably be unnecessary, provided the specification was followed attentively. This view had negated the possibility that systems might have a changing effect on their environment, which in turn would raise the requirement for re-tuning and re-adjusting them. The followers of this approach had also overlooked the fact that real business, which these systems were supposed to serve, never remains constant. It changes, thereby changing the original requirements. This, in turn, would require readjusting or even scrapping the system. Finally, the idea that users could specify precisely their requirements seems to have been largely a fallacy, negating the basis on which quite a few systems had been built.

Third, the maintenance effort is likely to increase as the system portfolio grows. It is misleading to assume that a percentage increase in the maintenance load is in itself a sign of failure, mismanagement or bad practice. Progressing from the state of having no computer system to the point of saturation means, that even in a slowly changing environment and with precision development methods, there would be an ever-decreasing percentage of work on new development and a slow but steady increase of the activities dealing with systems already built.

Nevertheless, the documented backlog of system requests grew alarmingly, estimated by the beginning of the 1980s at two-to-five years worth of work in major DP departments. This backlog evolved to be a mixture of requests for genuine maintenance, ie fixing errors, adjustments and enhancements to existing systems, and requirements, estimated at several-times the visible one. The invisible backlog there was an ever-increasing volume of 'invisible', undocumented backlog of requirements estimated at several-times the visible one. The invisible backlog consisted largely of genuine requests that disillusioned users were no longer interested in entering into the queue.

As a response to these problems, several new developments occurred. Quality assurance, quality control and quality management of system development emerged, advocating regular and specific tests and checks to be made on the system during its development (Fagan, 1980). Walkthroughs and inspections were inserted into analysis, design and programming activities to catch 'bugs' as early (and as cheaply) as possible.

The notion that systems should be made to appeal to their users in every stage of development and in their final form, encouraged the development of 'user friendly' systems, in the hope that early usability would reduce the requests for subsequent maintenance. Serious attempts were made to encourage an iterative form of development with high user involvement in the early stages, so that specifications would become as precise as possible. The idea of building a prototype for a requirement before the final system is built and asking users to experiment with the prototype before finalising specifications, helped the system development process a great deal.

By now the wide-ranging organisational effects of computer systems were obvious (Keen, 1981; Peltu, 1982). Methods for including organisational considerations in system design started emerging (Checkland, 1981). A group of far-sighted researchers, Land and Mumford in the UK, Agarin in the USA, Bjorn-Andersen in Denmark, Ciborra in Italy and others, put forward far-reaching ideas about letting systems evolve within the organisational environment, thereby challenging the hitherto 'engineering type view' of system development. The first time since the history of computing began, it was pointed out that computerised information systems were, so to speak, one side of a two sided coin, the other side being the human organisation where these systems perform. Unless the two are developed in unison, in conjunction with each other, the end-result is likely to be disruptive and difficult to handle.

Despite these new discoveries, official circles throughout the world had successively failed to support developments in anything but technology itself and the highly technical, engineering-type approaches. It seems as if the major official projects were mounted to support successive problem areas one phase behind the time (Land, 1983). For example: before micros became widespread, it was assumed that the only possible bottleneck in using computers would be the relatively low number of available professional programmers. Serious estimates were made that if the demand for new systems were to increase at the rate shown towards the end of the 1970s, this could only be met by an ever-increasing army of professional programmers. As a result, studies were commissioned to find methods for increasing the programmer population several-fold over a short period of time.[1] Wrong assumptions tend to lead to wrong conclusions, resulting in misguided action and investment, and this seems to be hitting computing at regular intervals. Far too much attention is paid in the major development programmes of the 1980s to technology and far too little attention is paid to the *application* of the technology.

NEW TYPES OF SYSTEMS

The 1980s have brought about yet another series of changes. It has become clear that sophisticated hardware and software together can be targetted in different ways towards different types of application areas. New generic types of systems emerged on the side of data processing systems and MISs. Partly, it was realised that the high-intelligence content of certain systems can be usefully deployed. Ideas originally put forward by the Artificial Intelligence (AI) community, which first emerged in the late 1950s as a separate discipline, became now realisable (Rich, 1983). Systems housing complex rules have emerged as rule-based systems. The expressions 'expert systems' and 'intelligent knowledge-based systems' (IKBS) became fashionable to denote systems which imitate the rules and procedures followed by some particular expertise. Partly, it was assumed that computers would have a major part to play in supporting decision making processes at the highest levels of companies and the concept of decision support systems (DSS) evolved. When remembering the arguments about management information systems, many academics and professionals have posed the question whether 'decision support system' was a new buzzword with no content or whether it reflected a new breed of systems. Subsequent research showed that the computerised system is only a small part of the arrangement that needs to be put

[1] This approach is reminiscent of the famous calculation in the 1920s predicting the maximum number of motor cars ever to be needed on Earth. The number was put at around 4 million on the basis that not more than that number of people would be found to act as chauffeurs for those who could afford to purchase the vehicles. It had never occurred to the researchers in this case, that the end-user, the motor-car owner, might be seated behind the wheel, thereby reducing the need for career chauffeurs.

in place for supporting top-level decision makers (Keen and Scott Morton, 1978).

Manufacturers in the meantime got busy providing advanced facilities that were made available by combining office systems, computers, networks and by employing the facilities provided by keypads, television and telecommunications. Electronic mail systems appeared, teleconferencing and videotex facilities shifted long-distance contact from the telephone, and – besides the processing of data – voice, text and image processing moved to the forefront. The emphasis shifted from the provision of data to the provision of information and to speeding up information flows.

IMPORTANT NEW ROLES FOR INFORMATION SYSTEMS

The major task for many information systems (IS) departments in the early 1980s was making information available. The problems of interconnecting and exchanging information in many different forms and at many different places turned the general interest towards telecommunications (Dickson et al, 1984). This interest was likely to intensify as more and more people gained access to, or were provided with, computer power and technologically pre-processed information.

As a result of recent technological improvements and changes in attitudes, the role of both DP professionals and users changed rapidly. More systems were being developed by the users themselves or in close co-operation with the users. DP professionals started taking the role of advisers, supporters and helpers. Systems were being more closely controlled by their users than was the practice previously. A new concept – the Information Centre – emerged, which aimed at supporting end-user computing, providing information and advice for users, at the same time as it also looked after the major databases and production systems in the background.

But the most important result of using computer technology was the growing realisation that technology itself cannot solve problems and that the introduction of technology results in change (Piercy, 1984). The impact of technological change depends on why and how technology is used. As management had now a definite choice in the use of technology, the technological choices could be evaluated within the context of business and organisational choices, using a planned approach. For this reason more and more companies started adopting a planned approach to their information systems. System strategy and strategic system planning became familiar expressions and major methods have been developed to help such activities.

By the mid 1980s new types of information systems emerged. From the USA came news of systems that helped companies achieve unprecedented results in their markets. These systems were instrumental in changing the nature of the business, the competition and the company's competitive position (McFarlan, 1984). The role of information systems in business emerged as a strategic one and IS professionals were elevated in status accordingly. At the same time the large stock of old systems became an ever-increasing burden on companies wanting to move forward with the technology.

It has been realised also that applying IT outside its traditional domain of back-room effectiveness and efficiency, i.e. moving systems out of the back-room and into the sharp-end of the business, would create in many cases distinct competitive advantage to the enterprise (Parsons, 1983). This should be so, because IT can effect the competitive forces that shape an industry by

- building barriers against new entrants
- changing the basis of competition
- changing the balance of power in supplier relationships
- tying in customers
- switching costs
- creating new products and services.

More and more researchers and practitioners were pointing towards the need for linking systems with the business, connecting business strategy with information system strategy (Somogyi, 1986). The demand grew for methods, approaches and methodologies that would provide an orderly process to strategic business and system planning. Ideas about analysing user and business needs and the competitive impact of systems and technologies are plentiful. Whether they can deliver in line with the expectations will be judged in the future.

SUMMARY

The role of computerised information systems and their importance in companies have undergone substantial transition since the 1950s. Over the same period both the technology and the way it was viewed, managed and employed had changed considerably. The position and status of those responsible for applying the technology in various organisations has become more prominent, relevant and powerful, having moved from data processing, through management services to information processing. At the same time, hitherto separate technologies converged into information technology.

As the technology moved from its original fragmented and inflexible form to being integrated and interconnected, the management of its use, both in terms of operations and system development, changed in emphasis and in nature. Computer operations moved from a highly regulated, centralised and remote mode to becoming more ad hoc and available as and when required. The systems effort itself progressed from concentrating on the programming process, through discovering the life cycle of systems and the relevance of data, to more planned and participate approaches. The focus of attention changed from the technicalities to social and business issues. Figure 1 summarises these changes.

Systems originally replaced clerical activities on the basis of stand-alone applications. The DP department's original role was to manage the delivery and operation of these, predominantly back-room systems. When data became better integrated, and more management oriented information was provided, the Management Services departments started concentrating on better management of their own house and on making links with other departments and functions of the business who

ERA	NATURE OF THE TECHNOLOGY	NATURE OF SYSTEMS OPERATIONS	FOCUS OF SYSTEMS EFFORT	CHARACTERISTICS OF SYSTEMS DEVELOPMENT
DATA PROCESSING	• CUMBERSOME MACHINES • LIMITED RELIABILITY • LIMITED INPUT/OUTPUT MEDIA	• CENTRALISED • REMOTE	• PROGRAMMING PROCESS	• EMPIRICAL
MANAGEMENT SERVICES	• LARGE MAINFRAMES • OPERATING SYSTEMS • SCREEN-BASED INPUT-OUTPUT • DATABASES • MINICOMPUTERS	• DISTRIBUTED PROCESSING • TRANSACTION DRIVEN OPERATIONS	• SYSTEMS ANALYSIS AND DESIGN • SYSTEMS LIFE CYCLE • INCREASING MAINTENANCE • DATA MANAGEMENT	• ANALYTICAL, STRUCTURED (separate trends for process and data) • PROJECT MANAGEMENT
INFORMATION PROCESSING	• CONVERGING TECHNOLOGIES • MINIATURISATION • PACKAGES • PCs/WORKSTATIONS	• USER/BUSINESS DRIVEN • INFORMATION CENTRE • BALANCE BETWEEN DISTRIBUTED/ CENTRALISED APPROACH	• INFORMATION MANAGEMENT • COMMUNICATION • END-USER INVOLVEMENT • LINK WITH BUSINESS STRATEGY	• PARTICIPATIVE • END-USER COMPUTING • PROTOTYPING • AUTOMATED TOOLS • IS PLANNING/STRATEGY
TRENDS	Fragmented ↓ Packaged & interconnected; addressing different forms of information (data, voice, text, image)	Unavailable, regulated ↓ Supportive, available	Technical Issues ↓ Business support Strategic issues	Ad hoc ↓ Methodical, social, business related

Figure 1.

ERA	REASON FOR USING THE TECHNOLOGY	CHARACTERISTICS OF INFORMATION SYSTEMS	TYPE OF APPLICATIONS	CHARACTERISTICS WAY OF APPLYING THE TECHNOLOGY
DATA PROCESSING	• ECONOMIES OF SCALES OF ADMINISTRATIVE OPERATIONS	• BATCH • STAND ALONE UNRELATED SYSTEMS	• SCIENTIFIC • COMMERCIAL: BACK-ROOM, ADMINI-STRATIVE SUPPORT	• AUTOMATION
MANAGEMENT SERVICES	• EFFICIENT OPERATIONS & CONTROL	• ON-LINE • REAL-TIME • INTERCONNECTED THROUGH DATABASES	• MANAGEMENT INFORMATION & CONTROL SYSTEMS • CORPORATE DATABASES	• MANAGEMENT SUPPORT • OPERATIONAL CONTROL
INFORMATION PROCESSING	• EFFECTIVE BUSINESS CONTROL & SUPPORT • STRATEGIC BUSINESS ADVANTAGE	• USER FRIENDLY • NETWORKED • MIX OF PRODUCTION SYSTEMS, MODELS AND WORKING PROTOTYPES	MIXED: • DECISION SUPPORT • USER MODELS • EXPERT SYSTEMS • ROUTINE PRODUCTION SYSTEMS & STRATEGIC APPLICATIONS	• BUSINESS SUPPORT • STRATEGIC WEAPON
TRENDS	Reducing costs ↓ Supporting the Business	Inflexible, Regimented ↓ Accommodating, Flexible	Operational ↓ +Tactical ↓ +Strategic	Technology Drive ↓ Business Need

Figure 2.

needed systems. This trend, combined with the increased variety and availability of sophisticated and easier-to-use technology, has led to the users taking a more active role in developing their own systems.

Lately, since it is realised that information is an important resource, which can be used in a novel way to enhance the competitive position of businesses, information technology and information systems are becoming strategically important for businesses. Information systems have now moved out of the back-room, low-level support position, to emerge as the nerve-centres of organisations and competitive weapons at the front-end of businesses. Figure 2 summarises how the focus of attention moved from being tactical to becoming strategic, how it changed the nature of systems and the system portfolio.

It is evident that activity in the information systems field will continue in many directions at once, driven by fashion and market forces, by organisational need and technological opportunity. But, it appears that the application of information technology is at the threshhold of a new era, opening up new opportunities by using the technology strategically for the benefit of organisations and businesses. It is still to be seen how the technology and the developers will deliver against these new expectations.

REFERENCES

1. Baker, F. T., Chief Programmer Team Management of Production Programming. IBM System Journal, Spring, 1972.
2. Boehm, C. and Jacopini, G., Flow Diagrams, Turning Machines and Languages with Only Two Formation Rules. Communications of the ACM, September 1966.
3. Brooks, F. R. Jr., The Mythical Man-Month. Addison-Wesley, 1972.
4. Canning, R. C., A Structure for EDP Projects. EDP Analyzer, Vol. II., No. 5., 1973.
5. Checkland, P., Systems Thinking, Systems Practice. Wiley, 1981.
6. Chen, P., The Entity-Relationship Model – Towards a Unified View of Data. ACM Transactions on Database Systems, 1976.
7. CODASYL Data Description Language. Journal of Development, US Department of Commerce, National Bureau of Standards, Washington, 1974.
8. Codd, E. F., A Relational Model of Data for Large Shared Data Banks. Communications of the ACM, 13(6), 1970
9. Dahl, O.J. Dijkstra, E. W. and Hoar, C. A. R., Structured Programming. Academic Press, 1972.
10. Daly, E. B., Organising for Successful Software Development. Datamation, December 1979.
11. Date, C. J., An Introduction to Database Systems. Addison-Wesley, 1980.
12. Davenport, R. A., Logical Database Design. The Australian Computer Journal, 11(3), 1979.
13. De Marco, T., Structured Analysis and System Specification. Yourdon Press, 1978.
14. Dickson, G. W., Leitheiser, R. L. Wetherbe, J. C. and Nechis, M., Key Information Systems Issues for the 1980s. MIS Quarterly, Vol. 8, No. 3, 1984.

15. Dijkstra, E. W., A Constructive Approach to the Problem of Program Correctness, BIT 8, No. 3, 1968.
16. Fagan, M. E., Design and Code Inspections to Reduce Errors in Program Development. Infotech State of the Art Review, 1980.
17. Galliers, R. D. and Marshall, P. H., Towards True End-User Computing: From EDP to MIS to DSS to ESE. Western Australian Institute of Technology, Bentey, W. A. 1985.
18. Gane, C. and Sarson, T., Structured Systems Analysis: Tools and Techniques. Improved System Technologies, 1979.
19. Grosch, H. R. J., High-Speed Arithmetic: The Digital Computer as a Research Tool. J. Opt. Soc. AM., April 1953.
20. Jackson, M. A., The Principles of Program Design. Academic Press, 1975.
21. Keen, P. G. W., Information Systems and Organisational Change. Communications of the ACM, Vol. 24, No. 1, January 1981.
22. Keen, P. G. W. and Scott Morton, M. S., Decision Support Systems: An Organisational Perspective. Addison-Wesley, 1978.
23. Kent, W., Data and Reality. North-Holland, 1978.
24. Land, F. F., Information Technology: The Alvey Report and Government Strategy. An Inaugural Lecture, The London School of Economics, 1983.
25. Lehman, J. H., How Software Projects are Really Managed. Datamation, January, 1979.
26. Lehman, M. M., An Environment of Program Development and Maintenance – Programs, Programming and Programming Support. Proceedings of the Sixth ACM European Regional Conference, ICS, 1981.
27. Manchester, P., Software Engineering Management at IBM, Computerworld UK, February 1981.
28. Mancinelli, T. B., Management Information Systems: The Trouble with Them. Computers and Automation, July 1972.
29. Martin, J., Principles of Database Management. Prentice-Hall, 1976.
30. McFarlan, F. W., Information Technology Changes the Way You Compete. Harvard Business Review, May-June, 1984.
31. Mumford, E. and Henshall, D., A Participative Approach to Computer Systems Design. Associated Business Press, 1979.
32. Myers, G. J., Reliable Software Through Composite Design. Petrochelli Charter, 1975.
33. Nolan, R. L., Computer Data Bases: The Future is Now. Harvard Business Review, September-October, 1973.
34. Palmer, I. and Rock-Evans, R., Data Analysis. Computer Weekly, October 1980.
35. Parnas, D. L., A Technique for Software Module Specification with Examples. Communications of the ACM, 15(5), 1972.
36. Parsons, G. L., Information Technology: A New Competitive Weapon. Sloan Management Review, Fall 1983.
37. Peltu, M., Computer Systems Can Go Wrong; Human Factors: Power to the People. Corporate Computing, 1982.
38. Piercy, N. (Ed). The Management Implication of New Information Technology. Croon Helm, 1984.
39. Rich, E., Artificial Intelligence. McGraw-Hill, 1983.
40. Seligman, B. B., Man, Work and the Automated Feast. (1964). In Seligman B. B., Economics of Dissent, Quadrangle, 1968.
41. Siegel, P., Strategic Planning of Management Information Systems. Petrocelli, 1975.

42. Somogyi, E. K., IT Related Strategies; in Earl, M. (Ed): Proceedings of the PA-Oxford Management Centre Conference on IT Strategy. October 1986. (To be published by Oxford University Press).
43. Sprague, R. H. and Carlson, E. D., Building Effective Decision Support Systems. Prentice-Hall, 1982.
44. Stevens, W. P., Myers, G. J. and Constantine, L. L., Structured Design. IBM System Journal, 1974.
45. Tofler, A., The Third Wave. Bantam Books, 1980.
46. Warnier, J. D., Logical Construction of Programs. Van Nostrand Reinhold Co., 1976.
47. Weinberg, G. M., The Psychology of Computer Programming. Van Nostrand Reinhold Co., 1971.
48. Williams, G. and Welch, M., A Microcomputing Timetable. BYTE, Vol 10., No. 9., September 1985.
49. Yourdon, E. and Constantine, L., Structured Design. Yourdon Press, 1975.
50. Zani, W., Blueprint for MIS. Harvard Business Review, November-December, 1970.

2. ORGANIZATIONAL PROBLEMS OF IMPLEMENTING A DISTRIBUTED SYSTEM*

Frank F. Land

Experience with the implementation of computer systems, centralized or distributed, suggests that the major causes of failures are connected with 'organizational' rather than 'technical' factors. If we align ourselves with management, we put the blame on poor or inadequate systems analysis and design. If we speak from the point-of-view of the computer professional, we speak of managerial inadequacies such as lack of vision, obstinacy, failure to move with the times, and so on.

The fact that organizational factors are associated with the perceived failure of many computer based systems leads to the question: are there special features in distributed systems other than those in other kinds of systems which give rise to special problems in their implementation? In practice, it will be found that many of the problems are common to all systems implementations, though distributed systems have certain features which lead to the escalation of some of the difficulties.

One useful method of analysing the kind of problems which may arise with the implementation of distributed systems is to look at the motives of the implementors of such systems.

The trend towards distributed systems stems in part from two kinds of reaction to the conventional centralized system. In the first place, there is the reaction of the user manager – in particular the line manager to the apparent tyranny and inflexibility of the centralized system.

Before computer systems were implemented to 'relieve' him of his data processing burden, he was responsible for, and in control of, most of the data processing activity related to his line functions. He understood his own information needs and had the means to satisfy them. He exchanged data and information with his fellow line managers, and had some control over the information passed up to senior management. However, when computer systems began to be discussed, the line manager saw them as an opportunity both to lose a troublesome and costly function (data processing) and to get 'better' information from the system. What he did not anticipate, was the extent to which he was left with the trouble-shooting end of his data processing activity. Indeed, error tracing and error correction became a greater burden because the manager was no longer in control of the system, and he and his people had only imperfect knowledge of the way the computer aspects of the system operated, and what the computer programs actually did. At the same time, his costs of data processing did not reduce to the extent expected in the first specifications.

* *Published in: Infotech State of the Art Report, Managing the Distribution of DP, Volume 2: Invited Papers, Infotech International, 1979.* See page 67 for a biography of Professor Land.

For the line manager who faced the outside world – customers, clients or suppliers – the situation often became very difficult. The system generated errors which he could not properly explain, but his responsibility vis-à-vis the customer had not altered.

An analogous situation developed in his relationship with his fellow managers. Furthermore, his communication with them often diminished so much so, that his knowledge of what was happening in the organization was reduced. Finally, he found that senior management received reports relating to his own live functions before he received that same information.

What the line manager had lost in giving up his data processing activity and with it a substantial part of his database (his files and records) is some of his power in the organization. Instead of being better informed, he is often less well informed. His ability to negotiate with his superiors, his peers and his subordinates is perceived to be less than when he had total control over his data and its processing.

Whilst the above account is in some senses a caricature of the real situation, in that it emphasises the negative points of centralized data processing on a computer, it does represent the viewpoint expressed commonly towards computer processing in many organizations. It is obviously true that a significant part of the problems outlined are not a consequence of centralized computer processing but are the results of poorly designed systems.

Nevertheless, distributed processing appears to some line managers to provide the possibility of regaining control over their database and data processing and hence to recapture their power in the organization, and at the same time to gain the benefits they first looked for in accepting computer processing at all. As a result, there has been strong departmental pressure in many organizations for a move away from centralized data processing, towards systems which provide facilities for local processing and even more important, for localized systems design and implementation. Typically, this movement has been most evident in organizations which have treated their central computer service as a bureau to which line management has had access very much on a first come, first served basis. In this type of organization the central service tends to operate with only weak central planning, and systems are more likely to be fragmented than in organizations where applications are developed on the basis of some corporate scheme.

The main organizational problems which may arise in situations where distributed processing is implemented as a result of departmental pressures, rather than as a result of corporate plans, are set out below.

THE RESOURCE ALLOCATION PROBLEM

In principle, resources should be allocated to projects – whether they be systems projects or other types of projects, such as developing a new product – in such a way that priority is given to projects which yield the highest return to the organization. In practice, this may be a difficult principle to implement because of the different degrees of risk associated with different projects, and because of the difficulty of measuring or quantifying non-monetary benefits. In the case of non-profit making organizations, where the objectives of systems change may involve factors such as the improvement of health standards, this difficulty is particularly important.

If the organization has a strong central planning authority, it can ensure that resources are allocated against common criteria, however the system is implemented. In organizations which allow distributed processing to proceed on the basis of departmental pressure, it is often the politically strong department which is allocated resources, rather than the departments with the best case. In the worst instances, decisions to utilize or allocate resources to distributed computer projects are not based on evaluation of that benefit to the organization but on the basis of a departmental assessment which could be counter productive to the organization as a whole, though it might appear to be of benefit to that department.

A good example of this kind of misallocation of resources occurred in the hospital service. The hospital had installed expensive laboratory equipment in order to facilitate the automatic testing of specimens from patients. The equipment however was only poorly utilized. It was established that the poor utilization was, in part, due to the poor communication between the doctors in the wards and the laboratories, and the consequent delays in reporting laboratory results to doctors. A new system was developed using linked minicomputers and terminals to speed up the handling and processing of test demands and results. With a much improved service, the demand for tests rose rapidly, and laboratory equipment utilization improved. In terms of the departmental objectives of the laboratories, the system was a success. But in terms of the overall objective of the hospital, the system was only of doubtful value, because in only a few percent of cases did the treatment of patients alter as the result of all the extra tests.

All systems implementations can suffer from the misallocation of resources, if no adequate criteria for allocation are set up. But distributed systems, introduced on the basis of departmental pressure to escape centralized systems, are more likely to fall into the trap of sub-optimization.

FRAGMENTATION

One of the principal aims of systems designers has been to develop so called integrated systems. This aim is based on two basic premises. The first is to regard an organization as an analogue of a complex machine, made up of many interrelated parts. The machine, and like it the organization, exists to provide some objective – the manufacture of a part or the maximization of profit. Neither the machine nor the organization can achieve their objective efficiently if the parts or subsystems are not geared to identical objectives. Integration in this sense attempts to ensure that all the goals of the different parts or subsystems are harmonized.

In practice, it is not certain that the machine/organization analogue is all that useful. It may be important for the survival of an organization if some components achieve satisfaction through pursuing their own goals rather than that of the organization, even if, in the short term, these goals appear to conflict with those of the organization. For example, it may pay an organization to give some latitude to workers for choosing their own mode of working, even if in terms of strict cost accounting such a mode contravenes the principle of profit maximization; if as a result absenteeism and sickness are reduced. Hence it is possible that the development of independent departmental systems by means of distributed processing can, despite fragmentation, lead to a system which in total is more effective.

However, in general, great care needs to be taken in the design of distributed systems to ensure that the objectives of the system are properly harmonized. A sales order system developed independently on behalf of the marketing department, which aims to provide marketing management with the facility to place short-term orders on the factory, will quickly bring the organization into disrepute, if the factory management develops its own control system on a basis of long, stable production runs. Yet both departments may be working towards a goal of profit maximization.

The non-harmonization or fragmentation of systems goals is in reality another symptom of an organization without proper machinery for goal setting. In such an organization, distributed processing provides an opportunity for these organizational problems to spread.

The second premise, on which integration is based, is that the avoidance of duplication in processes, and in records and files, will yield significant cost savings. The aim of integration is then to avoid redundancy in processes and in files.

For example, in practice, the principle of cost saving and efficiency gains through the avoidance of redundancy, is not as clear as the exponents of corporate databases claim. In a purely deterministic world, the case for integration would not be challenged. However, in the world of uncertainty and the high probability of error, whether wilful (fraudulent) or accidental, redundancy and duplication of processes can provide a considerable degree of protection. Would the multi-million dollar computer fraud cases, frequently reported in the press, be possible if the systems had been distributed?

Integration can also lead to another kind of problem. A hidden assumption made by some of those who favour the idea of an integrated system, is that there is a common language in an organization for all its activities. But this may not be true. 'Sales' to the marketing department means orders taken by salesmen, invoiced sales to the accountants, and goods delivered from the warehouse to the production department. There is a risk that an integrated system will not clearly separate these different semantic categories, and lead to confusion and, worse, error.

An organization may devise some benefit from not taking integration too far. The kind of fragmentation in systems which can occur when distributed processing is the result of local user pressure, and is not moderated by any overall planning mechanism, can lead to gross inefficiencies. The benefits of systems developed under local initiative, and with high local motivation to their success, can be offset by the problems and costs when the local system has to communicate with another local system or the central system with which it is not compatible. Incompatibility can occur in many ways and at many levels. And each instance of incompatibility can lead to additional processes attempting to reconcile the differences, and will yield a crop of inaccuracies and error. Incompatibilities can occur when, for example, different product groups manufactured in different departments use a different basis for providing statistics and forecasts. In one case, a company's corporate 5-year plan was based on departmental statistics and accounts whose basis was significantly different. As a result, the overall plan had little hope of realization.

Incompatibilities in systems developed independently can make it impossible at a later stage to develop unified systems, even if in a subsequent reorganization the relevant departments are merged. An insurance company originally had separate departments for the marketing and handling of two branches of its business. Both departments developed their own system. Subsequently, the insurance company attempted to merge the departments, but found that the incompatibility in their processing systems made the merger difficult to achieve. The difficulties were partly technical – but the chief difficulty arose out of the reluctance of either department to change their system to that of the other department. This example occurred in separately developed, but not distributed systems. It is given here, because distributed systems are at risk if there is no adequate planning mechanism.

THE PROBLEM OF STANDARDS AND GOOD PRACTICE

Over the thirty-odd year history of data processing, the data processing professionals have slowly developed codes of good practice and standards of performance. Practices such as structured and modular programming, the use of specification standards, and project control techniques have mainly been developed in the large centralized processing units in industry. These methods have not eliminated the problems of developing complex computer systems – the problems of reliable resource and time budgeting, the problems of building robust systems, the problems of reliability and accuracy – but they have gone a long way towards bringing these problems under control.

The trend towards distributed processing and the related trend of departments developing their own systems, threaten to reverse this process.* As a consequence of the user taking charge of their own systems development, and playing a more active rôle in the detailed work of analysis, design and even programming, and as a consequence of the diminished rôle of the DP professional, many of the practices developed over the past thirty years have to be relearned, and even reinvested. There is a risk too that good practices developed in one department do not get transferred to other departments. It is wrong to equate distributed processing with an impoverishment of standards of practice and performance in system development and implementation. But any organization which allows itself to be driven to distributed processing by user reaction against centralized systems, has to take a great deal of care if good professional practices are to be preserved.

One technique to gain the benefits of more user participation in the development of systems, and at the same time to preserve and even develop good practices and standards, is to implement a matrix organization. In this, those concerned with systems development in a department are responsible to their own departments for the

*Still continuing today. (Ed.)

systems under development, but are responsible to a central professional organization for the use of standards and methods.

THE LIFE-CYCLE PROBLEM

In an ideal world, systems would be designed to take account not only for present needs, but also to be able to cope with the requirements of the future. As it is not possible to forecast the future with the required degree of precision, systems should be designed with sufficient flexibility to survive in changing circumstances, at least until they have yielded their expected return.

Because distributed systems have to deal with localized demands only, the problem of flexibility and forecasting the future should be less, than for large centralized systems. In the first place, the scale of systems development tends to be smaller, and hence systems can be implemented faster. Instead of a design/implementation cycle taking three to five years, a typical distributed system can be implemented in perhaps one to one-and-a-half years. The cut-over date for the system is therefore much nearer the present than for a centralized system. In addition, the local management may be more aware of future trends for their department, than if the same system was developed centrally for a number of departments.

But the developers of distributed systems may be unaware of major company plans extending far to the future, because they are not at the level in the organization which makes them privy to such plans. The manufacturing division of a company making engineering products developed a distribution system based on a central store. The systems developers were not told that the senior management of the company had hired consultants who had advised them to change from a system of centralized distribution to a system of distribution based on many branches. The new distribution system would not come into effect for at least three years, whereas the planned computer system was to be implemented in less than two years and have a life-time of at least five years. The company plan and the divisional plan were unco-ordinated and in the event incompatible. Locally driven distributed systems face the risk that systems devised for immediate local needs, will be incompatible with the future plans of the organization.

A further problem which could occur, is that of widely different rates of progress between different departments. Those departments which are reluctant to develop their own systems or are satisfied with centralized data processing, can hamper the development of company-wide distributed systems. And such departments fail to build up the expertise in systems development acquired by departments which are ahead of them.

THE PROBLEM OF INFORMATION FILTERING

In a well regulated system, information flows are matched to the needs of the control system. A model of the organization suggests what information is needed at each control level, in order to facilitate the smooth functioning of the organization. The higher levels of the organization pass down instructions (or responsibilities) to the levels below, and the lower levels pass upwards details of performance at the lower levels. At each level, information is received, processed and passed up as reports of activity carried out, and down as instructions for further activity.

In a distributed system, developed on the basis of local pressure, it is possible for the locally designed system to be used to censor the information passed upwards. Local processing can be utilized to filter information in such a way as to distort the control mechanism of the organization. Indeed, one of the motives to centralize data processing was to avoid this kind of filtering. There are examples of organizations in which the senior management were systematically prevented from knowing the extent of failure in certain departments, with, in some cases, disastrous results for the organization. Distributed processing may, if it is not adequately controlled, provide opportunities for information filtering.

The problems outlined above can arise where distributed processing is undertaken as a result of pressure from user management to take advantage of technological developments which can liberate them from the tyranny of centralized systems. The problems are a consequence, not of the technology, but of the lack of planning and control in its implementation. As far as the user manager is concerned, the key to distributed processing is that it returns control over the database and the data processing activity to him.

PRESSURE FROM DP PROFESSIONALS

The second reaction that has led to the development of distributed systems is that of the professional computer systems designer. His reaction is based on three observations, which set out below.

The first is that the success of systems is critically due to the extent to which they win acceptance from those who work with and use the systems. This is associated with the realization that confidence and hence acceptance of systems is directly related to the degree to which those who work with and use the systems have been able to play a part in the evaluation and design of the system. Study after study has demonstrated that the more remote design is from the user, the less the system wins approval, and that the more the user is involved in design, the more chance there is that the system will be approved and be allowed to have a long life. Even systems, which for pure technical reasons may be inferior, prove to be more stable and better used when developed by those who work with the system, than theoretically better systems developed by a remote agency.

Distributed systems are seen as a method of providing facilities for a user to do his own processing and play a part in the development of his own system. The professional computer systems designer sees the development process as a partnership, in which he provides technical assistance (design expertise) whilst the user provides knowledge and understanding of the systems requirements. Such a partnership requires a great deal of sensitivity and tolerance from both parties. If this is present, it has been shown that a user group can design its own system, even if it has no prior technical understanding of computers at all.

Problems can occur where the responsibilities of the partnership are not clear. The computer professional has to give up his dominant rôle in systems design and take on an advisory rôle. In practice at least three groups become involved:

- The group of computer professionals (analysts, and programmers)
- The users for whom the system is developed (mainly managers)
- Those who work with the system in processing data.

All three groups have to participate, not only in the design and implementation of the system, but in setting the system's goals.

Failure to recognize the three-fold partnership can lead to conflict and to building a system which fails to win the approval of all parties. Where distributed systems cross departmental lines, the problem of possible conflict between different groups increases and it becomes important to set up the correct organizational institutions to cope with systems developments. Suggestions as to the form of such institutions are set out in the conclusion to this paper.

The second observation is that the cost of centralized systems was escalating as their complexity grew as a consequence of:

- Very heavy systems software overheads of the large mainframes needed for centralized systems
- The delay in obtaining the expected payoff from systems because of the length of the development cycle for complex centralized systems
- The hidden costs of the network of informal systems which typically compete with and sometimes supplanted the formal centralized system
- The high cost of error correction and error recovery of complex systems
- The high cost of maintaining complex systems
- The high cost of protecting the centralized system and the organizations which use such systems against failure.

It is possible for distributed systems to reverse this cost trend, as has been demonstrated, by amongst others, Citibank of New York. But the possibility of fragmented development, of extended communication networks, and of poorly designed local systems can offset or lose the hoped-for cost advantages.

The final observation is, that the trend in large organizations is away from centralization and towards techniques of profit centre management, and management by objectives. These techniques are oriented towards the distribution of responsibility within an organization, and towards groupings based not on functions or processes, but on customers and products. For example, a bank which had been departmentalized on the basis of types of transaction, decided to reorganize itself on the basis of customer groupings. In the original set-up, a single customer would be dealt with by a range of departments. In the new organization, whatever his transaction, the customer would have to deal with only one department.

Some managers saw that this trend in the organization of business could be supported by the new technology of mini and microprocessors embedded in distributed systems.

The main problems faced in the implementation of these concepts stemmed from the very different perception of the new wave of responsible managers. Taking advantage of their newly delegated powers, different managers took widely different views of the way to proceed. In many cases, they proceeded to develop the systems as expected by the organizational planners, whilst others insisted on maintaining manual methods, thereby breaking the chain of the distributed network. Some managers wanted to be pioneers in the development of distributed systems, some wanted to wait and see. In some organizations distributed processing, whilst broadly successful, suffered from many of the problems previously noted in centralized systems – cost escalation, systems which do not have the confidence of its participants, the growth of informal systems.

CONCLUSIONS

Computer-based business systems, whether centralized or distributed, face problems of implementation which stem from the nature of machine computing, from the nature of its human users and from the nature of business organizations themselves.

The computer can only operate on the basis of predetermined rules embodied in a computer program. Such rules can only be based on a model of the business process. This model is bound to be a crude approximation of reality. It cannot accurately reflect the true behaviour of those engaged in the organization's activity today, and even less the activity which will take place tomorrow and the day after. Hence it is impossible to design a perfect computer system for an organization.

Distributed systems, in that they can reduce the distance between the designer (the model builder) and the user, and that they give the user the opportunity to become the designer, provide the possibility of building systems based on more accurate, more perceptive, models of reality. And this should lead to more satisfactory, more robust systems.

It is further possible to suggest a number of steps an organization can take to reduce some of the problems outlined in this paper. Most of these steps would also help to produce better centralized systems.

1. Ensure that all systems proposals are evaluated using common guidelines or criteria for the measurement of costs and benefits. A common procedure for carrying out feasibility studies should be established which allows for the evaluation of systems goals by all those who are affected by the system.
2. Set up a mechanism for the long-term planning of systems change. All systems proposals must conform to the plans, but the plans must be flexible in the light of new ideas and changing conditions. A useful tool is a senior committee which comprises representatives of financial interests, staff and employee interests, customer or client interests, the interests of management, and perhaps even the community at large.
3. Establish a centre of excellence for the development of standards, methods and good practice. Ensure that responsibility for the technical quality of systems design and implementation is vested in the centre. The centre should also be responsible for training.

4. Develop the practice of monitoring all systems to ensure that they are achieving the cost and benefit targets set in the design study.
5. Regard all systems development as a branch of experimental science. Most new systems can be regarded as an innovation in the context of the organization which implements the system. There is as yet no way in which the designer can predict with precision the effect of the system on those who work with it and use it. Hence it is necessary to develop an approach to systems development which allows for the use of experimental methods such as surveys, models and simulation, controlled experiments, and pilot implementations.
6. Establish for each project a planning horizon which sets the time frame in which the system will operate. Ensure that the system is designed to meet future as well as present needs by engaging in a systematic analysis of those aspects in the environment to which the system is most sensitive.
7. Set up systems development teams, comprising the three principal partners – the user, those who work with the system, and the computer professionals. Give the user and those who work with the system the opportunity to take a major share in the design of the system. Ensure that the development team includes representatives of all those who will be affected by the new system.

This list of guidelines is not exhaustive. As set out above, it suits large organizations more than small organizations, but even small organizations can benefit from following the suggestions. Of course, many organizations use many of the guidelines already in their systems developments.

There is no way of avoiding all problems in systems development, but they can be minimized. The problems, to which distributed systems can be prey, have been outline above. It is hoped that by following the guidelines given in the conclusions, some of the problems can be avoided.

3. INFORMATION RESOURCE CENTER: a new force in end-user computing*

Robert V. Head

It has taken two decades for the information systems (IS) department to evolve within most companies into an important service organization. Today, its capabilities are well established and its limitations well known. This traditional IS department is now being augmented through the creation of a new, smaller and intrinsically *different* kind of organizational entity which, in this discussion, shall be referred to as the information resource center (IRC).

To understand the role of the IRC in the modern, computer intensive business organization, it is necessary to understand what has been happening to data processing technology in the recent past. These developments include:

- Rapid advances in computer technology, especially in microcomputers.
- Growth of significant workload backlogs within the application development section of the systems department.

Equipment technology trends show dramatic improvements in the price versus performance capabilities of processor hardware. The most striking aspect of this continuing improvement has been the emergence of the personal computer. The availability of microcomputers alone, however, is not the key phenomenon. These devices would be almost useless in the hands of nonprofessionals if they were not supported by significant amounts of software that facilitate their practical usage. There is today an overwhelming variety of 'user friendly' software in many categories.

Despite advances in both hardware and software, the IS department continues to struggle with a growing backlog of system development projects. Even though the mainstream transaction processing jobs of the organization – the bread and butter accounting systems – have been automated for years, there is a growing interest in further exploiting computer technology to support all aspects of the business.

In part, this explosion in new requirements has been fueled by cost performance improvements in equipment; and it has also been abetted by easier-to-use software packages. But there are other contributory factors. It is now widely recognized that,

* Reprinted from: JOURNAL OF SYSTEMS MANAGEMENT Vol. 36, No. 2, Issue 284 Feb. 1985

Robert V. Head is President and Principal Consultant of CAPIT, a Company for the Analysis and Planning of Information Technology, which he founded in 1981. During 1980–1981, he conducted independent research in information resources management as a Fellow at the Brookings Institution, a private research organization. He previously held several key positions as a computer executive with the U.S. government. He is the author of four books and more than 100 papers in the field of business systems. His most recent book, *Strategic Planning for Information Systems*, was published in 1982.

despite 25 years of development and growth in the company applications portfolio, we have barely scratched the surface with respect to the powerful usages to which the computer can still be put in almost every segment of the business.

EMERGENCE OF END-USER COMPUTING

The evolutionary factors just identified have coalesced to encourage a phenomenon known popularly and widely as 'end-user computing.' End-user computing can be defined as the direct assumption of system development and data processing tasks by the user of the service for his own direct benefit. This is in contrast to the traditional approach to computing in which user requirements are identified and defined and then turned over to professional system designers and programmers for implementation, with the end user a relatively passive participant in the process.

The traditional approach to system development has many drawbacks, despite the best efforts of systems professionals to improve the methodology of system development. Figure 1 illustrates the traditional process whereby a manager who has

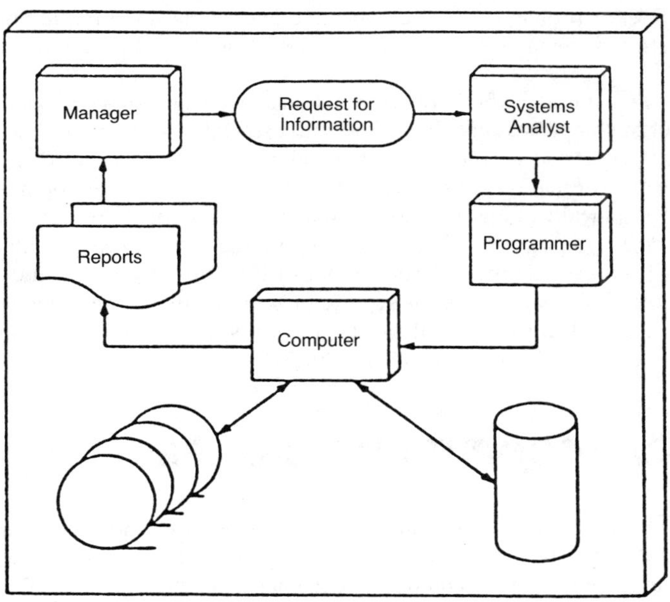

Figure 1. Traditional End-User Support

an information processing request must convey this to a systems analyst who in turn documents it in the form of a logic diagram or specification suitable for programming. The programmer completes the system development job, which is then turned over to operations and, eventually, the system produces the output requested by the manager.

There are two obvious drawbacks to this approach. First, there is the problem that something may be 'lost in translation' of the problem as originally formulated by the requestor and as it is implemented by the computer specialist. We have heard much about the 'communications gap' between computer professionals and non-professionals, and this can aggravate a problem that exists *whenever* requirements must be translated into action through successive stages of organizational activity.

The second principal drawback to this approach is that it can take a long time. How much time depends, of course, on the nature of the problem being tackled. If the system development staff can find a packaged solution to the problem request, shortcuts can be achieved. Or if they can fulfill the request based on their experience with handling similar requests from other users, time may be saved. In many cases, though, a protracted system development cycle may have to ensue before the user request can be satisfied. In extreme cases, on some large systems projects, *years* may elapse between initial request formulation and actual system operation.

Thus, the traditional approach to satisfying user requirements suffers from the dual drawbacks of problems in communicating and acting upon requirements and a time lag between when a request is submitted and the requisite output can be delivered.

End-user computing, whether performed on a mainframe or a personal computer, is an attempt to compensate for the deficiencies associated with the traditional system development process. It permits the individual manager or office worker to interact directly with an information system, utilizing user friendly software support tools. This is suggested graphically in Figure 2, in which a manager is able to retrieve information directly from a computerized data base without the intervention of human intermediaries. Of course, computer professionals are still necessary but they act in an indirect, supporting role. They must acquire or provide the software needed for end-user computing and must be available to aid users in their efforts at information retrieval and computerized problem-solving.

END-USER COMPUTING INCREASES

Actually, as users become directly involved in computation, and become more adept at it, the distinction between traditionally designed and programmed systems and those resulting from end-user computing becomes somewhat blurred. Though many users may never go beyond simple forms of interaction using the most rudimentary software tools, others will go on from this base level to more ambitious forms of problem-solving. As he becomes more adept at computation, a user may undertake the solution of larger and more complex problems. He may progress from the relatively limited realm of the desktop personal computer to utilize the higher capacity

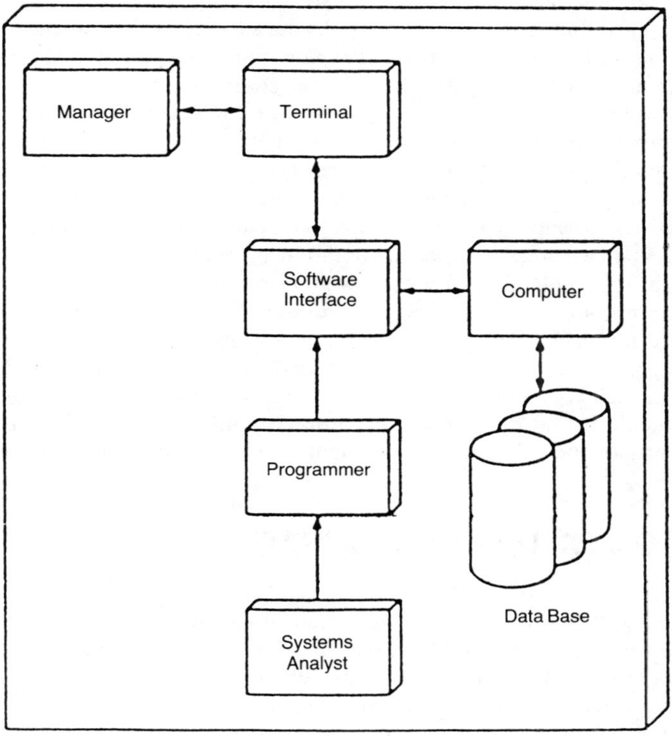

Figure 2. Contemporary End-User Support

and faster facilities of a mainframe, perhaps by converting his personal computer into an on-line terminal.

The user may also advance from reliance on 'menu-driven' types of commands and become adept at using not only the simpler programming languages like BASIC but proceed to master more powerful languages like COBOL. He may begin to take advantage of data base management software to construct data bases both for his own personal usage and perhaps for others in his department.

There are advantages and drawbacks to end-user computing that must be kept in mind as the organization draws up its plans for an information resource center. Tradeoffs must be weighed and priorities established based on the nature of the systems that are needed. Clearly, there will always be a significant role for the tools, techniques and disciplines associated with professionally developed systems. These systems are needed as much today as in the past for large volume transaction processing operations, especially those that reflect companywide requirements or involve more than one major component of the organization. The need for processing efficiency attainable only through large mainframes handling high volume transaction oriented applications remains important. End-user computing, on the other hand, provides a *new* option that permits rapid exploitation of computational capabilities by individual managers to meet problem solving requirements.

It is desirable, as a planning objective, to categorize computer applications throughout the organization and identify those that are large and important enough to remain within the purview of the professional system development staff. These can be separated from individual problem solving requirements that can best be satisfied through end-user computing. For example, companywide payroll processing should obviously remain a centrally managed operation as should accounts receivable in most organizations. It is unlikely that a bank would want to distribute the maintenance of savings accounts or customer loan accounts to small computers or that an airline would consider decentralizing its passenger reservations processing. Conversely, applications like word processing, calendaring and individualized spreadsheet analysis clearly belong in the realm of end-user initiated and controlled computing. But there is a large middle ground. Inventory control, for instance, might be handled differently in different parts of the organization; so might purchasing and accounts payable.

WHAT DATA TO CENTRALIZE

One good approach to categorizing applications according to their preferred development mode and assigning responsibility for maintaining them is to look at the applications from a data base standpoint. Where does the *ownership* of the data reside? Some elements of information are of company-wide importance and should be maintained by a central staff at a central facility. Access to such information, and the authority to update it, should be rigorously controlled both for security reasons as well as to maintain the integrity of the data. General ledger accounting is an example of this kind of application.

On the other hand, there may be data elements that are of no interest whatsoever to anyone other than the individual who creates and stores them on a floppy disk for his personal usage.

An attempt should be made to identify those data elements that have company-wide significance. This should include an identification of which organizational units and which individuals have the authority to create, to modify and to retrieve each data element. Thus, codes designating geographic locations would be standardized company-wide as would customer account numbers.

In short, a clear line of demarcation must be drawn between applications and data bases that are the 'official' property of the organization and those that are not. If this is not done, there will be ambiguities in managing end-user computing such as those having to do with 'ownership' and proprietary rights to programs and data generated by an employee as an adjunct to his official duties. How should these be documented and protected in the event the employee leaves? Are they important enough to be of concern to anyone beyond that employee and perhaps his immediate supervisor?

WHAT IS AN INFORMATION RESOURCE CENTER?

An information resource center is a facility dedicated to technology transfer. Its role is to facilitate the introduction of new hardware and software into the organization through training, demonstrations and consultation. Though the IRC is grounded in technology, it is less a 'technical' organization than a new *kind* of educational entity.

Perhaps the most widely used term is 'information center' which was originated during the 1970's by IBM in Canada. Originally, the information center concept focused on facilitating end-user access to data bases stored in large mainframes and did not emphasize end-user computing using stand alone micros. Today, the term information center is being applied to both end-user access to large mainframes as well as to facilities that aid a user in his computational tasks regardless of whether these are micro or mainframe oriented.

I have chosen not to use the term information center because many 'information centers' are devoted to dissemination of information to the public, e.g., 'office of information and public affairs', 'public and customer information center'. The term information center in many organizations is associated with these public relations activities.

Other terms used to designate the information resource center include 'information technology center' and 'computer store.' In Washington, one of the best known facilities is the U.S. Department of Agriculture's Information Technology Center which has served as a model for other facilities within the Federal Government. Also in Washington can be found the first of General Services Administration's computer stores which, while end-user oriented, have a different function and purpose from an information resource center as we are defining it. The computer store is designed to make it easy for U.S. government officials and employees to procure computer hardware and software.

It should be noted that in the case of the GSA computer store, which is officially known as 'Office Technology Plus', equipment and software can be purchased *only* for official use and not for the personal use of the government employee. Response to the GSA computer store, which opened in late 1983, has been very strong, and GSA has announced plans to open similar facilities around the country.

EVOLUTION OF THE IRC CONCEPT

The idea of an information resource center to facilitate end-user computing predates today's enormous level of interest in the personal computer. As has been mentioned, the notion was originated by IBM to describe a facility to aid users to interact with large computer center facilities. Thus, while in the popular mind there is an identity between end-user computing and personal computing, in actuality end-user computing as an alternative to traditional forms of system development predates the advent of the personal computer.

There are good reasons why this has been so. These have to do with planning and management problems that have beset large computer center operations since the early 70's. As suggested by Figure 3, the mature data processing organization has had to assume an increasingly heavy maintenance burden over the years as the company's applications portfolio expanded in size and complexity. Dozens or even hundreds of operational systems must be maintained and enhanced, and this siphons off an increasingly large proportion of IS resources that otherwise would be available for new application development. Yet there has been no abatement in the demand by users for additional computer services. In fact, as users have gained experience with existing applications, and as popular understanding of the capabilities of computers has become more widespread, the demand on the system development staff to undertake new projects has increased markedly.

As can be seen from the figure, management must contend with a classic resource allocation dilemma. Resources available for IS are finite and limited, yet demand for additional computational capabilities is on the rise. At the same time, the maintenance burden is absorbing a growing percentage of the resources that *can* be made available.

Various managerial and technical approaches have been taken to deal with this problem. There has, for example, been considerable effort over the past ten years to improve the *maintainability* of information systems. The term 'software quality assurance' has come into currency to connote a hightened emphasis on better designed and more reliable computer programs. A carefully constructed methodology known as 'system development life cycle management' has evolved to inject greater discipline into computer project management with the objective of husbanding those

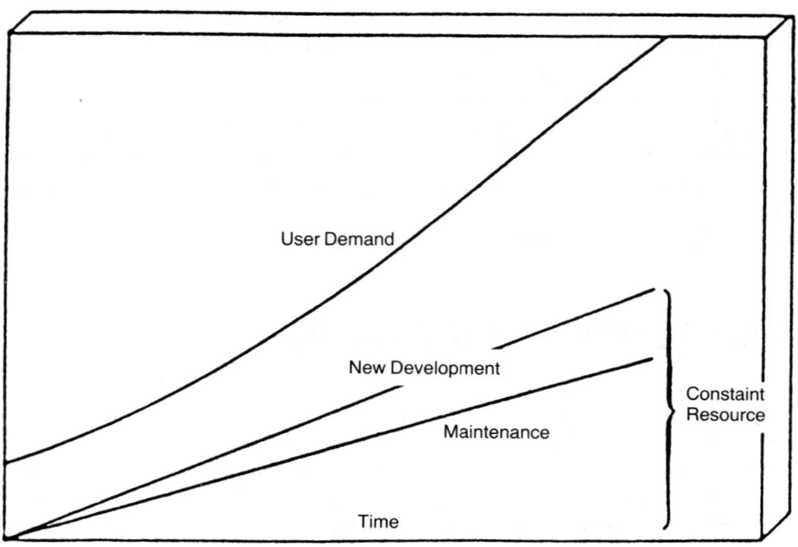

Figure 3. IS Resource Allocation

human and machine resources that are available for new project work. The basic idea behind all these techniques is to enhance programming productivity.

We have also witnessed the introduction of productivity aids such as structured design and structured programming methodology. The goal here is to boost the productivity of computer professionals by means of computer supported programming aids. By using these, the typical applications programmer might reasonably be expected to produce, say, eight instructions per hour rather than five, or to be able to complete testing and validation of a program more quickly.

GROWING USE OF APPLICATION PACKAGES

Another element in the search for greater efficiency in the usage of systems resources can be seen in the widespread acceptance of application packages. Commercially available application packages have constituted a growing subsegment of the computer software industry over the past few years. Packages for payroll, accounting and personnel information are widely available and their use is increasing. The same is true of packages for general ledger accounting and accounts receivable. These application packages are being acquired and applied not just by small companies; they are being put to use by the giants among the Fortune 500. These large companies are, of course, fully capable of developing their own general ledger or payroll systems, but they are finding it cost effective to acquire general purpose packages so that in-house system development staff resources can be assigned to more demanding and specialized applications.

These typify the measures that have been taken to improve the responsiveness of the IS department. Despite these efforts, though, the gap between user demand and the ability of the IS department to satisfy that demand continues to grow. A commonly accepted rule of thumb is that there is an applications backlog of two to three years awaiting attention in the typical information systems department. Where this is the case, there are bound to be dissatisfied users. No matter how fairly and carefully priorities are assigned, some important work must be deferred or left undone. This situation has contributed to the growing interest in end-user computing.

What steps must be taken before end users can assume a more contributory role in the system development process? Heretofore, users had the relatively passive task of defining their requirements, usually working with a trained systems analyst. After the system development cycle was accomplished, they interacted with the resultant system as originators of inputs and recipients of system outputs. One goal of an information resource center is to get end users involved directly in *all* stages of the system development process. Projects that lend themselves to this approach are usually small, though not invariably so. And, as we have mentioned, these computational projects may not be exclusively microcomputer oriented.

Regardless of the size or nature of the project, there are two essentials to achieving active and effective end-user involvement:

- Easy to use software packages that support user needs and interests.
- A managerial climate that encourages and supports end-user computing.

User friendly packages first appeared in the main-frame environment. Many of these were, and are, data base oriented in that they facilitate information retrieval and analysis by end users of data maintained at the information center. In some cases, these data bases contain the official records of the company, for example, customer account information included in a marketing data base. In other instances, data bases have been created specifically for usage by individuals or groups of end users, and in still other instances the end users actually create the data base, either supplying information that they themselves have generated or extracting data from larger company maintained data files.

Information creation, retrieval and display are but a few of the user support functions that can be facilitated by the IRC. Modeling is another important area. Here, the user is assisted in constructing his own simulation model or using a general purpose simulator for problem solving. Modeling has long been a mainstay of problem solving using large mainframe facilities. Under the IRC approach, the interaction with the model is direct and immediate without the assistance of technical specialists for the most part. The microcomputer based spreadsheet packages so prevelant today offer a form of modeling capability. Here, users enter a variety of accounting, financial or other quantitative data and by varying the parameters and giving computational and manipulative input instructions to the spreadsheet packages, they get answers on an assortment of 'what if' questions.

But no matter how up to date the hardware, and no matter how powerful the software packages made available, most end users cannot achieve a desirable level of proficiency if left strictly on their own. The information resource center must offer not only hardware and software but must provide expert and sympathetic technical assistance. One or more highly personable and proficient technical staff people must either be hired for the IRC or must be reassigned from other duties.

NEED FOR TECHNICAL SUPPORT PERSONNEL

The assignment of proficient technical support personnel to the IRC is reflective of the second major ingredient needed for success: an organizational and managerial commitment to aid end users in attaining proficiency in systems technology. Hardware and software are simply not enough. No matter how powerful the IRC capabilities or how inviting the work setting, it must be made clear that use of these facilities has the encouragement of top management.

This can be demonstrated in several ways. First, of course, top management must provide material support by making available the facilities, equipment and staff to set up and operate an attractive center. Sometimes, this requires action to overrule the information systems department, as not all IS directors are enthusiastic about encouraging users to begin doing things on their own.

Second, the commitment on the part of top management must be highly visible. A letter from the CEO to all employees announcing the opening and availability of the center is a good expression of support. Having the company president and vice presidents participate in a 'grand opening' of the center is another good device.

Beyond the fanfare of an initial opening announcement, top management could provide a role model for other managers by visiting the IRC and personally using its facilities.

If management genuinely believes that there is a payout in end-user computing, both by enhancing individual productivity and by relieving the developmental workload of the IS staff, this attitude must be demonstrated. Some benefit will come of simply setting up an IRC and adopting an 'open for business' approach, but the truly successful information resource centers must be actively 'marketed' throughtout the organization.

To summarize, the IRC concept has evolved through two distinct, though not incompatible, phases:

- An effort to deal with mainframe processing bottlenecks.
- An effort to demonstrate and train end users in microcomputers.

In an era in which personal computers are being used both in stand alone mode and at least part of the time as intelligent terminals on-line to a remote computer, these two objectives can be quite powerfully complementary.

4. STRATEGIC MIS: PROMISES UNFULFILLED*

Dr. Andrew C. Rucks and Peter M. Ginter

In the last decade there was substantial growth in the use of computers to aid business management decision-making. Computer based management information systems (MIS) have been designed to help managers assimilate information in order to respond to increasingly dynamic and complex environments. More specifically, recent advances in hardware and software technology have improved information processing capacity, provided more thorough situational analysis capability, and provided solutions for many complex, but well structured, tactical problems. For instance, a computer based MIS can easily identify project slippages, cost over-runs, personnel requirements and measures of product quality.[1]

With the introduction of business application oriented data base management systems (DMBS) and distributed data processing systems (DDPS), a wealth of information became available to managers. Yet, even with these advances in MIS technology, the predictions of computer based strategic decision-making systems made in the 1960s and 1970s remain largely unfulfilled.[2] While the current literature provides many examples of the application of computers in 'strategic management' and makes suggestions for future use, the level of decision making typically discussed is tactical (operational) in nature.[3,4] It is therefore the intent of this paper to briefly discuss the nature of strategic management, delineate the limited use of computer based MIS and review the major factors contributing to the limited development of software models of strategic management decision making.

* *Reprinted from: JOURNAL OF SYSTEMS MANAGEMENT, MARCH 1982.*

Andrew C. Rucks is Assistant Professor of Data Processing and Quantitative Analysis at the University of Arkansas. He holds a Ph.D. degree from North Texas State University. Dr. Rucks served four years in the U.S. Army with the U.S. Army Concepts Analysis Agency. Prior to joining the University of Arkansas, Dr. Rucks was employed by Auburn University. His research interests include management information systems, business strategy and policy, computer system acquisition and system simulation.

Peter M. Ginter is Associate Professor of Management at the University of Arkansas. He is involved in teaching, research and writing in the fields of organization theory, business policy, and marketing. He has published in such journals as the California Management Review, Business, Environmental Science and Technology, and Bulletin of Business Research, Prior to coming to the University of Arkansas, Dr. Ginter taught at North Texas State University and worked as a cost analyst for South Central Bell Telephone Company in Birmingham, Alabama.

While strategy has been variously defined, the following definition encompasses all of the generally accepted frameworks. Strategy is '. . .the process of deciding the basic mission of a company, the objectives which it seeks to achieve and the major policies governing the use of resources at the disposal of the firm to achieve its objectives.'[5]

The need for strategic management and its major component, strategic planning, in business organizations is widely accepted. The rationale underlying the installation of formal strategic management systems in organizations is simple and logical – in order to survive and prosper in a highly competitive and changing environment, every organization must develop and maintain an acceptable alignment with its environment. Environmental alignment is guided by an explicit strategy and provides integration for internal operations.[6] Moreover, a majority of management theorists and practitioners relate the process of strategy formulation to organizational performance.[7,8] While the need for strategic management has been recognized, how it is accomplished is subject to wider debate.

MIS PROMISES UNFULFILLED

In the 1960s and 1970s managerial expectations for MIS were inflated by advocates of this developing discipline. Managers were convinced that data processing could be transformed into information processing and the resulting MIS would satisfy all of their informational needs. For instance, Dearden observed that management expected 'to have in each executive's office a remote computer with a data base containing all of the relevant information in the company'.[9] By the mid-1970s top management was to be receiving substantial assistance from computers in strategic decision making.[10]

This expectation was not realized. What occurred was a broadening of tactical applications and limited development in the sphere of top management decision-making systems.[11] Operational level support was expanded beyond accounting systems to include material requirements planning (MRP), traffic routing, word processing and physical facilities management.[12] While computer assistance at the operational level has made a major contribution to the productivity of firms, in many cases it may have diverted resources from the development of strategic decision-making systems.

IMPEDIMENTS TO SMIS DEVELOPMENT

While MIS applications have remained operational in nature, there continues to be interest in SMIS development. Top managers, operating in complex and dynamic environments, increasingly are calling for strategic decision-making support. According to a Citicorp official, today's top executives need what top executives have always needed: 'Exactly enough of the most relevant information at precisely the right moment to produce an infallible management decision. . .'[13] Unfortunately there are some impediments to SMIS development. Major among these obstacles are: (1)

organizational structural deficiencies; (2) management – data processing personnel communication problems; and (3) strategic-management model deficiencies.

ORGANIZATIONAL STRUCTURAL DEFICIENCIES

The formal relationships established through organizational structure serve to direct and, yet, delimit the range and scope of organizational activities. The data processing (DP) function has traditionally been located within the accounting department. During the infancy of data processing, this organizational alignment was logical because the majority of early DP applications supported the accounting function. However, the placement of the DP function within the accounting department restricted applications to operational-level problems.

As the organizational significance of data processing became apparent, many organizations created separate DP departments.[14] This organizational evolution broadened computer applications to other functional areas but the scope of the data processing function remained unchanged.

Distributed data processing systems are the newest trend in organizing the DP function. DDPS shift operational responsibility for DP from an organization's central administration to its divisional elements. Under this DDPS philosophy, a centralized information systems unit controls the distributed (divisional) systems and provides specialized programming support for users.[15] While DDPS provides many organizational benefits (e.g. lower data communication costs, increased access to DP facilities, greater satisfaction of local DP needs), it too works against SMIS development. Each node of a DDPS exhibits a natural tendency to concentrate on local problem solving rather than organizational strategy model development. Until a corporate element is established with explicit SMIS responsibilities, MIS applications development will remain tactical in nature.

MANAGEMENT – DP PERSONNEL COMMUNICATION PROBLEMS

The literature is replete with references to the existence of communication problems between management personnel and DP personnel.[16,17] Communication problems are often caused by dissimilar educational backgrounds and a resultant lack of knowledge regarding the content and context of one another's jobs.[18,19] Top managers are concerned with long-range, external variables and must function in an unstable, unpredictable and political environment, while DP personnel are subject to short-range, internal variables and operate in buffered, stable and largely apolitical surroundings. Therefore, managers often leave system designers and programmers to operate in an ad hoc manner. Such managerial negligence results in a Gresham's Law of computing – easy to develop applications drive out the difficult to develop ones.[20] Without cross training (DP personnel trained in management skills, management personnel trained in DP, systems analysis and design) to provide mutual understanding, SMIS development is rather improbable.[21,22]

BUSINESS STRATEGIC MANAGEMENT MODEL DEFICIENCIES

Comprehensive strategy models tend to be extremely complex. As suggested above, normative or rational approaches to strategy suggest that strategy is explicit, developed consciously and purposefully, and is made in advance of strategic decisions. However there is considerable evidence suggesting that strategic management processes are not well-defined, logical and explicit. Rather, strategies may be unintended, incremental, and political.[23,24,25,26,27] Simple, normative, anecdotal models, while providing conceptual anchors for hypothesis formulation, may not reflect reality.

The organizational strategist (typically the chief executive officer) must concurrently consider the impact of a variety of interrelated external environmental forces and correctly assess organizational strengths and weaknesses. These analyses must culminate in the forging of a distinct, meaningful and preservable competitive advantage which then must be effectively and efficiently implemented.[28] Additionally, these activities are subject to the vagaries of the decision maker's value system and frame of reference.[29]

Given the highly contingent nature of strategic management, it is no wonder that there is considerable criticism of the generally available models of business strategy formulation. These models, predominantly flow diagram type models, are conceptually appealing, but far too simplistic to provide the necessary and sufficient basis for the development of a computer-based strategic decision-making system. Some scholars believe genuine strategic decision models of the firm are not possible.[30] Popular attempts to build such models in order to train potential managers currently reflect this belief.[31]

However, there has been some progress in the development of SMIS and related strategic scenario ('What if?') decision-making models. For instance, methodologies are emerging for dealing with illstructured, complex problems;[32,33] greater sophistication can be seen in the utilization of the computer at the strategic level,[34] requirements for developing an effective SMIS have been delineated,[35] and design of computer-based planning systems has been undertaken.[36] Unfortunately most of these efforts have been piece-meal in nature.

CONCLUSIONS

Human nature causes decision makers to seek the simplest possible solution for even the most complex problems. In this regard, it has been assumed that the answer to the strategic decision-making conundrum is somewhere embedded in the myriad of data gathered in efforts to know all there is to know about problems of strategy. The ability of computers to process vast amounts of data fostered hope that the environment of strategic decision making could be simplified. This hope has continually generated promises from MIS professionals that the development of computer based SMIS is imminent. Perhaps because of the pressures from all levels of business or because of the squishy nature of strategic decisions, SMIS development has not progressed to the extent that it can be applied to the 'What if?' questions often posed by strategy formulators. Ultimately the usefulness of SMIS can only be measured by the degree of success perceived through application.

REFERENCES

1. N. Statland, 'Information Processing: Fact, Fiction and Future', Data Processor, 8: February, 1966, pp. 20–23.
2. C. Litecky, 'Corporate Strategy: MIS', Journal of Systems Management, 32: 1981, pp. 36–39.
3. P. Kingston, 'Generic Decision Support Systems', Managerial Planning, 29: 1981, pp. 7–11.
4. M. S. Morton, 'Perspectives in Computerized Management Decision Making Systems', COMPSAC Proceedings, 1977.
5. G. A. Steiner, 'Top Management Planning', London: Macmillan Co., 1969, p. 513.
6. C. C. Snow and D. C. Hambrick, 'Measuring Organizational Strategies: Some Theoretical and Methodological Problems', Academy of Management Review, 5: 1980, pp. 527–538.
7. P. F. Drucker, 'Management: Tasks, Responsibilities, Practices', New York: Harper & Row, 1974.
8. D. R. Wood and R. L. LaForge, 'The Impact of Comprehensive Planning of Financial Performance', Academy of Management Journal, 22: 1979, pp. 516–526.
9. J. Dearden, 'Myth of Real-Time Management Information', Harvard Business Review, 44: May-June 1966, p. 123.
10. R. H. Brady, 'Computers in Top-Level Decision Making', Harvard Business Review, July-August 1967, pp. 67–76.
11. 'Computer Support for Managers', EDP Analyzer, 17: May 1979, pp. 1–13.
12. M. E. Walsh, 'MIS – Where Are We, How Did We Get Here and Where Are We Going', Journal of Systems Management, Nov. 1978, pp. 6–21.
13. 'What Does a Corporate President Expect From MIS?', Infosystems, June 1979, p. 27.
14. R. V. Head, 'Systems Organization and the Technology of the Future', Journal of Systems Management, Aug. 1979, pp. 6–11.
15. Ibid.
16. C. J. Bacon, 'Conflict Management in the Systems Environment', Journal of Systems Management, February 1980, pp. 32–37.
17. M. K. McAlister, and S. F. Hallam, 'Bridging the DP Management Communications Gap', Infosystems, March 1980, pp. 92–98.
18. Ibid.

19. Bacon, op. cit.
20. W. S. Anderson, 'The Expectation Gap', Journal of Systems Management, June 1978, pp. 6–10.
21. Bacon, op. cit.
22. R. C. Young, 'A Strategic Overview of Business Information Systems', Managerial Planning, March/April 1980, pp. 28–37.
23. H. Mintzberg, 'Patterns in Strategy Formulation', Management Science, 24: 1978, pp. 934–948.
24. C. E. Lindblom, 'The Science of Muddling Through', Public Administration Review, 19: 1959, pp. 77–88.
25. J. B. Quinn, 'Managing Strategic Change', Sloan Management Review, Summer 1980, pp. 3–20.
26. D. Miller and P. H. Friesen, 'Arche types of Strategy Formulation', Management Science, 24: May, 1978, pp. 921–933.
27. L. Fahey, 'On Strategic Management Decision Processes', Strategic Management Journal, 2: January-March 1981, pp. 43–60.
28. S. E. South, 'Competitive Advantage: The Cornerstone of Strategic Thinking', Journal of Business Strategy, 1: Spring 1981, pp. 15–25.
29. M. A. Lyles, 'Formulating Strategic Problems: Empirical Analysis and Model Development', Strategic Management Journal, 2: 1981, pp. 61–75.
30. Dearden, op. cit.
31. D. L. Eldridge and D. L. Bates, 'The Business Strategy and Policy Game', Dubuque, IA: Wm. C. Brown Company, 1980.
32. H. I. Ansoff, 'Strategic Issue Management', Strategic Management Journal, 1: 1980, pp. 131–148.
33. I. I. Mitroff and R. O. Mason, 'Structuring I11–Structured Policy Issues: Further Exploration in A Methodology for Messy Problems', Strategic Management Journal, 1: Oct.-Dec. 1980, pp. 331–342.
34. R. D. Buzzell and F. D. Wiersema, 'Successful Share-Building Strategies', Harvard Business Review, Jan.-Feb. 1981, pp. 135–144.
35. S. Neumann and M. Hadass, 'DSS and Strategic Decisions', California Management Review, 22: Spring 1980, pp. 77–84.
36. T. H. Naylor, 'Corporate Planning Models', Reading, Mass., Addison-Wesley Publishing Co., 1979.

5. CONTROLLING THE EVOLUTION TOWARD INFORMATION MANAGEMENT*

John R. Vacca

ABSTRACT: The introduction of end-user systems and standalone microcomputers into business organizations can result in a serious loss of control over information resources. DP management must retain control and coordination over these resources to avoid such problems as inadequate systems design by users and duplicate or inaccurate data. This article recommends several strategies for integrating the DP department into the planning of corporate information resource use.

PROBLEMS ADDRESSED

The shift from transaction processing to such user-oriented systems as strategic planning and decision support has decreased the DP manager's ability to influence the management of corporate information. In addition, the information has migrated from the control of the DP department to individual users through the use of standalone microcomputers and purchased software packages. These trends have resulted in several problems that can only be exacerbated by further uncontrolled migration; for example:

- Inadequately trained end-users introducing serious technical errors into the systems
- Redundant information resources
- Fragmented and incomplete information
- Incompatible hardware and software.

A solution to these problems is to establish a policy of integrating corporate information resources. The DP department, with its technical expertise and range of experience, is the prime candidate for assuming control of the integration process.

Such integration ensures that information is used optimally to promote continued growth, competitiveness, and profitability in the increasingly complex business environment in which most organizations are functioning. For successful integration, DP goals and strategies must be structured to match end-user needs and corporate objectives. Achieving this coordination requires implementing the following strategies:

John R. Vacca is a freelance writer and a former data base technician for one of the Western Railroads in Topeka KN. The author is grateful to D. P. Thompson for support of this work and earlier related efforts.

- Adopting new roles
- Developing an information management policy
- Penetrating the organization
- Planning business information
- Extending functions
- Forecasting technological trends.

This article discusses how to apply these strategies to establish a controlled information resource management system.

ADOPTING NEW ROLES

As information needs change, the role of DP management must become flexible enough to accommodate new end-user priorities. The following positions briefly describe emerging DP responsibilities:

- Change agent – Discovers and promotes opportunities for improving the effectiveness of information.
- Coalescence planner – Identifies, coordinates and combines information resources throughout the organization.
- Chief information officer – Establishes corporate information policy, standards and management control over organizational information resources. This is a senior-level position.

DEVELOPING AN INFORMATION MANAGEMENT POLICY

An information management policy should include the development of standards, procedures, protocols and systems that link diverse information resources. The development of standards for distributed processing is a logical place for the information manager to start, because these resources must be coordinated to facilitate consolidation and transmission of information. The DP department should then supervise and manage the distributed processing standards.

DISTRIBUTED PROCESSING STANDARDS

Especially in large organizations, the backlog of major systems in the DP department has encouraged many user departments to purchase microcomputers and minicomputers for small systems requirements. Microcomputer and minicomputer systems are often less expensive to develop than equivalent systems designed to run on mainframes and can be implemented quickly and without senior-level authorization.

DP management must ensure the compatibility and efficiency of these systems.

The timely establishment of distributed processing standards can avoid the problems caused by:

- Multiple computers dedicated to single applications
- Large numbers of special-purpose machines
- Involvement with multiple vendors
- Incompatible software languages and operating systems
- Different – and expensive – maintenance contracts.

An information management policy establishes the ground rules for distributed computer use in the organization. The policy indicates which computers can be acquired, what approvals are necessary, and the standards to which resources must adhere.

A manual of distributed processing standards should be issued to systems users. To ensure that distributed processing resources adhere to corporate long-range plans, are used efficiently, and are adequately protected, the standards should specify:

- DP responsibility for planning and coordinating automation
- Criteria for developing an application for a microcomputer or minicomputer rather than for the central mainframe
- User responsibility for operating and controlling the minicomputers in user areas
- Acceptable vendors
- Hardware and software selection criteria
- Security of physical facilities (i.e., the site and computer media)
- Contract negotiation guidelines
- Data communications network protocols
- Organizational data standards and issues
- Use of such outside resources as time-sharing, service bureau, consultants, and contract programmers
- Systems implementation guidelines.

Once data processing has prepared the standards, the physical plant officer, auditor, security officer and comptroller should review them and make recommendations. The standards should then be tested for adherence to corporate guidelines and, once implemented, can be used to audit distributed sites.

Because the trend toward distributed processing is accelerating, standards governing the acquisition and use of these information resources are increasingly important. Well-written standards help ensure that a fully integrated information network can distribute information to various parts of the organization quickly and easily.

PENETRATING THE ORGANIZATION

Although operations activities traditionally have relied heavily on the DP department, high-level management decisions involving millions of dollars are often made with little or no support from information management resources. Integrating a corporate-wide information strategy includes identifying functions and divisions that are inadequately supported by information management resources. The policy should be to reallocate scarce resources to users with the greatest potential contribution to corporate performance. Several penetration strategies can help identify underserviced departments and convince them of the benefits of using data processing.

The first step is to transfer systems personnel to departments in which the application of systems technology has met a lack of interest or resistance. Instead of senior management forcing these departments to automate, the systems expert should present DP services as a risk-free experiment to improve ongoing information management practices. Target divisional managers can usually be convinced to add a resident systems specialist to the staff if the strategy is supported by senior management.

The information specialist can assume direct line-management responsibility or supervise systems planning for that department. The initial projects should be small enough to implement and learn quickly, thus gaining early departmental support for the efforts. Once users in the department begin to work with the systems specialist, their resistance to DP concepts decreases. The implementation of a successful system – no matter how small – further enhances user perceptions of technology. Identifying these departments and training them in the use of information resources is also advantageous for DP management because new users are inoculated with a sense of corporatewide data resources from the initial experience with the technology.

BUSINESS INFORMATION PLANNING

Because information managers are not always involved in corporate planning, a practical alternative is to plan business information systems with user management. The DP department can work with the users to identify new applications of systems solutions to business problems by using a structured planning strategy. Users assign priorities to systems requirements, and DP provides ongoing systems support to user business plans. Eventually, the business information planning group moves from short-term, high-priority project identification with user departments to long-range planning at the corporate level.

Business information planning combines top-down analysis and bottom-up development strategies. Top-down analysis includes:

- Identifying needs through executive interviews
- Defining priorities by ranking systems in terms of such criteria as return on investment
- Determining systems support availability.

Bottom-up development includes:

- Identifying information data base needs
- Developing systems solutions
- Establishing implementation goals (e.g., scheduling and staffing requirements).

The basic steps of business information planning are to:

- Determine the scope of the project

- Select users and DP staff members to determine the magnitude of systems backlog, adequacy of current information management resources, and priorities for backlogged projects
- Identify new project opportunities by determining user business needs and urgent priorities
- Rank systems requirements, including basic descriptions and preliminary cost/benefit analyses
- Obtain approval of systems studies
- Plan the next level of systems needs.

The establishment of a long-range plan for evolving toward information management and a short-range plan for implementing the highest-priority systems first are the main objectives of business information planning. This function, however, is active in the planning phase only; its relationship to development is illustrated in Figure 1. Business information planning activities constitute 10 percent of a total systems project; the remainder is used by the development group once a first-draft project definition has been completed.

Ideally, the members of the business information planning group should understand both computer technology and business needs. The planning staff should strive to move from reactive to proactive planning activities (see Figure 2).

The first phase of business information planning meets new regulations and other requirements at the reactive end of the scale. Rewriting obsolescent systems is the next step. Emulating successful new systems installed in other organizations is proactive but does not involve users or senior management. User input results in a list of ranked

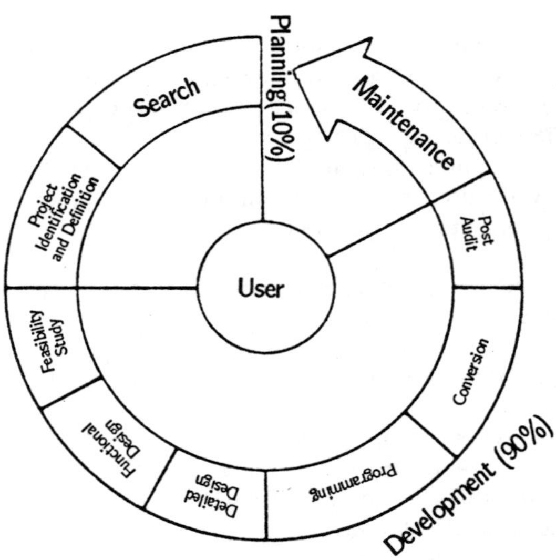

Figure 1. Project Life Cycle for Business Information Planning

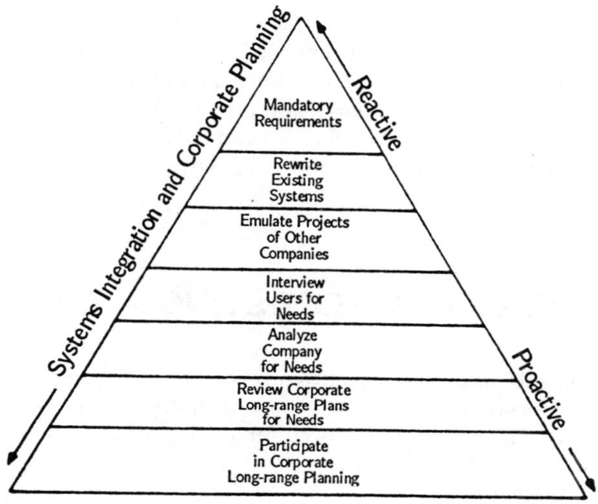

Figure 2. Project Identification Approaches for Business Information Planning

requirements, which provides a more structured and manageable method of planning information systems.

Financial, trends, and environmental analyses constitute the next stage of project identification. Higher-level staff support functions (e.g., the finance division of corporate planning) are required to coordinate long-range organizational plans. Senior management is needed to collaborate in formalizing long-range corporate plans and systems support requirements. At this point, information resource management has achieved full integration.

The business information planning function should be treated as a corporate research group whose time is charged to corporate overhead – not to the user. Users who may otherwise be reluctant to pay internal consulting charges are thus encouraged to use the research group to plan business systems. If implemented properly, a business information planning group can foster close user relations as well as excellent systems planning.

FUNCTION EXTENSION

Extending the information management function can be quickly achieved by incorporating the existing information resources in one larger department. For example, telecommunications and office information systems are excellent candidates for incorporation into an information management department because their technologies and applications are currently converging. The DP department should serve as the core of this new service because it involves several information management disciplines – computers, communications, systems and information processing.

Creating new opportunities for automated products and services can extend the information management function. Imagination and planning are requirements of this approach. Technological forecasting is another effective source for developing ideas and opportunities.

TECHNOLOGICAL FORECASTING

Anticipating the impact of technological trends on the organization is crucial to the corporate planning process and protects the organization from obsolescence and competitive inroads. The following five-step forecasting strategy is recommended:

- Identify key technological trends.
- Analyze impact on industry.
- Analyze impact on organization.
- Identify the information manager's role as a change agent.
- Develop appropriate strategy.

The current trend toward electronic banking provides an example of technological forecasting.

TREND ANALYSIS

In 1979, more than 40 billion checks were processed annually by the U.S. banking systems. Electronic funds transfer systems (EFTS) were developed to reduce annual check volume and improve customer service and bank efficiency. EFTS, however, is only part of a broader trend toward electronic banking, which incorporates the following key technological trends:

- Electronic money cards
- Funds transfer systems
- Automated clearinghouses
- Automated tellers
- Home banking.

INDUSTRY IMPACT

The success of electronic money cards and bank credit cards may soon lead to debit cards, which can substitute for checks, withdrawal orders, standing orders, etc. Full-transaction electronic money cards may emerge from the credit and debit cards; some companies already provide customers with money services usually available in a bank. The banking industry has therefore increased automated customer service and concentrated its personal services on large depositors. To accelerate processing transfers, banks have also upgraded their in-house services (e.g., switching from paper-tape to electronic systems).

ORGANIZATIONAL IMPACT

Although the impact of technology on a bank varies depending on competition and management goals, many leading banks are moving aggressively in the following areas:

- Electronic money cards
- Terminals in retail outlets for routine banking transactions
- Minicomputer-based money-transfer systems for domestic and international corporate funds
- Bank-at-home services.

INFORMATION MANAGEMENT'S ROLE AS CHANGE AGENT

An appropriate role for information management is as a developer of electronic banking systems. The information management department and business information planning group should show tangible benefits of electronic banking systems, including:

- Increased productivity
- Lowered costs
- Improved customer service
- Greater market share
- Clear competitive advantage.

STRATEGY DEVELOPMENT

Two strategies are appropriate in the current banking environment: support of self-service banking systems and integration of diverse electronic banking systems. Self-service banking reduces labor costs and increases productivity while providing the convenience customers demand. Because customers view banking as a package of financial services, integration of diverse systems is needed. Banking services should be consistent at all branches, subsidiaries, and international offices. Standardization, compatibility and consistency can be ensured by building these systems under a coordinated master plan.

Figure 3 outlines the process for technological forecasting and trend analysis.

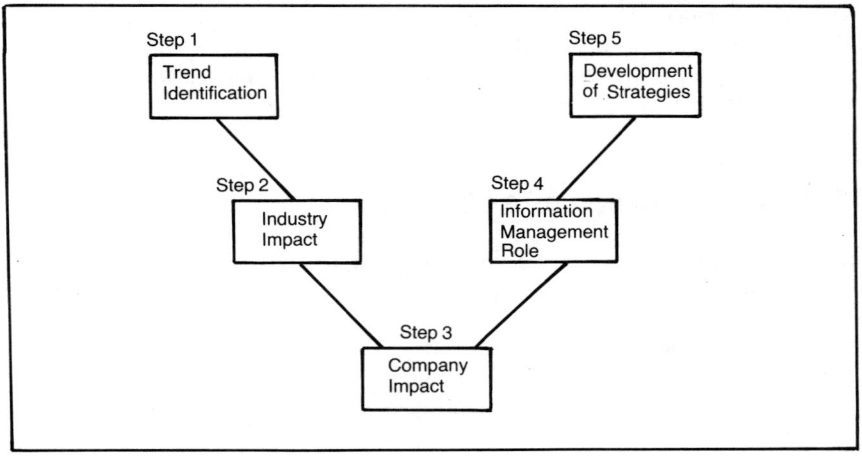

Figure 3. Technological Forecasting

RECOMMENDED COURSE OF ACTION

Information resources should be managed jointly by the information management department and users. The key to the success of a systems project is user involvement, especially in an environment of distributed information resources. On the other hand, the DP department cannot afford to surrender control of vital corporate resources to inexperienced users.

Two strategies are recommended to effect shared management of information resources. First, users should not need to become DP experts; shared management of dedicated information resources should give them the access needed. Second, users must be involved in systems planning, development, and implementation. This involvement can be achieved through the business information planning group.

If DP is to evolve into a more influential information management role, DP personnel must learn the organization's business to select and present useful information concerning corporate priorities, goals, and competition. Staff members therefore must become business managers first and information professionals second. Technical personnel who have never been exposed to management courses and techniques should:

- Complete management courses (e.g., corporate finance, marketing, organizational behavior and development, personnel management, effective communications).
- Study management styles and techniques.

• Learn how to make effective presentations.

The information manager should work toward becoming the chief information officer – not the chief DP officer. The information manager should educate management to view corporate information as a resource that must be coordinated and managed, and requires technological and user integration, but which must remain the domain of the information manager.

The information manager should build systems for senior managers as well as clerks. Chief executives are more likely to support and cooperate with DP when directly benefiting from DP services.

REFERENCES

1. *Business Week*. 'The New Planning: Computer Games that Planners Play.' (December 18, 1978): 66.
2. S. M. Davis, *Matrix*. Reading MA: Addison-Wesley, 1978.
3. P. F. Drucker, *Managing In Turbulent Times*. New York: Harper & Row, 1980.
4. ——. *Management: Tasks, Responsibilities, Practices*. New York: Harper & Row, 1974.
5. C. W. Getz, 'Coalescence: The Inevitable Fate of Data Processing.' *MIS Quarterly* (June 1977): 28.
6. P. G. Keen, *Decision Support Systems: An Organizational Perspective*. Reading MA: Addison-Wesley, 1978.
7. E. R. McLean, *Strategic Planning for MIS*. New York: John Wiley and Sons, 1977.
8. R. L. Nolan, 'Business Needs a New Breed of EDP Manager.' *Harvard Business Review* (March-April 1976): 123–133.
9. J. F. Rockart, 'Chief Executives Define Their Own Data Needs.' *Harvard Business Review* (March-April 1979): 81–93.
10. W. R. Synnott, 'Strategic Planning for Information Management Effectiveness.' *Infosystems* (October 1979): 70–82.
11. ——. 'Total Customer Relationship.' MIS Quarterty (September 1978): 16.
12. Umbaugh, R. 'EDP Managers Put on Business Suits.' Fortune (November 6, 1978): 69.

CHAPTER II

MANAGING INFORMATION

INTRODUCTION

Managing Information

Robert D. Galliers

Chapter I identified some key trends and issues associated with the introduction and utilization of information systems in organisations and concluded that managing information as a resource has perhaps emerged as the key issue facing organisations in the 1980s. Chapter II discusses information management in some detail, identifying some of the major issues and problems associated with this aspect of our topic.

A problem that immediately presents itself when attempting to provide effective information systems to support managerial activity, is the constantly changing nature of management's information requirements. The first paper in this chapter provides a discussion of the problems associated with the temporal quality of information. It introduces the concept of 'forecasting horizon' when proposing a means by which information systems can be developed in such a way as to become more adaptable and flexible in the face of changing information requirements.

It has also become evident that it is appropriate to regard information as a resource, requiring proper management, in much the same way as other organisation resources, such as personnel and equipment. This is a theme taken up by both the second and third papers in this chapter. The former notes that because management information systems (MIS), as traditionally conceived, did not provide the necessary tools for the adequate management of the information resource, it became necessary for a transition in thinking to take place, from an era concerned primarily with the technical aspects of MIS design, to one which is conerned with managing the information resource in the organisational context.

This realisation, combined with the often-experienced situation, whereby organisations are faced with a reduction in productivity within the information systems function and a concurrent increase in demand for an increasingly wide range of information systems services, has led to the view, expressed in the third paper of this chapter, that information should be managed as a corporate asset. Rather than perceiving corporate information requirements as being divided into various vertical application areas, the asset management approach suggests a horizontal structure, comprising the acquisition, storage, manipulation, retrieval and distribution of data and the development of strategic information units. These are designed to provide information which would cut across more traditional application area boundaries.

Another aspect of information management which has been increasingly recognised as the current decade has progressed, is the need to plan for the adequate provision of information and for the acquisition of appropriate information technology and associated resources. Information Systems Planning is not a trivial activity and requires a range of skills and expertise. The final paper summarises the results of a research survey undertaken in the United Kingdom into the range of approaches to information systems planning that are being attempted and the impact of these efforts on the ability of organisations to manage their information resources.

1. ADAPTING TO CHANGING USER REQUIREMENTS*

Frank F. Land

ABSTRACT: Systems which have the capability of adapting to changing user requirements must be founded on accurate and perceptive models of the organisation in which they have to function. Design methods based on active user participation and the use of experimental and prototyping methods help to ensure accurate models. But because systems are expected to survive even when circumstances change, the designers have to have a view of what the future world will look like. A technique which helps to provide such a view is called '*future analysis*'. However, even designs based on the best prediction technique cannot guarantee a fit between the currently designed systems and future needs. Hence it is important to design systems with built-in flexibility. A number of methods have been developed which reduce the disruption caused by the amendment or even replacement of a system or system's component.

INTRODUCTION

Information Systems have to operate in a turbulent, dynamic world. Despite the common view about people – that they are conservative, that they dislike innovation and react adversely to the prospect of change – people as processors of information have a very high capacity to adapt to changing circumstances. Information systems based on manual processing have shown themselves to have a considerable degree of flexibility, and, where it has proved necessary, have adjusted rapidly to changing needs. Manual systems have also shown the capacity to evolve through time, but without the kind of disruption and high and costly use of resources observed when computer systems have been subjected to unforeseen changes.

* *Reprinted from: © North-Holland Publishing Company, Information & Management 5 (1982) 59–75*
A version of this paper was prepared for the 'Infotech' State of the Art Report 'Life Cycle Management' 1980.

Frank Land is Professor of Information Systems at the London Business School. After graduating in Economics from the London School of Economics he joined the group working on the LEO Computers in 1953. He remained with the group as programmer, systems analyst, consultant and marketing manager until 1967, when he returned to the London School of Economics. The NCC had awarded the School a grant to establish teaching and research in Systems Analysis, and the school invited Frank Land to join them. There he was responsible for setting up undergraduate and graduate courses and establishing a research group developing methods for systems analysis. In 1986 he joined the London Business School. Frank Land is active in the British Computer Society and IFIP.

Computer based systems are inherently less flexible. It follows from the way computers have to be programmed, that any change which involves a change to the program requires an elaborate sequence of steps to be taken which can be time consuming, costly, and disruptive. Indeed, some changes, even changes which appear trivial to the non-expert user, cannot be incorporated in the system without a substantial redesign of the computerised parts of the system. Hence, the standard model of a computer application postulates a systems or application life cycle.

A project is conceived, requirements are analysed, feasibility is established, a series of design are conceived and embodied in specifications, hardware is selected, the system is constructed and tested and finally implemented. The new system operates until it no longer effectively meets the needs of the organisation, either because new technological opportunities have made the existing technology obsolete, or changing user requirements cannot be satisfied by the existing design. At that point a new system is required, a new system is conceived, and a new life cycle gets under way. Because the life cycle process is costly and disruptive, users and computer professionals have looked for methods:

- of increasing the life of the system by building flexible, changeable software.
- of replacing the life cycle approach of systems implementation by an evolutionary approach more akin to that applicable to manual systems.
- which make the construction of systems less dependent on particular hardware and which make it possible to transfer systems developed on one type of hardware to a different hardware.
- of improving the designer's model of the world in which the system will have to operate by making it a more accurate representation of the real world.
- which provide a systems planning strategy which enables the implemented system to more closely fit the real requirements as revealed when the system begins to be implemented.
- of design and construction which so reduce the cost of these processes, that a system which no longer meets the needs of the organisation can be discarded and rapidly replaced by a new system. The life cycle model is changed to a model based on the concept of expendable, replaceable systems.

In this paper some observations are made on each of the above methods, but the main concentration will be on methods of improving the designer's model of the world in which the system will have to operate. However, before dealing with the various methods, some observations are made on the life cycle model.

TIME AND THE LIFE CYCLE MODEL

The time taken to design, construct and implement a system will depend on the scale of the planned application and the resources available to implement the system. Even quite small systems require substantial time and resources, whilst the implementation of major systems may require a period measured in years. Time cycles ranging from eighteen months to five years are quite common for the period between the start of an information systems project and bringing the system into operational use. Large scale systems, such as those found in public administration or defence, may take much longer that that, and implementation times exceeding ten years are not unknown.

The life cycle is illustrated by Fig. 1 [19].

A major system may take three years to design, program, test and implement. After a further five years of systems operation it becomes apparent that the system no longer effectively meets the needs of the organisation, despite the fact that a great deal of resources have been devoted to maintain the system in an attempt to keep it viable. However it takes a further two years to develop a new system to replace the first system. The system which was conceived at time A therefore has to meet the requirements of the organisation not only as far as time B–three years after the project was initiated – but also at time C–eight years after initiation – and at time D–ten years later. In other words, those who design the system must be capable of either foreseeing the needs of the organisation ten years later, or of designing the system so flexibly that it can meet unforeseen needs for an operational life of seven years (B → D).

A computer based system, unlike a manual system, is normally planned on the basis of an expected life span. The system's designers estimate the resources and time needed to develop and implement the application. Often the expected operational life of the system is determined by economic (or accounting) considerations, rather than

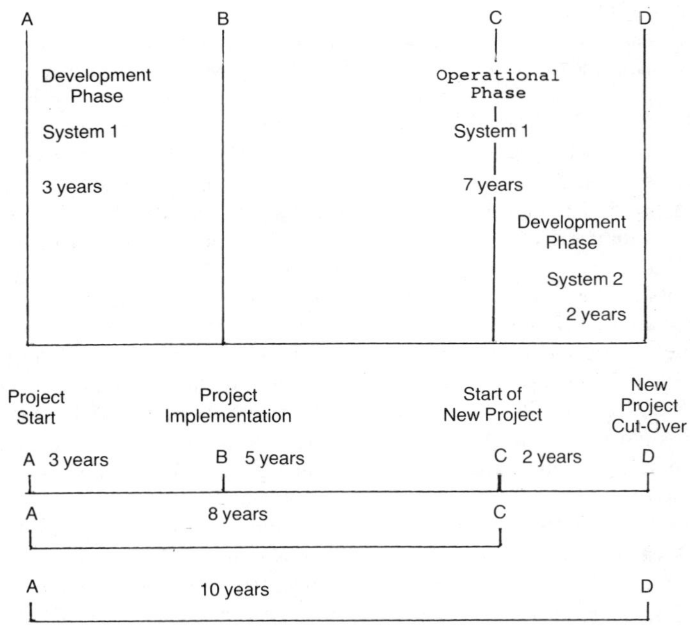

Figure 1. Application life cycle.

by technical or organisational factors. To recover the cost of development and to cover the costs of operating the system while providing an adequate return on the capital employed, the system has normally to have an operational life of several years. If it is expected to cost $\$x$ to develop the system, and $\$y$ per year to operate it, and the expected net annual return is $\$z-\$y$, then the life of the system has to be t years to return r, the required earning on capital invested, taking account of the cost of money and the rate of inflation.

If, as frequently happens, the development costs turn out higher than expected, and the tangible net benefit turns out to be somewhat below expectations, the hoped for life of the system is raised, without regard to technical or organisational factors. For example, a well known large scale application had its life extended to seventeen years in order to provide reasonable looking annual returns on capital employed! In practice, there is little chance of the system in question surviving for anything like that time.

Because it is inherently impossible to build a completely flexible, completely portable system capable of coping with any change, the system's planners have to define in some way the extent of change it is possible to accommodate. The further the planners look into the future, the more they are faced with uncertainty regarding the changes and their potential impact on the system. At some time in the future, the uncertainty becomes so great that the system's designers cannot conceive of any design that can cope with the possible range of requirements at a permissible cost. This is the *forecasting horizon*.

In practice, the forecasting horizon will vary from organisation to organisation and will be different for different applications. Some will be less affected by changes, whether they stem from circumstances outside the organisation, or from changes within. The forecasting horizon may vary in different time periods or epochs. At times of rapid technological change, such as the current period with the widespread availability of microcomputers and computer communications technology, the forecasting horizon is closer to the present than at times of greater technological stability. A similar effect is noted in times of economic or political turbulence.

One determinant of the forecasting horizon is the expectation of changed requirements of the system, together with uncertainty regarding these changes. The other important determinant is the extent to which the designer can build in flexibility. At any time, the designer has only a certain number of techniques and tools available at reasonable cost. It is generally cheaper to build a dedicated, highly specific system than a generalised, flexible one. It is, however, worth noting that a more general purchased application package may be cheaper for an individual user than a dedicated, tailor-made system. The higher costs of producing the generalised package is spread over a number of purchasers.

Because of limitations in the tools and techniques, it is not possible to design systems which provide infinite flexibility. This is illustrated in Fig. 2.

Here, line AB represents the technical possibilities of building flexibility into a system. Above the line it is not possible to provide further flexibility, at least at reasonable cost. The line is shown as rising because it can be expected that such techniques will be improved, or be reduced in cost even for systems designed at an earlier time.

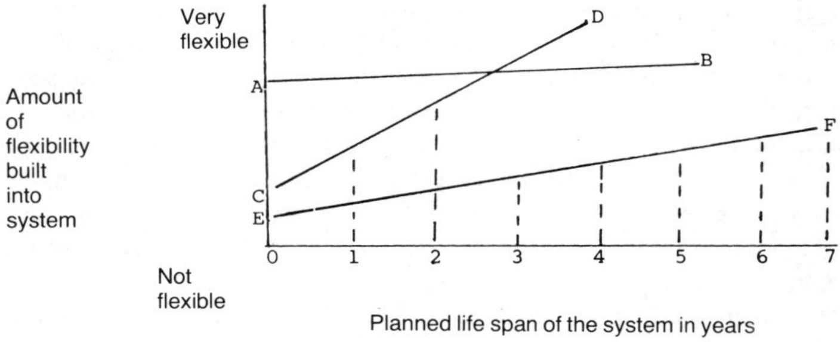

Figure 2. Planned life span of the system in years.

Line CD represents the extent to which flexibility has to be built into a particular system to meet unforeseen changes in requirements. The system is one which exists in a changing, uncertain environment. Given the available technical/cost possibilities, the system runs out of flexibility options in just under three years. For this application, the forecasting horizon is less than three years beyond the present.

Line EF represents the amount of flexibility needed to achieve different life spans for an application existing in a much more stable, predictable environment. The forecasting horizon for the system lies beyond seven years, and is therefore not an important factor in determining the *planning horizon* for the system.

For all applications, the systems designers have to decide on the life span targetted for, and the extent to which the system should have flexibility. As a general rule, the planning horizon should fall within the forecasting horizon.

THE DESIGNER'S MODEL OF THE REAL WORLD

A system's designer designing a computer based information system, has to provide the system's constructors – the programmers – with a model of the system they must implement. The model is embodied in the system's specification which depicts the designer's understanding of the functional activities, data structures, information flows, and decision processes. By implication, it also mirrors the analyst's conception of how the users behave and will behave given the new system. To enable the programmers and those responsible for the planning of the manual procedures to develop an efficient system, the model is supported with a range of statistical information – activity rates, volumes, distributions of peaks and troughs, seasonal trends, response requirements, etc. The model then is made up of assumptions about behaviour, statistical facts, and information about the organisation derived from the process of systems analysis.

If the analysis process yields accurate data, (i.e., data which portrays the state of the real world with precision), the designer has a good chance of constructing a realistic model of the organisation and its requirements – at least, as it is at the time the analysis was carried out. But even the best model based on an analysis of the state of the organisation as it is now and incorporating the view of the future as seen by the management at this point of time, loses precision when it has to predict the state of the organisation in two or three years, and even more so when the model is expected to provide the basis for the construction of a system which has to survive for many years.

The first task is to adopt better methods for modelling the present set of user requirements. The standard methods for creating the model are based on four common techniques of analysis:

i) Interviewing members of the user community to establish the requirements of the new system and the 'facts' about the existing system.
ii) Carrying out surveys by questionaire to establish the same information as by interview.
iii) Observing the system in operation to find out how it works and to measure specific attributes of the system, such as the size and duration of queues at peak times.
iv) Studying documentation and procedure manuals relating to the system in order to discover the formal rules which govern the operations of the system.

Using these techniques, the analyst/designer builds up a picture of the system in present use and defines the requirements for the operation of the future system. Most systems analysts recognise that at least some members of the user community are not totally neutral with regard to replacement of the existing system with a new one – some may be expected to resist change, whilst others may desire change simply because it may increase their own power or status. Whatever bias they have is bound to colour their responses to the analysis process. Hence good analysts attempt to validate their model by cross checking, for example by interviewing more members of the user community and using observation as a check on responses to surveys or interviews.

But a major hidden assumption of the conventional analysis process is that the analyst is neutral. Studies by Hedberg in Sweden and Mumford in the U.K. [14] have shown that this is not so. They found that many professional D.P. people have beliefs and values which significantly affect the way they set about the analysis process, which distort their model of what the real world is like, and which influences the designs they prefer. The studies show that systems analysts tend to think of organisations and of information systems in terms of scientific rationality and in terms of engineering principles. They tend to describe an information system as an information providing machine (see for example the extensive literature on MIS) and think therefore that improvements to the machine can best be achieved by the application of further technology. As a result, they tend to neglect the social and behavioural factors which in practice are often most important in distinguishing between effective and less effective organisations or systems.

Checkland [6] defines such systems as '*Human Activity Systems*', and has developed a methodology of analysis and design based on the recognition that the different participants working within, or in association with, the system view the system from a different perspective and, as a result, have a different understanding of the system and different expectations and objectives. Sir Geoffrey Vickers [31] vividly describes the different perspectives, when he describes a school as a system for educating children as viewed from the perspective of a teacher, but as a system for generating sewage when viewed from the perspective of a sanitary engineer.

Dew and Gee [10] showed in a study of the way managers described existing management information systems, that there was a very wide divergence between different managers of the same organisation as to the purpose of the system. Middle managers tended to believe that a budgetary control system designed to give them information on budget variances in order for them to take action, had been designed to give more senior management control over them. Senior management tended to assume that the function of the system was to help middle management take action. Even amongst managers of the same level there were wide divergences in ranking the most important attributes of the system.

Argyris and Schon [1], in the course of comparing managers' statements relating to their activities, with observed behaviour of the same managers, found wide discrepancies. Managers may say that they take action on the basis of an 'espoused' decision process with the help of specified information. In practice, they take decisions in a very different way, using perhaps different information. The implications for the systems analyst are far reaching. To the extent that the analyst's model of real behaviour and real requirements is based on what the user tells, the research of Argyris demonstrates that the basis is inadequate and can be very misleading. Unfortunately, the analyst is not helped a great deal by his back-up technique of observation, because it has been shown – the 'Hawthorn effect' – that where the respondent is aware of being observed, normal behaviour is modified for the period of observation.

The analyst faces a further difficulty, revealed by recent research. All organisations function on the basis of a mixture of formalised systems, with defined relationships and roles, specified rules and regulations, clear boundaries and clearly demarcated responsibilities, systematised predictable information sources; and informal systems, with loose relationships and structures, varied often unexpected information sources, informal groupings and alliances and ad hoc processes. The rational scientific ideology, prevalent amongst systems analysts, tends to drive them to reject the informal system in favour of the formal and this attitude is strengthened by the fact that the technology, which is their stock-in-trade, can only cope with systems based on rules. As a result, systems designed for computers tend to strip away the informal element in systems and retain only the formalisable, programmable aspects.

Earl and Hopwood [11] and Mintzberg [21] report on research findings which suggest that organisations which rely on a significant level of informal systems, out-perform organisations which have attempted to replace the informal by formal. These findings are supported by studies carried out by Burke and George [5] on a large sample of Canadian managers, which indicated that where managers have the possibility of using a computer-based MIS, they tended to prefer to use one of their subordinates as their information source. Any model of user requirements has to take into account the need to preserve the informal element in information systems.

The single, most widely noted problem area identified by surveys which have attempted to find out the extent to which computer-based information systems are regarded as successful by users and DP personnel, is the problem of communication between the user and the DP specialist. An example of such a study is one carried out by the British Computer Society in 1978 [3]. There are many reasons for communication difficulties [18] and some have been referred to above. The most important reasons are:

1) The different ideologies and perspectives of the different interests involved in a systems study. This problem is made worse by the different languages which different professions have developed for communication amongst themselves. This can cause wide variations in interpretations and ultimately distorted models.

2) The uncertainty, on the part of the user, regarding the way the designer operates, and hence what information the designer will need. Often this results in misplaced emphasis and omission of details which are important to the designer but irrelevant or trivial for the user.

3) Uncertainty on the part of the users, regarding the impact the final system will have on their individual roles in the organisation and on them personally. They may doubt their ability to cope with the new system, or fear redundancy, or that their jobs may be deskilled or routinised. These fears can attack managers as well as lower level employees. This can result in a defensive attitude and a deliberate withholding of information from the analyst. Users develop a range of counter-implementation strategies designed to preserve the status quo. Keen [16] outlines the 'games' users play in their attempt to inhibit (or subvert) change. But the most widespread strategy for protecting the user from having to cope with the unknown new system, is the development of unofficial, informal systems.

4) The observation that the user operates with informal systems and that the formal procedure of the existing systems have been overtaken by less formal (but often more effective) unauthorised procedures. Many users will be reluctant to tell enquiring analysts the way they actually work because the analyst is regarded as a representative of authority. The difference between espoused systems and systems in action have also been noted above.

5) The fact that those who are involved in the analysis process – DP specialists and users – are often not aware of strategic decisions made by senior management which could have an important bearing on the workability of the system. Corporate planning is often separated from information systems planning and senior management themselves are not necessarily aware that their corporate decisions are relevant to the design of the information processing system, and for reasons of security and confidentiality, do not make even senior subordinate managers privy to all decisions.

6) The problem facing both users and analyst/designers is, that new systems almost certainly include innovations. This happens, for example, with respect to management reports. The problem is, that neither the user nor the analyst/designer can predict the manager's response to the new style of report. In any case, different managers may respond very differently to the same report, and whilst one manager can become more effective, another manager, equally effective with the old system, will find the new system less useful. Conjectures about peoples' behaviour are no substitute for knowledge and in the case of innovating systems such knowledge is not ordinarily available.

IMPROVING THE DESIGNER'S MODEL OF THE REAL WORLD

The best DP practitioners are aware of the problems referred to above and have developed their own methods of analysis to ensure their designs are based on better models of the real world. But many systems fail to yield expected benefits or may even have to be abandoned long before the end of their expected life span because the designer's model was unrealistic and the communication barrier made it difficult for users and DP professionals to recognise the defects in the model. The fact that the designer has produced a comprehensive specification and that the user has 'signed off' the specification after due study, is not a guarantee that the designer has understood the user's needs, or the user, the designer's specification. There is a need therefore for new approaches to systems analysis and design which enable the designer to create more accurate, more perceptive models of the real world as it is at the time the analysis is performed, and which permit the designer to more reliably model the future.

One such approach is that of Peter Checkland, working in the Lancaster University Systems Department [6]. In the methodology, developed by Checkland, the analyst first searches for alternative 'root' definitions of the system subjected to analysis. The alternative definitions are derived from the different viewpoints of those who have an interest in the system. On the basis of the root definition, conceptual models are created which define the activities necessary for each view of the system to work. The analyst compares the models with each other and with an analysis of what actually exists. Finally, the analyst confronts the different interest groups with their different models and the implication of the differences, and from the resulting debate, attempts to get an agreed, or at least clarified analysis of the situation, and the beginnings of a specification of desirable and feasible changes.

Checkland, his colleagues and students have applied the methodology in a number of situations, and progress of the work is reported in the Journal of Applied Systems Analysis (Vol. 3, No. 2, pages 87–117, 137–148, Vol. 4, No. 1, pages 40–51, Vol. 5, No. 1, pages 75–83, Vol. 6, pages 51–68, Vol. 7, pages 123–130, Vol. 8. pages 101–114).

Particular attention is focussed in this paper on the socio-technical approach and the participative methods associated with it. Like the Checkland method described above, the socio-technical method explicitly recognises the importance of the different interest groups concerned with one system, and the method seeks to discover the social, technical, economic and organisational objectives as perceived by the different groups.

However, the socio-technical approach applied as part of the conventional process of analysis and design carried out by professional specialists cannot overcome some of the major communication problems, vis-avis the user, described earlier. These problems can be eliminated or at least reduced, if, in association with the socio-technical approach, members of the user community at all levels are involved in the analysis, design, evaluation, and implementation of the computer based system, and if they are allowed to take the main responsibility for the system.

Participation in, and responsibility for, design and implementation can result in the elimination or reduction of the problems listed above:

1) By setting up a design team which contains representatives of all the major interest groups, it becomes possible for the different ideologies and perspectives of the participants to be made explicit, and for the different members of the group to learn from each other's different viewpoints. The whole process is enriched by the interaction of the group and results in a far more sensitive and perceptive model of the world.

2) In order to participate in the design process, the user has to learn and become familiar with design methods. As a result, the user is no longer uncertain. The users who are not members of the design team (and it is rare for more than a small proportion of users to be directly concerned with design) must be given the opportunity to learn from their peers on the design team, how the process is cararied out.

3) The user is concerned with the setting of objectives for the system, and is involved in the detailed design work, and the planned redesign of jobs and work organisation called for by the new system. As a result, the uncertainly as to the impact of the system on the user is reduced, as are the defensive strategies thought up by users to thwart the conventional systems designer. Once again the users who participate in the design team have the responsibility to communicate with their colleagues outside the design team. In the conventional design process the designer concentrates his attention on the computer part of the system, and though the new design may change the tasks users have to perform, little attempt is made to change the way the work is organised. With the participation of users in the design team, more attention is paid to work organisation, in an effort to achieve both the efficiency and social goals set for the system.

4) If the users are directly responsible for the design of their own system, they will be less concerned with covering up the use of non-standard procedures and unauthorised short cuts.

5) The problem of senior management security is more difficult to solve. One technique is to involve senior management in a steering group for the new project. The steering group has particular responsibility for setting the global objectives of the system, defines the resources available for the project and the constraints to which the design team have to work. A further role of the group is to act as umpire in the case of conflicts or unresolvable problems in the design team. If senior management are prepared to involve themselves in this way, they become more aware of the possible impact on the system of their strategic decisions.

6) The problem of predicting future behaviour in the context of an innovative information system can only be reduced if the systems design process is seen as experimental. But the users can play an important part in designing and participating in the experiments.

The socio-technical approach was first developed at the Tavistock Institute for Human Relations which saw that a new technology could only be effectively introduced into industry if the designer attempted to integrate the social requirements of those who have to work with the new technology with the economic and technical requirements of the management.

The ideas at the Tavistock in the 1950's have been adopted in many parts of the world, and more recently have began to be used for the design and implementation of DP systems. The socio-technical method has been applied to a number of computer systems projects, for example, in the USA, for example, by Taylor [30], in Italy by De Maio [9] and his team at the Polytechnico of Milan, in the U.K. by Mumford and her colleagues [22], and in Germany by the BIFOA organisation [17].

The importance of the socio-technical method is that it includes the analysis of social requirements in the process of understanding an organisation and its requirements, thus ensuring that the analyst's model has a better chance of reflecting the real needs of the organisation. At the same time, it provides techniques for carrying out the analysis of social requirements, thus giving the designer the opportunity of building a system which addresses itself to meeting social as well as efficiency and economic objectives. Systems which result from such an analysis are likely to be more robust.

Participation techniques are being employed more frequently in the design of computer based systems and a number of interesting cases have been reported [2, 17, 22, 28] from many parts of the world. All these examples encourage the belief that, despite problems and difficulties, the socio-technical approach combined with extensive user participation plays an important role in the design and implementation of better systems. Nevertheless, the approach can only produce satisfactory results if the right tools are available. Such tools and their development are described in several papers [7, 9, 19].

The approaches discussed above provide a sound starting point for the design of systems capable of a long and effective life. The model of an organisation's requirements, derived from these approaches, is likely to yield a design which incorporates more real knowledge of all needs, including the elusive social needs and, as a result, has a better chance of receiving approval and support from all members of the user community, than systems based on the more conventional methods of systems development. But to design systems capable of meeting a wide variety of changing user needs, the designer has to employ other techniques, as well.

CHANGING USER REQUIREMENTS

All planning activities face the problem that, that which is being planned lies in the future, and hence is subject to uncertainty. How can the planner produce a design which is not made irrelevant or obsolete by unforeseen changes in circumstances?

One approach is for the planner to attempt to predict the changes which could occur over the expected life of the system, and which could have an impact on the system in question. Such 'future analysis' is discussed in more detail in the appendix. In this analysis, the design team – aided by coopted 'experts' and using a variety of techniques ranging from 'Delphi' methods and 'brainstorming' to statistical analysis and simulation modelling – identifies the main areas in which change is possible.

One important feature of the analysis is that it tests what the impact of a conceivable change in requirements could have on the system. The designer then has the choice of modifying the design to enable the system to cope with such a change, perhaps by allowing spare file space or by parameterising the relevant algorithm, or if the nature of possible changes is so imprecise that no design strategy can be envisaged which would enable the program to adapt, the designer may decide that the life span for which the program was originally designed has to be reduced.

'The extent of the future analysis would depend on the kind of system under consideration. If the system is central to the organisation's existence, and a failure could imperil the whole enterprise, the future analysis must be very detailed. In such projects as the Apollo Moon shot, the analysis of all possible contingencies was very elaborate indeed' [18].

The principal outcome of the analysis is a list of systems features which are vulnerable to possible changes. This list gives the designer valuable information as to which aspects of the system have to be protected by making use of the many techniques now available for achieving flexibility. Such tools include modular construction, structured design, parameterisation, providing spare capacity, data dictonaries, data base management techniques and table look-up methods. The problem of where flexibility is needed is illustrated by the following real example.

Two major airlines merged. Each had, at the time of the merger, comprehensive airline reservation systems and in each system, the flight number was used as the principal key for accessing the data base. The management of both airlines had stated categorically that a three digit flight number would be adequate for identifying all services for the foreseeable future. As a result, the systems designers had implemented a large suite of programs at each airline, in which the three digit flight number was a major means of access to the files. However, one of the airlines used a four digit number in place of the flight number as an indicator that some special action was required. When the airlines merged, it became necessary to go to a four digit flight number. The change from a three digit flight number is conceptually trivial, and would have required only a little clerical effort to implement before the systems came onto the computer. However, the change to a four digit number with the computer system took a great deal of programming effort and time. The incident gave rise to considerable disruption, high costs, and consequent loss of confidence which might have been avoided if the kind of structured analysis set out in the appendix had been used.

But the designer has to be aware that building flexibility into systems can also be expensive, both in terms of design effort and operational performance. The designer is involved in a trade-off between the extra development and operational costs of designing a system which is adaptable and flexible – a very general system – or of designing a very specific system dedicated to the needs existing at the time of implementation, but which may be incapable of modification, and may have to be replaced if requirements change.

Podger [25] suggests a way in which the designer can be helped to determine where to build flexibility into the system. He points out, that any application area or system can be analysed, to discover in terms of those who are associated with the system, which features of the system tend to be deep rooted and invariant or subject only to slow change, and which features are less permanent and more likely to change. He uses an accounting system as an example. To the professional accountant, the content and method of construction of the basic accounting reports – the balance sheet, the profit and loss account, the fundamental method of double entry book-keeping, are invariant. On the other hand, he can readily envisage repeated changes in the layout and to some extent the content of the various transactions which give rise to the accounts. Podger suggests the construction of a map of the system showing the interconnections between the many activities of the system. He notes that those aspects of the system which are deep rooted in the structure of the application tend to be highly connected but to have a low volume of activity, whilst those features which are less dependent on the principles which govern the organisation of the application area, and hence are more readily subject to change, are less connected but tend to have much higher activity rates. From this analysis he postulates that any system can be divided into:

- An inner zone of basic values and principles, which it would take a revolution to change.
- An intermediate zone of general procedures which are subject to change but where the lead time between the change being formulated and required is quite long.
- An outer zone of specific procedures, subject to more rapid and frequent change.

The conventional model of the systems life cycle assumes that an analysis and feasibility stage precedes the detailed design stage and that this will be followed by a specification and agreement of the specification for the system. At that point the design of the system is often frozen. For a typical information system the stages preceding the design freeze take between 20% and 35% of the total time required for the development of the system. For between 65% and 80% of this time the design of the system is not to be modified, even though the 'world' is changing all the time. In practice, even a frozen design gets modified if the system is seen to be becoming irrelevant to real requirements. Further, inconsistencies in design are discovered during the construction phase as a result of 'systems queries' (which as Waters [32] shows are often due to poor specification methods.)

An alternative to the conventional approach is one which seeks to defer design decisions up to the point at which further deferment would hazard the completion date for the system. Instead of having a single freeze date for the system, often quite early in the life cycle, some aspects of the system would remain open for re-design in the light of further information, almost up to the implementation date. Whilst this approach makes project control more difficult, it enables the system to be tailored more nearly to the requirements as they are at the time of implementation. Gosden [12], after many years of responsibility for implementing information systems, argues very strongly for a design philosophy based on 'creeping commitment', and of keeping design options open for as long as possible. One consequence of this approach is that throughout the development phase of a system the designer can continuously refine the model of the real world. In other words, creeping commitment implies an ongoing process of analysis and evaluation which is carried out in parallel with design and construction. In this way, the whole process of development is accompanied by a reduction in the designer's uncertainty, and as the implementation date is reached, the level of uncertainty becomes very low.

Rosenhead [26, 27] observed that many planning processes are based on an assumption of a particular and specified future. The designers rely on a single model of requirements for the future. At the same time, they design the system so that it will operate at maximum efficiency with those requirements as a basis. If the future should turn out to be different, the system which has been tuned for one set of circumstances, may operate in a degraded manner with another set of circumstances. Rosenhead suggests that in order to build systems which are robust – systems which are not degraded by changing circumstances – the designer has to consider alternative futures. At each stage of the design process, the design chosen should be the one which can cope with the largest number of possible futures. He perceives a sequential design process through time, and as the project advances towards the implementation date, and knowledge increases, it becomes possible to reduce the number of futures the system has to be prepared for. The approach recommended by Rosenhead sacrifices an optimising design (based on a single model of the future) for a design which can cope at a satisfactory level of performance with alternative models of the future. He defines the robustness of a design in terms of the number of alternative futures the design can cope with.

Uncertainty as to the effectiveness or relevance of the system being designed may be the result of the turbulent, dynamic environment into which the system must fit. It may also be due to the difficulty of predicting how those who will use or work with the system will behave when they are confronted with a system in action, rather than the system in words – the system as described in the specification. The only way the designer has of reducing the uncertainty regarding the users response to the system is to choose an experimental approach to systems design.

Brittan [4] describes a development strategy which replaces the conventional sequential development process by one of successively refined prototypes. The function of each prototype design is to test the assumptions on which a design is based in real world conditions. Brittan suggests that it is cheaper to build one or more prototypes of a system, which pays little regard to performance, than to build a finely tuned system which turns out to be unusable or only usable at a low level of effectiveness. The prototype development process, suggested Brittan, has the following phases for each prototype:

1. Project proposal
2. Preliminary study
3. Full study
4. Systems specification
5. Systems construction
6. Implementation impact
7. Implementation
8. Monitor, review, evaluate
9. Project closure.

The prototype approach is, however, only one of many possible experimental design strategies the designer can use. These include building simulation models of the system. For example, the LEGOL project of Stamper [8, 15] can be used to simulate the operations of alternative designs of administrative or legislative rules, prior to the implementation of such rules. In this way inconsistencies and unforeseen consequences of the application of the rules can be identified. Simulation models can also be used as part of a strategy exploring behaviour by means of management type games. Hawgood and colleagues [13] describe the construction of a game, COMSI-COMSA which models, for example, the existing inventory control system, and a proposed inventory control system. The game is played by the stock control management team using the two models and the results of each game are compared against criteria for efficient inventory control. This enables the designer to choose the inventory control system which produces the best results in the game.

Other experimental techniques, useful for the designer, include field experiments with new systems components or prototypes of such components, as for example, simulated exception reports, and attitude surveys by questionnaire. It is possible to test the effect of new systems on job satisfaction by the use of survey techniques supplemented by interviews, as described by Mumford and Weir [24].

The assumption underlying the life cycle model of an information system, is that (once implemented) the system adapts to changing user requirements by successive modifications until such time as the cost of maintenance and modification becomes so high that it is cheaper to replace the system. The model reflects the way systems were managed in the era when, to take advantage of the economy of scale (Grosch's law), systems tended to be large, complex, integrated and centralised structures. Modern technology, with mini and micro computers and communication networks, favours distributed systems or systems using small dedicated processors. It is possible to identify two types of application which are supported by the trend in technology:

1. Applications with a high content of generalised but unchanging processes. A good example of such an application is word processing. It is possible to specify a set of generalised word processing functions which are not likely to change significantly in the foreseeable future. The Podger model [25] helps to identify the generalisable invariant aspects of systems. Because such applications do not change a great deal, the problem of adapting to changing requirements is not severe. More and more of this kind of application will be implemented in the form of application packages.
2. Highly specific applications, subject to change. The cheap new micro computer technology suggests a possible change in approach to such systems. Instead of large, complex, integrated systems this type of application may be split into separate functions, corresponding to separate organisational units, with each function processed on a dedicated micro computer. The size of programs would be relatively small, corresponding to a few modules of a large modularised integrated system. Systems will adapt to changes in requirements not only by modification but also by replacement. Because each system is dedicated, the process of replacement will have a relatively small disruptive effect on the organisation as a whole, and because the systems are small, the replacement system will be relatively cheap. Even today it has been found that it is cheaper to replace programs written in a very high level language, like APL than to modify them [20]. Newer developments using application generators such as NOMAD [29] enable prototypes to be generated quickly and cheaply. It becomes possible to discard parts of systems and replace them with new versions without causing great disruption to the system as a whole.

CONCLUSION

One of the vital problems facing the designer of computer-based information systems is that of ensuring that the system continues to meet the changing need of the user, and at the same time taking advantage of the opportunities offered by the rapid developments in the technology.

The analysis of the problem given above suggests a few guidelines for the designer:

- Base the system on as accurate model of the real world as possible. To do this, it becomes necessary to adopt methods of analysis, design and evaluation which involve a far higher degree of user participation than is customary in conventional systems analysis and design methods.
- Use design methods which permit experimentation or prototyping in order to check how an innovative system might operate.
- Attempt to identify those aspects of a system which are deeply embedded and hence change only slowly, and those aspects which are volatile and subject to frequent change.
- Avoid commitment to a particular design too early. Practice as far as possible 'creeping commitment'.
- Design systems which can cope at adequate level with a range of possible requirements scenarios, rather than choosing a design which optimises on the basis of a single (perhaps most probable) vision of the future.
- Attempt to second guess the future by engaging in a systematic future analysis.
- Build flexibility into the system through well known construction techniques which enable the system to be modified without major disruption.
- Take advantage of trends in technology – both hardware and software – which enable the designer to develop small, dedicated replaceable systems.

These guidelines are not applicable to all situations. The designer has to choose those which are most relevant to the current application and fit with the organisational environment. Nevertheless, the use of the guidelines should help the designer to overcome the problem of adapting to changing user requirements.

REFERENCES

1. C. Argyris and D. Schon, 'Theory in Practice: Increasing Professional Effectiveness', (Jossey-Bon, San Francisco, 1974).
2. P. Blokdijk, 'A Participative Approach to Systems Design', in: H. Lucas, F. Land, T. Lincoln, K. Supper, eds., 'The Information Systems Environment' (North Holland Publ. Comp., Amsterdam, 1980).
3. British Computer Society, 'User Requirements in Data Processing' (Hayden & Son, London 1979).
4. J. Brittan, 'Design for a Changing Environment', The Computer Journal, Vol. 31, No. 3, (Feb. 1980).
5. F. E. Burke and R. E. George, 'How Top Executives Perceive their Choices

Among Information Sources of Decision', IFIP WG 8.2 Working Conference, The Information Systems Environment (June 1979).
6. P. Checkland, 'Systems Thinking, Systems Practice' (John Wiley, 1981).
7. H. Clausen, 'Concepts and Experiences with Participative Design', in: N. Szyperski and E. Groschla, eds. 'Implementation of Computer-Based Information Systems' (Sijthoff & Noordhoff, 1979).
8. S. Cook and R. K. Stamper, 'LEGOL – a Tool for the Study of Bureaucracy', in: H. Lucas, F. Land, T. Lincoln, K. Supper, eds., 'The Information Systems Environment' (North Holland Publ. Comp. Amsterdam, 1980).
9. A. De Maio, 'Socio-Technical Methods for Information Systems Design', in: H. Lucas, F. Land, T. Lincoln, K. Supper, eds., 'The Information Systems Environment' (North Holland Publ. Comp., Amsterdam, 1980).
10. R. B. Dew and K. P. Gee, 'Management Control and Information' (Macmillan, New York, 1973).
11. M. Earl and A. Hopwood, 'From Management to Information Management', in: H. Lucas, F. Land, T. Lincoln, K. Supper, eds., 'The Information Systems Environment' (North Holland Publ. Comp., Amsterdam, 1980).
12. J. A. Gosden, 'Some Cautions in Large Scale Systems Design and Implementation', Information and Management, Vol. 2, No. 1, (Feb. 1979).
13. J. Hawgood, F. Land, E. Mumford, C. M. Reddington, 'Evaluation and Management of Computer Based Systems: An Interdisciplinary Approach', in: 'Information Processing '71' (North Holland Publ. Comp., Amsterdam 1972).
14. B. Hedberg and E. Mumford, 'The Design of Computer Based Systems: Man's Vision of Man as an Integral Part of the Systems Design Process', in: E. Mumford and H. Sackman, eds., 'Human Choice and Computers' (North Holland Publ. Comp., Amsterdam, 1975.
15. S. Jones and P. Mason, 'Programming the Law', in: H. Lucas, F. Land, T. Lincoln, K. Supper, eds., 'The Information Systems Environment', (North Holland Publ. Comp., Amsterdam, 1980).
16. P. G. W. Keen, 'Information Systems and Organisational Change', Communications of the ACM, Vol. 24, No. 1, (Jan 1981).
17. F. Kolf and H. J. Oppeland, 'A Design-Oriented Approach to Implementation Research: The Project PORGI', in: N. Szyperski and E. Groschla, eds., 'Design and Implementation of Computer-Based Information System' (Sijthoff & Noordhoff, 1979).
18. F. Land, 'User Requirements and Involvement', in: 'User Friendly Systems', INFOTECH State of the Art Conference, (March 1979).
19. F. Land, J. Hawgood, E. Mumford, 'Training the Systems Analyst of the 1980's: Four New Design Tools to Assist the Design Process', in: H. Lucas, F. Land, T. Lincoln, K. Supper, eds., 'The Information Systems Environment' (North Holland Publ. Comp., Amsterdam, 1980).
20. E. R. McLean, 'The Use of APL for Production Applications: The Concept of Throwaway Code', in 'APL 76: Conference Proceedings' (ACM 1976).
21. M. Mintzberg, 'The Structure of Organisations' (Prentice Hall, 1979).
22. E. Mumford and D. Henshall, 'A Participative Approach to the Design of Computer Systems' (Associated Business Press, 1978).
23. E. Mumford, F. Land and J. Hawgood, 'A Participative Approach to the Design of Computer Systems', Impact of Science on Society, Vol. 28, No. 3 (1978).
24. E. Mumford and M. Weir, 'Computer Systems in Work Design: The ETHICS Method', (Associated Business Press 1979).
25. D. N. Podger, 'High Level Languages – A Basis for Participative Systems Design',

in: N. Szyperski and E. Groschla, eds., 'Design and Implementation of Computer-Based Information Systems' (Sijthoff & Noordhoff, 1979).
26. J. Rosenhead, 'Planning under Uncertainty: 1. The Inflexibility of Methodologies', OR, The Journal of the Operational Research Society, Vol. 31, No. 3, (March 1980).
27. J. Rosenhead, 'Planning under Uncertainty: 2. A. Methodology for Robustness Analysis', OR, The Journal of the Operational Research Society, Vol. 31, No. 4, (April 1980).
28. M. Saaksjarvi, 'Framework for Participative Systems Long-Range Planning', in: H. Lucas, F. Land, T. Lincoln, K. Supper, eds., 'The Information Systems Environment' (North Holland Publ. Comp., Amsterdam, 1980).
29. J. Sharkey, 'Systems Prototyping', Proceedings Management Conference, (Butler-Cox Foundation, Dec. 1981).
30. J. C. Taylor, 'The Socio-Technical Approach to Work Design', in: K. Legge and E. Mumford, eds., 'Designing Organisations for Satisfaction and Efficiency' (Gower Press, 1978).
31. G. Vickers, 'Education in Systems Thinking', Journal of Applied Systems Analysis, Vol. 7, (April 1980).
32. S. J. Waters, 'Towards Comprehensive Specifications', The Computer Journal, Vol. 22, No. 3, (Aug. 1979).

APPENDIX

FUTURE ANALYSIS

The analysis can be carried out in four stages.

STAGE 1

The *first* stage is concerned with an attempt to discover the kinds of change which may have an impact on the system under consideration. There are two broad classes of change the design team has to consider:

- Change which may affect the logic of the system
- Changes in the 'traffic' the system has to cope with – changes in volumes, in frequencies, e.g., peaks, numbers of elements etc.

Changes also need to be classified as:

- Transient or short-lived
- Permanent or long-lived.

Note should be taken of how frequently the changes occur over the lifetime of the system.

Changes can be classified into a number of major categories, and the design team has to consider the system in relation to each of these categories. The major categories are:

Changes in Available Technology

The technology referred to may be information-processing technology such as computers or communication equipment, or it may be technology which is embedded in the object system itself, such as, machine tools, production processors and so forth. Changes in technology can have a number of important effects on systems:

- They may make the chosen technology obsolete – manufacturers will no longer provide maintenance or spares.
- They may provide similar capabilities at very much lower costs.
- They may make it possible to achieve systems goals which were out of reach with the chosen technology.

In general, in times of very rapid technological change, the planning horizon for a system would shorten, and the technology chosen should, as far as possible, be modular and replaceable.

Changes in Legal Requirements

Many aspects of company law, tax law, industrial relations law and now privacy laws, can have a profound effect on systems. A feature of changes required to meet new legislation is that the changes are mandatory and have to be implemented to a strict externally determined timetable. If the changes are not implemented in time, the organisation concerned may be subjected to legal sanctions. Changes in legal requirements can arise from domestic legislation, from international regulations such as those promulgated by the EEC, and from changes in administrative practice permitted under enabling legislation.

Changes in Economic and other Environmental Factors

Changes in the economic environment have an impact on the rate of growth or decline of organisations, and on their competitive place in the market. At the most trivial level, such change can have a large effect on the level of activity and hence movement of messages through a system, and on the peak traffic the system may have to provide. At a more profound level, it can lead to major changes in organisations, affecting the product range, the method of distribution, the policy on stockholding, wages policy and questions relating to the ownership of the enterprise itself. Some of the most profound effects on systems are seen when companies are taken over or merged.

Some systems are almost immune to the kind of change brought about by changing economic circumstances, e.g., the census system in the U.K. But even such systems may have to be protected against some of the consequence of changing economic circumstances, such as strikes and other forms of industrial action.

Change in Attitudes, Expectations, Tastes, or in Climates of Opinion

Attitudes towards technology, and in particular to computer based systems, have changed over the past decade and will continue to evolve. Attitudes towards the role of government, towards industrial democracy, towards devolution and many other features of life are constantly undergoing change. Some of these changes are short lived, others remain dominant for long periods. Some are localised, affecting only a particular group in a factory or a particular district in a country, others are competely general. Changes in expectations of what kind of work is rewarding or satisfactory can have an important impact on the effectiveness or even workability of a computer system.

Most of the change categories discussed so far concern themselves with changes over which the organisation has no control. Changes are triggered by events outside the organisation, and the organisation and the systems within it must respond at best they can. But other categories are concerned with changes originating within the organisation itself and therefore to some extent controllable by the organisation.

Changes within the Organisation

All commercial and administrative organisations have a tendency to change their structure and style of management. It is sometimes suggested that these changes are cyclical from centralisation to decentralisation and back again, from authoritarian to democratic and back again. In reality organisations evolve under the pressure of external changes, and some of these will lead to an apparent cyclical effect. Thus the development of large mainframe computers coincided with movements towards centralised management; whilst the advent of the new mini- and micro-technology is paralleled by organisational philosophies of distributed responsibility. There is no doubt that changes in managerial personnel, in management techniques, in management style, in the control system and procedures, and in organisational structure can have large impacts on information systems. The effects are two-fold:

- They may give rise to requests for systems changes to conform to the new pattern of requirements.
- They may affect the extent to which systems are perceived as successful: a system may be seen to be successful by the manager who was instrumental in having it implemented, but may be seen as a failure by the succeeding manager.

The *first* task of the design team is to consider which category of change could be relevant to the systems under consideration. The *second* task is to identify the people most likely to contribute knowledgeably to a discussion of future trends in each relevant category.

For an evaluation of technical change, the discussions with the design team could involve:

- Suppliers of computer equipment and software
- Members of the computer or management service staff
- Members of the organisation's research or R and D department
- Outside consultants.

For consideration of the second category, legal changes, the important authorities to consult would include:

- The company secretary
- The chief accountant
- The personnel manager or industrial relations manager
- Officials of trade unions
- The organisation's legal advisers.

The *third* category, changes in the economic environment, is perhaps broadest, and in many ways, most difficult. Since many of the issues resulting from changes in economic circumstances are matters of highly confidential policy, for example, issues related to mergers or takeovers, it may be impossible to obtain information even where such information exists. Those who should be involved in discussions may include:

- Top management representatives
- Corporate planners (if they exist)
- The chief accountant
- Marketing management
- Management services
- Outside consultancies.

If the *third* category presents most difficulty, the *fourth* category, changes in attitudes and expectations, gives rise to the greatest uncertainty regarding the impact of such changes on the system itself. Those who may help to resolve the uncertainty include:

- Representatives of user departments
- The personnel or industrial relations manager
- Members of the management services staff
- Shop stewards and union officials
- Outside consultants.

The *fifth* category, changes within the organisation, involves a great variety of different change types. Discussion on such changes could therefore be structured by levels in the organisation. Strategic and control systems changes could involve:

- Top management representatives
- Heads of major departments
- Management services
- Senior trade-union officials
- Consultants.

Changes in unit operations should be discussed by:

- Departmental managers
- Section heads

- Members of unit operation staff
- The personnel manager
- Shop stewards or union representatives
- Management services staff.

It should be noted that the change categories are not independent. A change in one category can trigger changes in other categories. A change in the attitude of the population at large to industrial democracy can trigger legislation which will lead to organisational change and a consequent change in the expectations of the people working in the organisation. Hence the groups of people identified to help in forecasting the future should always be organised in such a way that such triggering effects could be traced.

The *third* task is to select appropriate tools to help in the future analysis. Job satisfaction analysis can help to give indications of attitude and expectation changes. These can be supplemented by other surveys designed to elicit attitudinal data. The identification of unit operations help to define the areas where organisational changes may arise. Further techniques include statistical forecasting methods for extrapolating rates of growth or decline, changes in volumes, changes in frequencies: economic modelling of the economy and the organisation itself to identify economic trends, and simulation methods to test the effect of various changes on the performance of the organisation.

To summarise: stage one categorises the types of change which could have an impact on the system under consideration, identifies those who can help in discussing future trends, and selects tools and techniques which can be used as an aid to forecasting.

STAGE 2

In stage two, the design team has to try to assess the kind of future which the system under consideration will have to face. With respect to each change category, the team, with the aid of the selected discussants and the use of the available tools, has to attempt to answer the following questions:

1. What future changes are conceivable at the present time, and when may they occur?
2. What impact might such changes have on the system?
3. Can the probability of such changes occurring be estimated? If so, what are the probabilities?

Take the case of a coronary heart unit for which a new system is under consideration. In category one the team might consider changes in medical technology which could affect the system, and changes in computer technology. With regard to medical technology it may be regarded as conceivable that a drug will be perfected which enables coronary cases to be stabilised without hospitalisation. Such a drug may be available within the next ten years. Its impact on the system in question may be profound but the team regard the probability of such a drug being developed as quite low. Nevertheless, it suggests to the team that the planning horizon for the system should be limited in the first instance to no more than five years. In practice the team will have to explore a large range of possibilities. Of these, only a few will be assessed as having an impact on the system, and therefore as affecting the design of the system.

In category *three*, economic and other environmental changes, the team may note that medical statistics indicate a constant rise in the rate of heart disease. This suggests that the system needs to be designed to cope with increasing loads, and in particular peak loads. On the other hand, the team may be aware of the possibility of future economic recession and cuts in public expenditure. How would the system cope with an increased demand for its services, but a reduced budget? If the team assesses the probability of such cuts being enforced in the future as high, is a design of the system possible which is less sensitives to cuts in expenditure?

In category *five*, the team may discover that a plan to merge two health authorities has been discussed and could be implemented within the next three years. Since both health authorities have systems for coping with coronary emergencies, the team may decide that a new design objective has to be set up – ensuring that, as far as possible, the systems of the two authorities remain compatible.

The chief methods employed in stage two are open-ended discussions between the design team and the people identified as capable of contributing to the discussion, using 'brain-storming' techniques, DELPHI methods, surveys, and a variety of forecasting and diagnostic tools. The extent of the future analysis would depend on the kind of system under consideration. If the system is central to the organisation's existence and a failure of the system could imperil the whole enterprise, the future analysis must be very detailed. In such projects as the Apollo Moon shot, the analysis of all possible contingencies was very elaborate indeed.

The outcome of stage 2 is:

- A target life-span for the system.
- A revised list of design objectives.
- A list of systems features which may need to have flexibility built into them.
- A number of scenarios of the future which any design would have to cope with.

STAGE 3

Up to this point, the design team has concentrated on the kinds of change the system may face in the future. However, there is no way in which a team can make precise predictions about the future, and even with the best possible future analysis, unexpected events will test the system. If the system is to be robust, a further diagnostic procedure needs to be invoked. In stage 3 the design team has to systematically test the system under consideration to establish those systems features which are sensitive to any change in requirements, either in terms of the logic or the traffic. The team has to ask itself two questions:

1. What features of the system is sensitive to changed requirements or changes in traffic?
2. What will be the impact on the viability of the system as a whole if such changes occur?

The team has to consider the whole system – the computer sub-system and the manual sub-system. The process of analysis has to be structured in such a way that all aspects of the system are covered and reviewed.

To examine the computer sub-system, the team has to analyse each facet of the proposed system and test its sensitivity to change. The process of examination is in some way analogous to a structured walkthrough of a program design. A method proposed for such an examination analyses the following facets for each system:

Identifiers

Check what would happen to the system if:

- the range of identifiers were increased (or reduced),
- an identifier changed its characteristics – for example, the identifier code changed from 6 to 7 digits, or the identifier had a check digit added to it.

If the proposed design can accomodate such changes with minimum delay or limited use of resources, there is no further problem. If the change cannot be accomodated, the team has to check the consequences of delayed implementation and possible costs. If these prove to be unacceptably high, the proposed design may have to be modified to allow changes to be introduced. Note that the analysis is carried out independently of any assessment of the probabilities of such changes occurring.

Modification of the design usually involves the deployment of one of the many techniques which provide for flexibility in the system. In the case of changes of identifiers, these would include the possibility of leaving a redundant space for extending the identifier range or format, and the use of data dictionaries and indexes.

Input and Output Messages

Check what would happen to the system if:

- the content of messages were to change,
- the types of message were changed,
- the frequency, volume or expected response time of messages changed.

The analysis is carried out as for identifiers. Tools which may help to provide flexibility include the use of a modular design approach.

Algorithms or Procedural Rules

Check what would happen to the system if:

- the logic of the rules were altered,
- the rules were invoked more or less frequently,
- the values (constants) used within the rules were changed.

The analysis is carried out as for identifiers. Flexibility can be enhanced by techniques such as modular design, use of look-up tables and parameterisation.

Files (or the Database)

Check what would happen to the system if:

- access paths to files were altered,
- contents of files were altered,
- frequences of access to files or part of files were altered,
- distribution of variable elements in the file were changed.

The analysis is carried out as for identifiers. More flexibility may be provided by use of database management systems, the provision of redundant space, and the use of data dictionaries.

Identifier Relationships

Check what would happen new dependencies or relationships were required. Data analysis techniques are used to see what the effect of such changes would be. Database management systems could help to provide more flexibility.

The design team has to carry out a similar analysis of the manual system. For each manual activity the team has to list each task and role and consider the effect of changes in carrying out the task, or changes in roles. In addition to changes in logic and 'traffic', the team has to consider the effects of changes in behavioural variables, such as attitudes and motivation, and external factors, such as the availability of alternative employment.

STAGE 4

The design team has to see the extent to which the proposed system could be modified to make it less vulnerable if changes were to occur, however unexpected.

As a result of the stage 1 analysis, the design team can list those elements of the proposed system which are most sensitive to change, and those elements where such changes would have the greatest impact on the organisation. A particular element in the system may be very difficult to change in response to a revised need, but the effect of not accomodating the need may be trivial as far as the organisation is concerned. It may, for example, be possible for a manual procedure to be set up to cope with a new requirement which cannot be implemented on the computer system. The important list is the one which identifies the elements which could have important consequences for the organisation if they cannot be accommodated quickly (or cheaply).

In stage 4 the design team considers the output from stages 2 and 3 in order to make recommendations regarding the system's planned life-cycle and to decide how much flexibility to build into the system, and which scenarios to cope with. To do this, the team has to assess the possible damage to the organisation from failing to adapt to changes and two compare this with the cost of building in flexibility. To a large extent, the tradeoff has to rely on the judgement of the design team, since it is difficult to quantify precisely the cost of building in flexibility or of evaluating the damage from failure to adapt.

One further point needs to be noted. The extend to which a system responds to changes is a function not only of the way the system is constructed but also the type of organisation in which the system operates. Some forms of organisation are inherently more capable of responding to change than others. This applies to the organisation responsible for the design implementation and operation of the information system and the organisation of the enterprise itself. In considering the question of life-span and flexibility, the design team has to be aware of any constraints imposed by the style of management and the structure of the organisation.

2. INFORMATION ASSET MANAGEMENT*

Daniel S. Appleton

'If you can't manage assets to reflect their true value, you're inviting someone to do it for you.' This is a quote from Robert Anderson, chairman of Atlantic Richfield. He said it in response to takeover noises from T. Boone Pickens. What Anderson really meant to say was that poor asset management, i.e., the inability to recognize true asset structures and apply good asset management principles to them, should be punishable by death.

Information resource management (IRM) is today where business management was 20 years ago. It is just beginning to feel a need for asset management. That need is being driven by dramatic reductions in productivity, accompanied by even more dramatic increases in the volume and complexity of demand. It's not hard to figure out that there is something fundamentally wrong with the management equation that continues to allow this condition to exist, much less get worse.

Thomas Kuhn, in his popular book *The Structure of Scientific Revolutions* (The University of Chicago Press, 1970) explains that serious anomalies, like this, occur when there is a 'malfunction in the paradigm' that underlies existing values, processes and technologies. The paradigm must change before the anomalies can be cured. Paradigm changes occur as these anomalies become economically unacceptable, and people begin to break from tradition in search of new answers.

Kuhn even documents the sociology of such paradigm shifts. At first, proponents of the new paradigm are seen only as irritants. Next, they are scoffed at. Then they are decried. Finally, their ideas are nothing new: 'I've been saying the same thing for the last 10 years, but no one listened.'

But according to Kuhn, true believers in the new paradigm are 'like the man wearing inverting lenses. Confronting the same constellation of objects as before and knowing he does so, he nevertheless finds them transformed through and through in their many details.' It is extremely difficult for believers in the old paradigm to see through these inverting lenses and not get confused. Their brains tend to deinvert the inversions.

In the information resource management business, the anomalies we are

* *Reprinted from: DATAMATION, FEB. 1, 1987.*

Dan Appleton is president of D. Appleton Co. Inc., a Manhattan Beach, Calif., firm that specializes in data resource management methods and tools. He published his first DATAMATION article ('What Database Isn't') in 1974, and has since published 17 more, on topics ranging from data management (see, for example, 'Business Rules: The Missing Link,' Oct. 15, 1984, p. 145) to information resource management ('Data-Driven Prototyping,' November 1983, p. 259) to manufacturing automation ('The State of CIM,' Dec. 15, 1984, p. 66).

experiencing are what I have labeled very large projects. These anomalies are the result of plunging productivity in the provision of information services and products, accompanied by a dramatic increase in demand for them. The mere existence of very large projects signals the need for a paradigm shift, away from the tradition of standalone systems development and toward what I describe as the asset-based life cycle model.

There are still a lot of believers in the old paradigm. They find it difficult to recognize very large projects in their own world. They scoff at the concept, saying things like, 'Our projects don't even approach $5 million, so obviously they aren't what he's talking about.' But they are deinverting. Anyone who is surprised at the emergence of very large projects – or who doubts their existence – has either been too wrapped up in his own chapter of the IRM Framework of the Month Club, or has just not been playing attention.

The diseconomies of the traditional systems approach to IRM have been obvious to many people for a long, long time. As far back as 1972, John Dearden, in his landmark 'MIS Is a Mirage' article in the January–February *Harvard Business Review* blew the whistle on the old paradigm. He forecast that the strict application of the system approach to automating management's information requirements was leading inexorably toward a concept called 'the management information system' (MIS). According to Dearden, 'The notion that a company can and ought to have an expert (or a group of experts) create for it a single, completely integrated supersystem – an MIS – to help govern every aspect of its activity is absurd.'

To Dearden, the MIS is the ultimate very large project, and he argued that any management that sought such a thing was embarking on 'a wild goose chase, a search for a will-o'-the-wisp.'

Again, believers in the old paradigm would say that they absolutely agree with Dearden. The MIS is a mirage. But their actions speak louder than their words. Most businesspeople and dp executives, most IRM consultants and gurus, while accepting what he says, have seen fit to ignore what he means. They have also seen fit to ignore the danger signals of very large projects. Instead, they have preferred to ride the traditional paradigm into the ground.

FORCES SHAPING IRM

There are, however, a few iconoclasts. In October 1985, 20 of them assembled in Fort Lauderdale, Fla., at the National Bureau of Standards Fifth Database Workshop. The group, which included 11 top-level dp executives, three senior academics, three wise vendors, and three brilliant (ahem) consultants, spent two and a half days discussing the basic economic, political, and technical forces that are shaping information resource management for the 1990s.

Within the first two hours, there was a fundamental agreement that 'the asset management mentality' is the strongest economic force within IRM. In fact, the group agreed that information asset management would become the dominant theme in information resource management (IRM). The group projected that as information asset management continues to evolve, it will have dramatic effects such as the following:

- The concept of the application system will change.
- Users will be treated as a free market.
- Dp as we know it may go away.
- The traditional systems development life cycle will be replaced as the standard approach to software management.

The NBS workshop participants spent a great deal of time examining the notion of information assets. They were able to conceptualize them as horizontal structures that transcend the vertical structures we currently think of as applications. They proposed that there are five horizontal asset structures, all of which share data as a common denominator. The five horizontal structures were data acquisition, data storage, data manipulation, data retrieval and data distribution.

The workshop proposed that over the next five to ten years, we would see a shift in management perspective from its current focus on the vertical applications structure, to a future focus on the horizonal asset structure as the dominant concept of information resource management. The effect of this transition would be to modify the way planning, organization, administration and control are performed for information resource management. Planning would be conducted with a priority on the horizontal structures; IRM would be organizationally aligned more closely with the horizontal structures; administrative procedures, such as financing concepts, would reflect the horizontal structures; and control concepts, such as the software management process, would be mapped closely to the horizontal structures.

Though believers in the old paradigm will have trouble recognizing the signs, the horizontal structures are already beginning to assert their influence over IRM. Of course, the increasing influence of data on IRM has manifested itself organizationally in the data and database administration functions, and in the planning arena through strategic data planning. It is not the dominant theme, but it is a theme that folks find quite interesting. The data retrieval structure is starting to flex its muscles through organizational concepts such as information centers, and through the concept of downloading data from operational systems to decision support systems on 4GLS (Fourth Generation Languages) and PCs.

Overall, there is an increasing movement toward what people are beginning to call data-driven or data-oriented information resource management, and that is having an effect on requirements definition and software development and maintenance procedures. These new data-driven procedures differ significantly from the traditional process- or application-oriented procedures in the way they deal with work definition, allocation, and control, and in the technological support that they employ. Their objective, of course, is to standardize and reuse asset structures that transcend individual project boundaries. To accomplish this, they reflect the asset-based life cycle model.

As the horizontal structures begin to take hold, the vertical structures are not just standing still. In fact, in some ways the changes talking place in the vertical structures are even more profound than those taking place in the horizontal structures. These changes are more directly a result of the frustration from very large projects.

To understand the full and future impact of these changes on IRM, it is only necessary for us to look at what businesses do when they encounter their equivalent of a very large project – that is, a market that is beginning to take off on its own.

In the early '70s, as traditional markets began to come unstuck, businesses began to employ a new concept of strategic planning and organization specifically focused around asset management. First developed by General Electric and later refined by the Strategic Planning Institute, the Boston Consulting Group, and eventually the Big Eight firms, this new approach was based on a concept of management called the strategic business unit (SBU).

SBU IS A NATURAL BUSINESS

Borrowing from Arthur D. Little Inc.'s definition, an SBU is a natural business. This is much more profound than it may at first appear, since the idea of this form of strategic planning is to divide an existing enterprise into several natural businesses. That's not an easy job for most incumbent business managers.

Each SBU is supposed to end up with its own markets, its own control structure, and its own resource structure. But SBUs are more than just profit centers. Each is supposed to have its own balance sheet. That makes it a business within a business. The objective of an SBU is to manage products and resources to service a specific free market while providing positive financial consequences to the parent firm.

A tremendous amount of research has been conducted on SBUs. They are the result of natural economic forces at work between free markets and free business structures. We have a lot of empirical evidence about their behavior. The Strategic Planning Institute in Boston has a database that tracks and monitors over 700 of them – in all flavors and colors. Perhaps the best explanation of the economic forces at work in them is presented by Oliver Williamson in his book *Markets and Hierarchies* (The Free Press, New York, 1975).

It is my belief that the SBU is an appropriate analogy to use in characterizing what is beginning to happen to the vertical structure of IRM. Applications will eventually get bunched into what I suggest might be called strategic information units (SIUs). Like an SBU, an SIU is an environment. It has a distinct market, a distinct control structure and a distinct set of resources.

Whether they are officially recognized or not, the seeds for SIUs are just as well planted as were the seeds for SBUs. SIUs are natural IRM businesses. For example, in most discrete manufacturing enterprises there are four SIU structures emerging:

1. Manufacturing planning and control – the information structures that support planning, scheduling, and materials acquisition.
2. Product and process definition – the information structures that describe the physical products, and the discrete processes needed to manufacture them and control quality.
3. Factory automation – the information structures needed to manage and control robots and machines, centers, and cells, in the factory itself.
4. General business management – the information structures that are employed for the management of finances, marketing, personnel, and so on.

CONNECTED BY COMMON NEEDS

Today, each of these environments consists of an interconnected group of islands of automation, forming what could loosely be called archipelagoes. Most fundamentally, the islands are connected by the common information needs of their users. There are other bonds as well. For example, there is usually some consistency in their data structures (that is, in their business rule); they generally have similar hardware, systems software and communications technologies; and the organization structure that administers and controls their financing and planning is distinct. Each archipelago contains strategic, management and operational control activities, and so, possesses capabilities to handle large transaction volumes and decision support functions. Each also has responsibility to manage data acquisition, data storage, data manipulation, data retrieval, and data distribution.

Archipelagoes, it seems, are very loose confederations of heterogeneous applications that are drifting toward each other because of natural business forces. It is up to IRM managers to recognize and transform these archipelagoes into SIUs. Under the traditional approach to IRM, this transformation would be attempted in the form of a very large project (or two, or three), and the economics of tops and bottoms would begin to have their way.

What makes an SIU distinct from a traditional application project, i.e., what prevents it from becoming a very large project? Perhaps the most important differences lie in the value systems of very large projects and SIUs. There are five major differences.

The first one involves how users are treated. In a very large project, they are treated as 'suppliers of requirements.' Their job is to help define requirements, and they can do so with varying degrees of involvement with the technical project team. Once they have defined requirements, they usually wait until the application is completed, and then implement it.

In a strategic information unit, users are treated as if they were customers creating demand in a free market. The SIU's job is to provide supply consistent with demand. Success in an SIU is a function of being able to economically service increasing demand, not in forcing the user to freeze his requirements.

The second difference is almost as bothersome as the first. It requires that the SIU develop a distinct notion of what its products are. These products must be distinct, and they must have predictable costs and lead times. They must also utilize SIU assets. These products must be forecast in units that will be delivered to the customers.

Traditionally, very large projects embrace no distinct concept of product. The hope is that they will produce an applications system, i.e., a single product or some deliverable modules that fit neatly together. Without the concept of multiple products, there is no mechanism for measuring productivity, since productivity is measuring a ratio of outputs to inputs. The very large project concept of productivity is to measure lines of code per hour, but lines of code are not products, especially in the eyes of the user.

The third difference between very large projects and SIUs is in the significance they assign to asset management. Very large projects are so interested in building the application that they have no time – or budget – to focus on the development of assets. They do not recognize that the development and utilization of assets, if properly done, will dramatically reduce development costs and lead times as well as maintenance costs and lead times.

Usually, the project folks are so focused on trying to get the application designed in detail before the requirements change that they have no time to build assets such as standard data structures and reusable code modules.

SIUs give assets top priority in their resource commitment decisions, and their control structures ensure that the assets get reused with the minimum customization. This means that some of the asset structures must be defined *before* requirements are finalized, and that requirements must be stated in the language of the SIU's assets.

The fourth difference between the SIU and a very large project has to do with how each relates to the various support staffs. Regardless of their size, very large projects tend to be subservient to support staffs such as data administration, planning, operations, etc. SIUs are not. The appropriate relationship between the SIU and its support staffs was described best by Williamson in *Markets and Hierarchies*, wherein he proposes that the optimum organizational structure for managing in a free market environment that is increasing in size and complexity is what he calls the M-Form organization.

M-FORM MANAGING STRUCTURE

According to Williamson, the M-Form, or multidivisional structure, was developed in the early 1920s by the Du Pont Company, under the leadership of Pierre Du Pont, and at General Motors, under Alfred Sloane Jr. 'This organizational innovation,' wrote Williamson, 'involved substituting quasi-autonomous operating divisions (organized mainly along product, brand, or geographic lines) for the functional divisions of the U-Form (Unitary) structure as the principal basis for dividing up the task and assigning responsibility.'

To be consistent with Williamson's thinking, an SIU should be given 'quasi-autonomous standing' as long as the SIU's efficiency performance can be monitored and it can be demonstrated that the SIU's output has a greater value than the cost of its asset formation and product delivery. The system for measuring this performance must be consistent for all SIUs (within, for example, an SBU) so that their performance can be compared. Establishing this system of measurement is a major obstacle facing information resource managers because most of the measurements required to operate in the M-Form structure depend on a solid understanding of the new asset management paradigm, and a good set of inverting lenses.

Information asset management occurs within SIUs, and it occurs among SIUs. Actually, information asset management is what SIUs are all about. The lessons learned by most businesses that have set up the SBU concept was that SBUs must be established proactively, not reactively. The SBU structure defines where the enterprise is headed strategically. The SIU should define where IRM is going in the future. It is doubtful that there should be only one SIU, and there should probably be no more than six or eight. But, once the IRM pie has been divided up among them, there should be nothing left over.

The fifth difference between the SIU and very large project value systems is undoubtedly the most difficult to accept. It is the notion that SIUs are not established for a specific time interval, whereas very large projects are established with the assumption that they will cease to exist once the application has been implemented. If they have a maintenance phase, it is usually perceived to be a completely different management issue from the original development project.

In most companies this distinction represents a very real cultural barrier to information asset management. The traditional approach to project justification requires specific user organizations to sign up for specific costs and benefits. Much of the cost of setting up an SIU – getting it into business, so to speak – is not directly related to those costs and benefits. The company has to come up with investment dollars to get the SIU rolling. These investment dollars must be spent every year to ensure that the asset structures (which depreciate over time) are continually upgraded. The investment dollars do not show a direct benefit in improved user efficiency or effectiveness – the traditional source for justifying project costs. They show a return in reduced SIU costs and increased SIU responsiveness in satisfying changing user requirements. From a financial perspective, setting up an SIU is no different from setting up an SBU.

There are two schools of thought about information resource management. One school believes that IRM is just a new phase of Alvin Toffler's 'Third Wave', the first couple of phases having been automated data processing and MIS. The other school believes that IRM is an ongoing process and that each business is immersed in its own struggle to improve the way it handles that process.

Regardless of which school you belong to, you will be faced during the coming years with the task of adapting your thinking toward an asset management concept. You will be hit from both the horizontal and the vertical directions, by asset structures and by strategic information units. You will feel the effects in planning, organization, administration and control. In order to make the best of things, you need to get some of those inverted lenses. And when you look through them, you have to resist the temptation to deinvert what you see.

3. FROM MANAGEMENT INFORMATION TO INFORMATION MANAGEMENT*

Michael J. Earl
and
Anthony G. Hopwood

ABSTRACT: Systems designers, managers and researchers increasingly recognize that there are problems in the development and operation of MIS. Frequently lack of management support and involvement are cited as causes of inadequate MIS and calls are made for managing information as a resource.

In this paper the authors argue that a new perspective is required, from a concern with management information as a technical phenomenon to a concern with information management as a substantive organizational phenomenon. Such a re-direction may depend on new metaphors, language and frameworks being derived first.

Among both researchers and managers there is an increasing realization of problems in the management information area. A recurring theme in the literature is that MISs have been disappointing in so far as they commonly have failed to meet expectations (Argyris, 1977). In management courses, sessions on MIS rarely want for lively discussion, heated debate and general concern. Managers frequently complain of information overload on the one hand and an information gap on the other. The professional information providers – systems analysts, accountants and management scientists – proudly describe their achievements and earnestly explain their current plans. The information users listen with mixed feelings ranging from hope to scepticism, from commitment to antagonism and from understanding to incomprehension. There are problems in the current state of MIS.

Meanwhile substantial sums of money continue to be spent on information processing. Companies commonly claim that their data processing budgets consume 2% of sales turnover. One major multinational company has estimated that 10% of its

* *Reprinted from 'The Information System Environment', ed. Lucas, Land, Lincoln and Sapper, North Holland Publishing Company, 1980.*

Michael J. Earl is with the Oxford Centre for Management Studies.
Anthony G. Hopwood is with the London Granduate School of Business Studies.

world-wide corporate turnover is spent on information processing. Ten percent of net assets on world-wide balance sheets are thought to be explained by hardware investment and a UK multinational's data processing budget is currently growing by 30% per annum compound. Top management understandably is becoming concerned with 'value for money'.

Gibson and Nolan (1974) have suggested that DP budgets follow an S-shaped curve, characterized by increasing management attention to planning and control of the computer resource. Concern with efficiency of information processing is expressed by productivity audits, performance monitoring and proliferation of controls. Effectiveness is emphasized by the introduction of steering committees, attempts at cost benefit analyses and charging for computer services. Maturity, they suggest, is reached only when the computer resource is fully integrated into everyday management practice and thinking. Our evidence would suggest that such a maturity has yet to be achieved however. While continual thinking and concern may be evident, it would be clear that we are a long way from gaining the full integration of the computer resource into management practice.

Meanwhile, information processing technology continues to advance. Mainframes and mass storage continue to approximate to Grosch's Law, providing more power for less money. Minicomputers, and many microcomputers, threaten to change the shape of data-processing and perhaps of MIS. 'Convergence' of computing, data communication and word processing will extend the scope of formal information processing. Managers and specialists are both excited and alarmed. The specialist contemplates new techniques and new applications. The DP manager sees new options and new anxieties. Managers wonder whether an opportunity has arrived to regain control or, more frequently perhaps, whether the technology will finally leave them stranded.

Yet despite some of the fundamental questions posed by these trends, investment in formal MIS continues. With the persuasiveness of so many interested parties, particularly the information providers, the appeal of sophisticated technology and the felt need to keep up with others, it is easy to justify ever more information systems. There is always an information need, the system always needs improving and incremental growth is generally invisible. Indeed, MISs perpetuate themselves: they are necessary because they are there. Professions and disciplines such as accounting, computer science and cybernetics are built around them. Other seemingly successful organizations have MISs and publicize them. Yet in transferring systems from other organizations, we fail to examine the context in which they originally operated, often implementing misfits as a result. Finally, we seek spin-offs, trying to satisfy management information needs on the basis of existing data-orientated systems (Zani 1970). In short, MISs are assumed to be good for us. After all, or so it is frequently claimed, is not information the raw material of decision making, the *sine qua non* of planning and control and the life blood of organizations?

Increasingly, however, the existence of any *a priori* relationship between formal MISs as commonly conceived and effective organizational performance is being questioned. In a planning context, for instance, Grinyer and Norburn (1975) found no significant relationship between formal information systems and financial performance. Instead, they found that use of both informal channels of communication and informal decision-making processes was associated with success. Lorsch and Allen (1973) found that complexity of management control information systems facilitated upward information flows, but not downward flows. However, both downward and upward flows were found to be associated with favorable financial performance with alternatives to formal MIS appearing to be essential.

Indeed, it is the 'newly poor' (Olofsson and Svalander, 1975) that invest heavily in additional mechanisms for internal visibility and control, although often in so doing they may further dislocate themselves from their problematic external environments as they consciously or unconsciously succumb to the demands of their ever more visible internal environments. Financially efficient, they may still walk to their economic grave (Hopwood, 1979). And the financially successful, on the other hand, tend to avoid many of the rigors of ever more sophisticated information and control systems (Child, 1973, 1974, 1975; Rosner, 1968; Turcotte, 1974). Seemingly they revel and flourish within the context of informal planning and assessment practices (Child, 1974), multiple and overlapping flows of information (Grinyer and Norburn, 1975) and continually renegotiated exchanges between organizational participants (Georgiou, 1973). Indeed, the hearsay evidence of many managers suggests that the information they use in critical decisions does not emanate from the formal MIS. As Mintzbert (1972) discovered, top managers select and prefer informal information processing in most of their work.

Thus with the past disappointments with information systems which explicitly have claimed to facilitate the process of management, the growth of expenditure on information processing and the newly emergent technological developments, pressures on both MIS designers and users are undoubtedly increasing. Concerns and dissatisfactions are being expressed and at least some are starting to probe for alternatives.

The theme of our paper is that a major constraint on both current practice and the delineation of alternatives is that information processing is viewed in too narrow and technical a manner. Information is still seen as a technical phenomenon, a 'thing' that has a seemingly problematic relationship to the intricacies of organizational processes and practices. And, as a consequence, our underlying information concepts and language tend to encourage the formalization, bureaucratization, standardization and mechanization of information processes – the very things which the recent studies quoted above suggest neither fit nor suit the realities of organizational activity. If this is the case, and we think that it is, then the alternatives to present practice may not be recognized because our existing MIS perspectives are outdated and not descriptive of even present organizational practice.

In this paper we argue for a new perspective, from a concern with management information as a technical phenomenon to a concern with information managment as a substantive organizational phenomenon. Our theme is not just a play on words or a mere evangelical call to put management back into information systems. The perspective which we seek is one that is concerned with a broader appreciation of information processing in organizations. We are urgently in need of some new and very different metaphors for considering the roles which information does, can and might play in organizational functioning. To illustrate this we start by examining the variety of ways in which organizations process information.

THE INFORMATION PROCESSING MIX IN ORGANIZATIONS

Despite the emphasis which has been placed on MIS, organizations have invested and continually do invest in a multitude of ways of processing information. One way of looking at the variety of approaches used in practice is to distinguish between routine and non-routine and official and unofficial modes of information processing. The resulting array of information possibilities is depicted in Figure 1.

	ROUTINE	NON-ROUTINE
Official	MIS Management Accounting Systems; Production Control Systems	Access Facilities; Task Forces; Liaison Roles
Unofficial	Black-books; Just in Case Files	The Grape Vine; Lunch Table Chats

Figure 1. The Information Processing MIX

The official, routine information processing box contains the MIS which have been emphasized so much. They are often the operational systems upon which our organizations depend from day to day. In some businesses they have even become a substantial part of the business itself; for example air-line reservation systems, production control systems in the engineering sector and transactions systems in banking.

The unofficial, routine category of information processing contains systems which serve local needs. In some cases these strive to compensate for the inadequacies of the routine systems; in other cases they are maintained as defensive information against attack from superiors and peers. It is evident from reseach (Hopwood 1973; Simon et al., 1954) and from discussions with managers that such informal, but nonetheless routine, approaches to information processing are ubiquitous. Hedberg and Johnson (1978) saw them as having value in creating and maintaining subcultures to question and challenge the status quo and stability. Also they suggested that they often provide more flexibility and discretion to managers than the official counterparts. Argyris (1977) suggests that unofficial, routine systems often represent actuality, provide concrete descriptions of unique situations, indicate true causality and provide private and tacit views. Earl (1978a) suggests that they may be attractive because they are simple and may serve as unofficial prototypes for subsequent official routinization.

The non-routine, official category includes purposive approaches to facilitating the processing of information such as investments in the capability to provide ad hoc information and mechanisms for furthering access to information. Also included in this category are those structural approaches to information processing which are effective because they are based on managerial actions and interpersonal activities through which 'things get done' and by which we can learn from experience. Such structural mechanisms provide means for crossing intra-organizational boundaries, for transcending levels of authority and influencing others by discourse and persuasion. Meetings, conferences and task forces provide channels of lateral and downward communication when often the routine MISs are predominantly upward. By being less formal and structured, non-routine and official 'information systems' may also help achieve 'control with' rather than 'control over'. They may perhaps offer top management a means of keeping 'in touch', when the formal and official MIS no longer represents the reality they once measured. Finally, they can often be created quickly and then killed when their purpose has been satisfied. Conversely, the routine, official forms of information processing take a long time to create and may never die.

The unofficial, non-routine category comprises many of the informal information systems upon which managers depend. These devices carry news quickly, convey nuances, and can process qualitative information. To discover what is important, one joins the grape-vine. To influence someone or break down the system, one sits at the right lunch-table. To try and make sense of complexity, we share the problem and construct our organization and world through, and with, each other. These forms of information processing are personal and private and accordingly fulfil purposes which the official or routine system could never attempt.

The reality of information processing in organizations is the vibrant and varied mix depicted by this framework. Organizations both have and require a balance of complementary information processing forms, including the more personal and structural varieties. However, it seems to us that so much of this reality does not influence or enter into legitimate professional discourse in the MIS area, and this may well be a major constraint on organizational adaptation or change. Investing heavily in routine, official MIS, we often forget and exclude investment in, and development of, competing, counter-balancing, overlapping and reinforcing information flows and processes. Just why does the emphasis on the formal and routine continue? What is at stake with the development of MIS as we now know them? What organizational roles do they really serve? To address such questions, let us consider further a key aspect of the interface between information and organization, namely the roles which information plays in decision-making. How is the development of MIS implicated in the very different types of decision-making processes which constitute organizational life?

INFORMATION AND DECISION

Many writers have seen MIS as servants of decision making and several authorities have devised decision-orientated strategies for MIS design (Ackoff 1967; Zani 1970; Mason 1969). The relationship between information and decision making has been an influential basis for the analysis, development and articulation of normative MIS 'solutions'. Indeed, some have even described MIS as Decision Support Systems (Gorry and Scott-Morton 1971).

However, one problem with the use of the decision-making perspective for the analysis of both information needs and information systems is that the relationship between information and decision has rarely been critically examined. The link has, in other words, been presumed rather than described and analyzed. A particular view of human rationality and the attendant relationship between information and decision-making has been uncritically adopted. We have tended to presume, for instance, that the specification and analysis of information precedes decision-making, that the roles played by information in decision-making are invariate across a multitude of different decision situations. Information is there to facilitate and ease rather than more actively influence, if indeed not frustrate, the decision-making process. Such presumptions are, however, little more than abstractions from the complex reality of information processing in organizations. While they might simplify the information system design process, their relationship to the realities of organizational life is questionable.

One way of looking at the relationship between information and decision-making in more detail can be based on the analysis of Thompson and Tuden (1959) which adds to the traditional view of the link between decision-making and uncertainty, by classifying various states of uncertainty and different types of decision-making processes. As can be seen in Figure 2, they distinguish between uncertainty (or disagreement, for that is the same at the organizational level) over organizational objectives and the uncertainty over the cause and effect relationships which are embodied in particular organizational actions. When objectives are clear and undisputed, and cause and effect certain, Thompson and Tuden highlighted the potential for decision-making by computation. As cause and effect relationships become uncertain, however, that potential diminishes and decisions start to be made in a judgemental manner. If the focus of uncertainty resides in the specification of objectives, however, decisions tend to be the result of compromise when cause and effect relationships are certain, and of a more 'inspirational' nature when even that clarity disappears.

<table>
<tr><td colspan="2"></td><td colspan="2">UNCERTAINTY OF OBJECTIVES</td></tr>
<tr><td colspan="2"></td><td>Low</td><td>High</td></tr>
<tr><td rowspan="2">Uncertainty of Cause and Effect</td><td>Low</td><td>Decision by Computation</td><td>Decision by Compromise</td></tr>
<tr><td>High</td><td>Decision by Judgement</td><td>Decision by Inspiration</td></tr>
</table>

Figure 2. Decision-Making and Uncertainty

By being based on a more detailed characterization of the ways in which uncertainties are perceived and located in organizations, we believe that such an array of decision possibilities is of real significance in trying to understand the emergence and functioning of information systems in organizations. Moreover, the framework relates to the views of those who have seen information processing as a means of uncertainty reduction (Galbraith, 1973) and information value as the degree to which uncertainty is reduced. However, rather than presuming the link between information and uncertainty, let us consider the roles which information processing and information systems might and do play in the different decision situations described by Thompson and Tuden.

First, we strive to articulate a normative view. Using an all-too unsatisfactory 'machine' analogy, Figure 3 outlines the orientations which information systems perhaps might adopt in the best of all possible worlds. Given low uncertainty on each dimension, we approach the management scientists' definition of certainty, where algorithms, formulae and rules can be derived to solve the problem by computation. Alternatively, it may represent Simon's structured decisions (1960) where the intelligence, design and choice phases are all programmable. In either case, stock control systems, credit control routines and linear programming models are all examples of what we call 'answer machines'.

		UNCERTAINTY ABOUT OBJECTIVES	
		Low	High
Uncertainty of Cause and Effect	Low	Answer Machines	Dialogue Machines
	High	Learning Machines	Idea Machines

Figure 3. A Normative View of the Relationship Between Information Systems and Uncertainty

Given clear objectives but uncertain causation, we need to explore problems, ask questions, analyze the analyzable and finally resort to judgement. Here, MIS cannot provide the answer but they can go part of the way, providing assistance through what Gorry and Scott-Morton (1971) would call decision support systems, Mason and Mitroff (1973) might call dialectical systems and Churchman (1971) calls inquiring systems. Examples of what we refer to as 'learning machines' are enquiry facilities, sensitivity analysis and 'what-if' models.

Given uncertainty or disagreement over objectives but relative certainty on causation, then values, principles, perspectives and interests conflict. In a rapidly changing economic, social and political environment, such bargaining situations may be increasing. Here, political processes are important where often the vital tasks include discussion, intelligence and problem-sharing to gather different points of view, seek conflict resolution or just keep talking. Examples of relevant information processing here might include 'think-tanks', information centers, consultative and participative processes, retreats and the like – all examples of what we refer to as 'dialogue machines'. The orientation is towards freeing channels of opinion and communication and toward polemics and debate, with the value of information being measured by the number of consistent points of view that can be persuasively argued with the data and within the context provided by the information system (Boland 1979).

Finally, given uncertainty in both dimensions, or decision by inspiration, we seek 'idea machines'. Here the formal MIS may provide multiple streams of thought which Koestler (1964) suggests triggers creativity. Other information processing forms may include the semi-confusing information systems suggested by Hedberg and Jonsson (1978) and the use of creativity techniques, such as Delphi processes or brainstorming. They will also include experience sharing and contact with other organizations or related thinkers. Certainly, fluid or organismic organizational design will be spontaneous, encouraging boundaries to be crossed and the fertilization of ideas (Burns and Stalker, 1961).

Most people will not argue with this exposition. When presented in such terms, they are prepared to acknowledge the variety of roles which information systems might serve and even the consequent variety of approaches to information system design and operation. However, although the analysis may be acceptable, it describes, we would venture to suggest, a set of circumstances which is very different than the reality of the relationship between information and decision-making which exists in many organizations. That reality which is so fundamental to our argument is illustrated in Figure 4.

		UNCERTAINTY ABOUT OBJECTIVES	
		Low	High
Uncertainty of Cause and Effect	Low	Answer Machines	Ammunition Machines
	High	Answer Machines	Rationalization Machines

Figure 4. Uncertainty Decision-Making and the Roles of Information Systems

On the whole we have learned how to develop MIS for decision by computation. While some problems may remain, quite successful 'answer machines' are in widespread use. Thereafter, however, organizational reality starts to diverge from the normative and all too appealing set of circumstances outlined in Figure 3. Rather than using 'learning machines' to confront the uncertainties inherent in cause and effect relationships, information system designers have sought to reduce or even camouflage them. Uncertainty, it would appear, is seen as a threatening rather than inevitable state of the world, which, rather than being exploited for what it is, needs to be masked by an enormous investment in tidy minded systems and in pushing down the boundaries of computational practice. So, in circumstances which cry out for information which can stimulate learning and the exercise of judgement, we find routine MIS which often assume the very certainties which cannot be found.

The management scientist seeks to develop optimizing models where descriptive models can only be appropriate. The same specialist promotes the use of probability models and modes of risk analysis where a sensitive use of deterministic models may better facilitate the exercise of judgement. The systems analyst prescribes enquiry systems which have specified answers rather than interrogation facilities for the user to select and develop, and the modeller seeks solutions as answers rather than frameworks for decision-making. All the above assume a certainty which the user has never readily experienced. Designers simply forget how much prior knowledge and insight their procedures require, or impute, and by so doing they are rarely, if ever, able to come to terms with the 'wicked' (Mason and Mitroff 1973) problems which constitute an important part of management practice.

In emphasising the more technical mechanisms for the improvement of information, designers so often ignore the complementary but equally essential investments which need to be made in interpretative and decision skills. In other words, our parent disciplines of computing, accounting and management science have sought for answers where the answer always be specified, aiming for technocratic solutions, regardless of the cost to either the user or the organizational environment.

Such approaches result in the presumption of states of quasi-certainty which do not exist and the use of particular forms of economic and scientific rationality which bear little or no relationship to those which are implicit in the processes of management decision-making.

Then, as we also suggest in Figure 4, far from creating a basis for dialogue and interchange, MIS tend to be used as 'ammunition machines' in decisions by compromise. By the use of this perhaps emotive term, we wish to point to the ways in which information systems serve to promote and articulate particular interested positions and values. Political processes in organizations give rise to the emergence and elaboration of information systems, as one party or interested group seeks to influence others. For, as Bariff and Galbraith (1978) point out, information systems may be used to perpetuate or modify decision-making processes and social structures. By influencing the accepted language of negotiation, such systems can help to shape what is regarded as problematic, what can be deemed to be a credible solution and, most important of all, the criteria which are used in their selection. In ways such as these, traditional management accounting systems and mechanisms for financial appraisal can be used to reduce the complexity of a decision environment into a simple uni-goal economic system that has a life of its own divorced from the broader realities of organizational functioning. As one manager put it: 'given a sensitive strategic decision (for example divestment), the information on the table is generally financial. Once the decision is made and we discuss its implementation, other information is used, such as engineering, marketing or personnel consideration'.

The 'idea machine' we suggested for decision by inspiration may appear to be the only contribution that MIS can make in the context of such extreme uncertainty. However, we suspect that that very uncertainty creates the need for other roles which they can and do serve. Rather than seeking to promote the creativity, inspiration and entrepreneurship which is so vital in such strategic contexts, MIS may more often than not operate as 'rationalization machines' seeking to legitimize and justify actions that have been decided upon. As Bower (1970) discovered, and as many managers have described to us, the widespread adoption of capital budgeting procedures has resulted in the availability of justification devices rather than the simple and unproblematic provision of information for, and prior to, decision-making.

We do not seek to question the necessity for rationalization machines, for organizations require mechanisms through which they can legitimize what is to be done and retrospectively create a rationale for action. What we do suggest is, that the information processing which is typical of such procedures, be recognized for what it is, and that more active acknowledgement be given to the fact that the creativity and inspiration, which are so necessary in such contexts, are more likely to spring out of socially interactive forms of information processing.

By introducing our rather strong metaphors for information and decision, we are calling for a re-orientation away from the exclusive emphasis on technocratic and bureaucratic forms of information processing which is so characteristic of today's information system practice. There is, we think, an urgent need to acknowledge the reality of information practice in its full diversity; to see, in other words, the processes which create the roles for information processing and give rise to information systems in their wider organizational context. Such metaphors point to both the present existence of, and extended future possibilities for, MIS designs which acknowledge the uncertainties of organizational life. Hedberg and Jonsson (1978), in prescribing semi-confuring information systems, called for a similar reorientation. Like them, we advocate a move to a process view of MIS rather than the structured view which has been prevalent hitherto. Such a view would be dynamic rather than static, emphasizing the roles which information processing plays on the actions and interactions through which and by which managers make sense of their environments and cope with uncertainty.

TOWARDS INFORMATION MANAGEMENT

In summary, we can state that many MIS specialists adopt a partial and rather idiosyncratic view of the role which information processing does and can serve in organizations. Emphasizing the importance of formal and systemic approaches, they invest heavily in a perspective and approach which can be, and often is, radically at variance with the way in which managers in their own organizations engage in the active and influential processing of information. Indeed, we frequently get the impression that the MIS function is increasingly operating in a rather isolated, albeit comfortable, organizational niche. That is not to say that it lacks influence. Isolated though it may sometimes be from the more active processing of information in organizations, it can nonetheless have an important influence on the delineation of the desirable and the possible. However, that influence stems not from the appropriateness of the MIS designs, but from the way in which the resultant information is taken up and used by those managers who strive to personally influence ongoing processes of organizational control. So, in the last resort, it may well be that it is the managers, or at least some of them, who put the management into MIS!

If these claims are valid, it becomes apparent that information management which emphasizes the development of conventional MIS in isolation from their organization context will only at best yield marginal gain. At worst, it might be dysfunctional, for it can perpetuate and strengthen information processing forms which neither represent the social reality of organizations nor the real complexity and uncertainty of the organization and its environment. Indeed, it is by no means unlikely that such a limited view of information processing may be impairing organizational performance and threatening organizational survival.

However, we should not overlook the fact that today's organizations do contain a mix of vibrant and varied information flows and processes. The routine co-exists with the non-routine, the official with the unofficial and despite the massive investment in formal MIS and the application of limited information-decision concepts, the undercurrents of the non-routine and unofficial have survived. Indeed, we would like at least to acknowledge the possibility that their survival is the result of under-emphasis and inattention. It could well be that if we attempt to plan, organize and control them too much, we may kill the very spontaneity, flexibility and informality on which their effectiveness depends. This is indeed a real possibility. Nevertheless, we are still convinced that if information management is to offer something of real benefit to organizations, it has to have a framework that can at least place the informal within its wider context. Otherwise a continued focus on the narrow, technical aspects of information processing may not only ultimately drive out these very necessary complements and counterparts, but also we may fail to fully exploit the real possibilities for the organizational processing of information which emerging technologies may offer (Earl, 1978b).

The wider, alternative and complementary forms of information processing which currently co-exist in organizations must therefore start to enter into the discourse of MIS designers, managers and even users. Indeed, a vital task of information management needs to be the explication of a broader framework for the consideration of information processing in organizations and an understanding of its implications for MIS analysis and design.

We can summarize our own, albeit tentative, suggestions for the outline of such a framework in the following way:

- New frameworks and metaphors are required to re-orient our information thinking.
- A major goal of such frameworks and metaphors is to explicate social reality and challenge technocratic wisdoms.
- Information problems do not necessarily require information systems; alternative forms of information processing can, do and should exist in organizations.
- Investment in organizational processes and structural forms of information processing are required to complement the MIS.
- We need to improve our understanding of how organizational decision-making and control is achieved, before major advances in MIS will be possible.
- Many MIS will need to generate frameworks rather than providing mere solutions.

With such a broader organizational perspective, tasks and responsibilities of *information management* will take on a very different form.

With the technical so explicitly linked to the organizational, no one management function can be, or should be, responsible for the whole of information processing. The role of the information specialist therefore will need to become that of a catalyst for change. The user, in contrast, will need to have the confidence to explicate and describe his own information environment, processing and problems. In such a context, progress in information management therefore will depend on *us*, as managers and users as much as, if not more than, on *them* as specialists.

REFERENCES

1. R. L. Ackoff, 'Management Misinformation Systems', Management Science, Dec. (1967), 147–156.
2. C. Argyris, 'Organisational Learning and Management Information Systems', Accounting, Organisations and Society, Vol. 2. No. 2. (1977), 113–123.
3. M. L. Bariff and J. R. Galbraith, 'Intraorganisational Power Considerations for Designing Information Systems', Accounting, Organisations and Society, Vol. 3. No. 1. (1978), 15–28.
4. R. J. Boland, Control, 'Causality and Information System Requirements', Accounting, Organisations and Society, Vol. 4. No. 4. (1979).
5. J. Bower, 'Managing the Resource Allocation Process', Division of Research, Graduate School of Business Administration, Harvard University, 1970.
6. T. Burns, and G. M. Stalker, 'The Management of Innovation', (London, Tavistock, 1961).
7. J. Child, 'Strategies of Control and Organisation Behaviour', Administrative Science Quarterly, (1973), 1–17.
8. J. Child, 'Management and Organisational Factors Associated with Company Performance – Part 1', Journal of Management Studies (1974), 175–189.
9. J. Child, 'Managerial and Organisational Factors Associated with Company Performance – Part 2', Journal of Management Studies, (1975), 12–27.
10. W. Churchman, 'The Design of Inquiring Systems', (Basic Books, New York, 1971).
11. M. J. Earl, 'Prototype Systems for Accounting, Information and Control', Accounting Organisations and Society, Vol. 3. No. 2. (1978a). 18–172.
12. M. J. Earl, What Microprocessors Mean', Management Today, September (1978b)67–71.
13. J. Galbraith, 'Designing Complex Organisations', Addison-Wesley, 1973.
14. C. F. Gibson, and R. L. Nolan, 'Managing the Four Stages of HDP Growth', Harvard Business Review, (Jan.-Feb. 1974), 76–88.
15. G. A. Gorry and M. S. Scott-Morton, 'A Framework for Management Information Systems', Sloan Management Review, (Fall, 1971), 56–70.
16. P. Georgiou, 'The Goal Paradigm and Notes Towards a Counter Paradigm', Administrative Science Quarterly. (1973), 291–310.
17. P. Grinyer, and D. Norburn, 'Planning for Existing Markets: Perceptions of Executives and Financial Performance', Journal of the Royal Statistical Society, Series A, (1975), 70–97.
18. B. Hedberg and S. Jonsson, 'Designing Semi-Confusing Information Systems for Organisations in Changing Environments', Accounting, Organisations and Society, Vol. 3., No. 1 (1978), 47–64.
19. A. G. Hopwood, 'Criteria of Corporate Effectiveness', in M. Brodie, and R. Bennet, (Eds.) 'Managerial Effectiveness', (Thames Valley Regional Management Centre, 1979).
20. A. G. Hopwood, 'An Accounting System and Managerial Behaviour', Saxon House, 1973.

21. A. Koestler, 'The Act of Creation', (Hutchinson, London 1964.
22. J. Lorsch and S. Allen, III, 'Managing Diversity and Independence'. Division of Research, Graduate School of Business, Harvard University, 1973.
23. R. O. Mason, 'Basic Concepts for Designing Management Information Systems', AIS Research Paper No. 8. Graduate School of Business Administration, University of California, Los Angeles, October, 1969.
24. R. O. Mason and I. M. Mitroff, 'A Program for Research on MIS', Management Science, (Jan. 1973), 475–487.
25. H. Mintzberg, 'The Myths of MIS', California Management Review. (Fall, 1972) 92–97.
26. C. Oloffson and P. A. Svalander, 'The Medical Services Change Over to a Poor Environment – 'New Poor' Behaviour', Unpublished Working Paper, University of Linkoping. (1975).
27. H. A. Simon, G. Guetzkow, G. Kozmetsky and G. Tyndall, 'Centralisation v. Decentralisation in Organising the Controller's Department', New York, Controllership Foundation Inc. 1954.
28. J. D. Thompson and A. Tuden, 'Strategies, Structures and Processes of Organisational Decision', in J. D. Thompson, et. al. (Eds.), 'Comparative Studies in Administration', University of Pittsburgh Press, 1959.
29. W. E. Turcotte, 'Control Systems, Performance and Satisfaction in Two State Agencies', Administrative Science Quarterly, (1974), 60–73.
30. W. M. Zani, 'Blueprint for MIS', Harvard Business Review, (Nov.-Dec. 1970), 95–100.

4. A FAILURE OF DIRECTION*

Robert D. Galliers

ABSTRACT: Many corporate systems fail to deliver the desired benefits. On the basis of his UK research findings, Bob Galliers outlines the factors which make for success and failure.

INTRODUCTION

Most British firms are wrestling with the problem of information systems investment. The recognition of its importance has dawned only recently.

How can companies ensure that their investment in information technology is reaping dividends? The evidence is that comparatively few British organisations have been successful in exploiting IT to anything like full effect. And even fewer have been able to align IT with broader goals.

These difficulties have led to increasing attention being paid to the need for effective strategic planning of IT investments.

In this paper, we turn the spotlight inwards to companies themselves, and publish the results of new research into how information system planning is actually carried out in British business. The findings are based on a survey of IS (information systems) management in 130 UK companies, conducted by Bob Galliers in 1986.

The survey provides a unique insight into the views of IS professionals and a small group of consultants on the current success of systems planning, revealing information not previously available. (Figure 1. indicates the sectors coveredby the survey.) It describes what companies hoped to achieve, the various approaches used, and whether the results matched up to expectations. In follow-up research it is intended to seek out the views of management, thus providing an opportunity for comparison between the opinions of the two groups.

The principal findings of the survey do not make comforting reading. They confirm what many senior executives have long felt, that there is widespread disagreement among the IS profession as to the objectives of IS planning, and how best to tackle it.

The very term 'IS planning' means different things to different people, ranging from strategy formulation to little more than IS project management. Indeed, in as many as 80 per cent of cases, no distinction is made between strategic and tactical planning, with consequent confusion over the desired outcome of the process, and the best means of achieving it.

** A version of this paper has been published by Business Computing and Communications, July-August, 1986.*

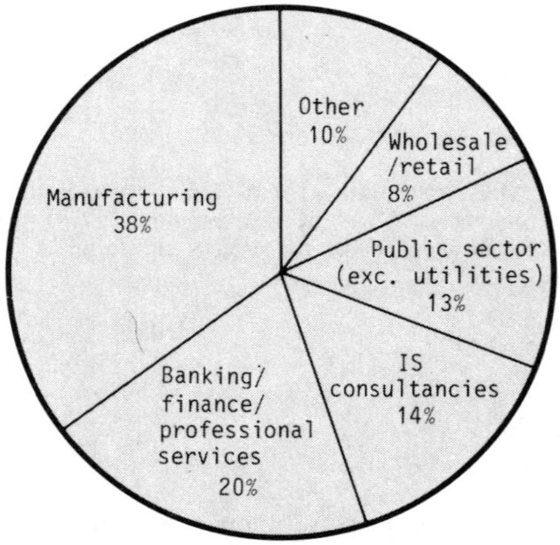

Figure 1. Sectors covered by the survey.

Even more worrying is the fact that only 20 per cent of companies appeared to have the desire to match information systems to business needs. Another damning statistic to emerge is that in up to 50 per cent of cases IS planning was either totally divorced from, or only tenuously linked to, the corporate business plan.

In view of these facts, it is perhaps not surprising that, when asked to evaluate the success of IS planning from the viewpoint of their senior management, 41 per cent of IS professionals admitted that it was unsuccessful.

But the blame cannot be laid at the door of IS departments. The need to involve senior management and users in the planning process is widely recognised. In fact it was ranked as the single factor most critical to the success of the IS planning process.

It seems, however, that IS staff frequently have difficulty in persuading their senior executives to take the reins when it comes to new technology. In only 20 per cent of cases were IS planning projects headed by senior management.

THE REASONS FOR IS PLANNING

Looking at the findings in more detail, one encouraging point to emerge is that the great majority of firms do at least appear to attempt to plan their IS developments. Eighty four per cent of those surveyed try to plan their information systems, and 61 per cent do so on a regular basis. Only four per cent have never undertaken IS planning nor intend to do so.

Even allowing for the likely bias in returns, it seems probable that most British firms are wrestling with the problem of IS investment. However, Figure 2 shows that

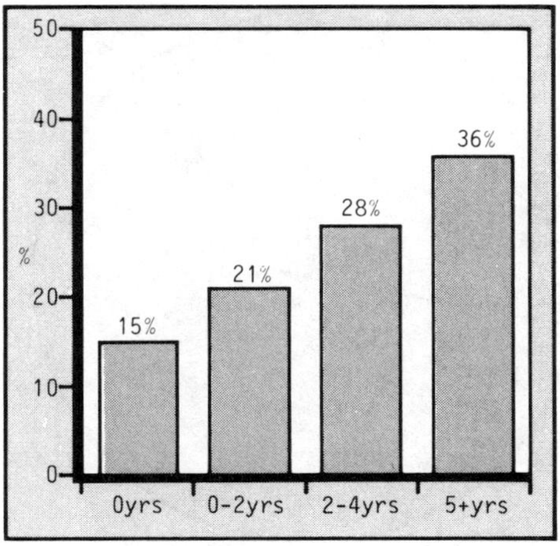

Figure 2. Length of IS planning experience.

the recognition of its importance has dawned only comparitively recently for most organisations.

The diversity of approach to IS planning is illustrated first by the remarkable differences in the composition of project teams (see figure 3). The number of personnel involved varies from just one or two to over ten, although in the majority of cases the number of team members is restricted to between three and five.

But the discrepancies go much deeper than mere headcount. There is a major divergence of opinion on such fundamental issues as: the reason for undertaking IS planning in the first place; the primary focus of attention, the actual approach or methodology, and the desired outcome. These differences are summarised in table 1.

As can be seen, the motivation advanced for IS planning varies from such nebulous sentiments as 'sound management practice' to more hardnosed goals such as 'improving information systems in support of business objectives.' However, it is clear that several of the principal reasons relate to the needs of the IS department itself.

For example there is the need to cost-justify (presumably ever-growing) IT budgets to a (presumably sceptical) management; the need to ensure a coherent technical strategy for IT investment, and to resolve conflicting demands for IT services from different user departments. It is these pressures, rather than the desire of senior mañagement to align IT with the business plan, which is likely to precipitate the planning process.

This fact is also reflected in the approach of many studies, which again vary dramatically. In broad terms 'homebrew', in-house approaches out-number the well-known, proprietary methodologies by over 3:1. (Previous research has shown that this is also the case in the US.) They actually account for almost 60 per cent of the total

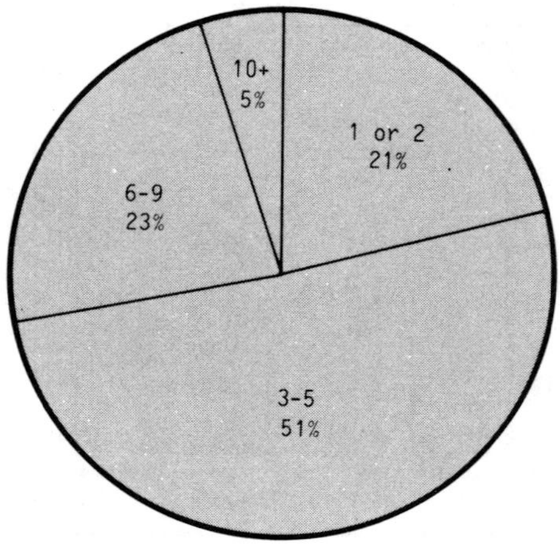

Figure 3. The size of IS planning teams.

(although these sometimes also incorporate aspects of proprietary approaches).

But of the in-house approaches, only roughly half are top-down in nature, driven by business strategy/objectives and involving any analysis of business processes. The rest are 'bottom-up' studies: reactive rather than proactive, assessing requests for IT or proposed IS developments in the light of available resources.

THE OUTCOME OF THE PROCESS

When it comes to stated outcomes of the IS planning process, there is a heavy emphasis on factors such as identifying the information needs of the organisation, and an associated, prioritised applications portfolio. Similarly, identification of the resources (finance, staff and equipment) required for the IS plan featured prominently.

What is interesting, however, is that lip service was also paid to the alignment of IS with corporate objectives – mentioned by some 85 per cent of respondents. This figure contrasts starkly with the mere 20 per cent who claimed that realignment of IT was a reason for undertaking an IS plan in the first place. It seems therefore to be regarded as an, albeit important, by-product of the planning process.

Other goals seen as desirable included, sensibly enough, identification of the organisational changes brought about by new systems, and the allocation of responsibility between user departments and the IS function – an area of growing concern to many IS managers. (In situations where there is sufficient expertise within a user department and the system to be developed has little impact on other departments, it would be appropriate for the users to develop the system themselves.

Table 1: Major aspects of IS Planning as undertaken in UK organisations.

Reason	Focus	Approach	Outcome
1. Matching IS to business needs (competitive advantage; strategic impact) **20%**	**1.** Identification of Applications Portfolio **68%**	**1.** Formal, commonly known or proprietary approach **31%**	**1.** Prioritised Applications Portfolio **86%**
2. Resource considerations (accountability; IS justification; ROI) **18%**	**2.** Business Requirements – Current **68%**	**2.** Formal, "bottom-up" approaches (eg. matching requests against resources) **27%**	**2.** IS closely aligned to corporate objectives **85%**
3. Coordination (consistent, corporate approach to IS) **16%**	**3.** Business Requirements – Future **67%**	**3.** Formal, "top-down" approaches (eg. bus. strategy-driven; analysis of business processes) **25%**	**3.** Identification of required resources assoc. with IS Plan **80%**
4. "Sound management practice" **10%**	**4.** Identification of software packages which may be acquired **39%**	**4.** Informal, ad hoc approaches **20%**	**4.** Identification of IT req's. for org. as a whole **78%**
5. Need for effective IS/Past failures **10%**	**5.** Allocation of responses for IS developments between IS & user functions **31%**	**5.** Data analysis approaches (focus on devel. of corp. data models) **4%**	**5.** Identifications of IT req's. for indiv. applications **65%**
6. Need to prioritise IS developments (increased demand for IS services) **8%**	**6.** Database design **22%**	**6.** IT-led approaches (focus on IT availability/ trends **1%**	**6.** Identification of req'd or change as a result of intro. of IT **61%**
7. External advice (eg. consultancy advice) or req'mt. (eg. HQ policy) **7%**	**7.** IT-led (focus on IT availability/ trends) **20%**		**7.** Allocation of respon. for IS development between IS & user function **59%**

Conversely, in situations where corporate information is involved, responsibility for the development is more appropriately invested in the IS function).

It is interesting to note that other, more immediately tangible outcomes such as a reduction in the development backlog or the costs involved in the IS development process, or actual/prototype IS, appear as outcomes in only a third or so of the cases.

Indeed, it would appear that specific goals rank very much as being of secondary importance compared to other factors such as senior management commitment to, and involvement in, the IS planning process.

FACTORS OF SUCCESS AND FAILURE

The process of planning itself, provided there is sufficient management involvement, is seen as being of prime importance, since improved relationships and communication are likely to result between management and the IS function. The factors deemed important by IS managers and consultants for the successful outcome of IS planning are summarised in table 2.

As can be seen, for both IS managers and consultants alike, six of the top ten success factors relate to the involvement of senior management in the IS planning process. In only one instance is there a specific outcome of sufficient significance which can be ranked as one of the top ten critical success factors.

However, one factor which ranks high in both the opinion of IS managers and consultants is the need to formally review both the process and outcomes of IS planning. Despite this recognition, it is unfortunately the case that a formal review takes place in only 11 per cent of all the cases in the survey – just 6 per cent if the responses from the consultancies are excluded.

Table 2: Views of UK IS Managers and Consultants as regards Factors Critical to Successful IS Planning.

Rank	IS Managers Success Factors	Rank	Consultants Success Factors
1.	Commitment of Senior Management	**1.**	Involvement of Senior Management
2.	Involvement of Senior Management	**2.**	= Commitment of Senior Management
3.	Involvement of Senior & User Mgmt.	**3.**	= IS Planning based on Corporate Objectives
4.	Improved Understanding between Management and IS	**4.**	Involvement of Senior & User Management
5.	Review of IS Plans	**5.**	IS Planning Approach Based on Future Scenarios
6.	IS Planning Approach includes Opportunity to Debate Alternatives	**6.**	Process/Outcomes Well Supported by IS Management Function
7.	Chief Information Officer part of Senior Management Team	**7.**	Review of IS Plans
8.	Process/Outcomes Well Supported by IS Management Function	**8.**	Improved understanding between Management and IS function.

Major pitfalls which require to be avoided are summarised in table 3. These, for the most part, are the converse of the critical success factors listed in table 2. Other factors contributing to failure, however, include the lack of planning experience and credibility of IS staff involved in IS planning; the lack of a clear business plan/direction for the company; reliance on bottom-up style IS planning (remember that this style appears to be used in over one quarter of the organisations surveyed); planner over optimism; and inflexibility in the IS plan itself.

A CRITICAL GAP

A key point to emerge from tables 2 and 3 is that a strong link between corporate/business planning and IS planning is an important contributory factor to the success of the latter. In practice, however, this connection is rarely made.

Participants were asked to rank on a scale of 1 to 4 the strength of the link between the two processes. In 16 per cent of cases they were totally separate, and in 43 per cent only tenuously linked. In only 10 per cent of companies surveyed was IS planning fully integrated with the business plan.

One reason for this state of affairs is shown in figure 4. The importance in IS management's eyes of the participation of senior executives and line management in IS planning shows up clearly. But business planners are found surprisingly rarely on IS planning teams, given the generally accepted wisdom of meshing together the IS and corporate plans.

Another paradox emerges when one examines the leadership of IS planning teams. Both IS managers and consultants believe that a senior executive rather than an IS representative should head up the team. On a scale of 1 to 4, IS respondents scored management 2.976 as opposed to 2.723 for themselves; while the emphasis was even more pronounced by the consultants: 3.000 to 1.353.

Table 3: Major Problems/Pitfalls in IS Planning, According to UK IS Managers and Consultants.

Rank	Problems/Pitfalls in IS Planning
1.	Lack of Management Commitment to Planning/Change
2.	Lack of IS Planning Experience/Credibility
3.	Lack of Business Plan/Direction
4.	Lack of Senior Management Support/Involvement
5.	Bottom-up/IT-led IS Planning
6.	Rate of Technological and Environmental Change
7.	Planner Over-optimism
8.	Inflexibility/Rigidity of the IS Plan

Despite their good intentions, however, in practice an IS executive is three times more likely to head the team: 63 per cent as opposed to 20 per cent, while middle/user managers took the chair in just 12 per cent of cases.

THE UK PRACTICE

Finally, let us take a look at how successful current IS planning appears to be (according to IS managers and consultants) compared to the initial efforts of the organisations concerned.

Respondents were asked to rank, again on a 1 to 4 scale, how successful they viewed their attempts at IS planning, from three distinct viewpoints: from the IS viewpoint, from senior management's viewpoint and from that of user/middle management. The responses to these questions are summarised in table 4.

In each case, there is a quite strong belief that IS planning has improved over recent years, particularly by the consultants who, interestingly, rank their current attempts at IS planning considerably higher than do IS managers. And while the former believe that their efforts have had the most impact at senior management level, the latter see the greatest benefits occurring within their own departments.

What table 4 does not show, however, is the proportion of respondents who believe that their IS planning endeavours have improved on earlier attempts, as against those believing the contrary. In fact, the majority of respondents who felt able to pass judgement on this question indicated that current efforts are no more or less successful than were their initial efforts.

A minority, but a not insubstantial number, of IS managers actually indicated that their efforts are *less* successful now than they were initially in relation to the impact of IS planning on the running of their own departments and on senior management. Respectively, 21.9 per cent and 19.5 per cent were of this view, while 43.8 per cent and 29.9 per cent believed that, on the contrary, things had improved.

As regards the impact of IS planning on user/middle management, the belief was that in six cases out of ten, things stayed the same, while there had been an improvement in 32.9 per cent of cases. Very few – 5.3 per cent – thought that their efforts were now less well received by user/middle management than was the case when IS planning was first attempted.

It is interesting to note that a formal review of the IS plans takes place in only 11 per cent of the cases.

CONCLUSION

All in all, it is reasonable to conclude that IS planning meets with a degree of success in a majority of organisations, but that these efforts are not particularly well received in far too many instances. Bearing in mind the likely bias in favour of IS planning on the part of respondents to the survey, this conclusion may well turn out to be an overstatement of the success of IS planning as currently undertaken in this country.

Table 4. Views of IS Managers and consultants as to the Relative Success IS Planning as it Impacts on Senior and User Management and on the IS Function.

	Snr. Mgmt. Viewpoint			User Mgmt. Viewpoint			IS Mgmt. Viewpoint		
	Successful	Unsuccessful	Mean (max 4)	Successful	Unsuccessful	Mean (max 4)	Successful	Unsuccessful	Mean (max 4)
IS M'grs.	42%	59%	2.41	37%	63%	2.24	46%	54%	2.48
Initially Cons'nts	93%	7%	3.36	72%	29%	3.07	64%	36%	2.86
IS M'grs.	59%	42%	2.59	55%	46%	2.58	66%	35%	2.74
Currently Cons'nts	93%	7%	3.57	86%	14%	3.21	100%	0%	3.21

Table 5: The IS Planning Team Membership.

	Never	Occasionally	Always
Senior Management	14%	24%	61%
User/Middle Mgmt.	10%	34%	56%
Business Planners	52%	33%	15%
External Consult's	33%	62%	4%

Improvements clearly need to occur. These may be achieved through greater understanding by IS staff of the business in which their organisation operates and of the intricacies of planning. Greater understanding of, and commitment to, IS on the part of management is also necessary. The IS planning process must be seen as a corporate exercise, not just as an IS one.

Finally, clear performance measures must be agreed upon prior to embarking on a planning exercise and the outcome reviewed in the light of these measures at appropriate intervals.

Without this clarification and management involvement, it is possible that IS planning will lead to worsened communications between the IS function and management. In an era where IT has the potential for competitive advantage and strategic impact, this could ultimately be disastrous to the continuing well-being of the organisation concerned.

CHAPTER III

LEARNING TO LIVE WITH THE TECHNOLOGY

INTRODUCTION

Learning to Live With the Technology

Robert D. Galliers

Chapter II dealt with the growing realisation that the information resource was something which required management and the inherent qualities of which required special consideration. In parallel, organisations in the latter half of the 1970s, and into the 1980s, were becoming increasingly aware that the technology itself presented a range of problems and issues with which they were unfamiliar and for which they were unprepared. In addition, a number of promises and expectations arising from developments in the technology remained unfulfilled. Organisations began to realise that the introduction of information technology required much more careful consideration than had previously been thought necessary. This chapter deals with a number of management issues associated with the organisational impact of information technology.

First, though, we take a critical look at a commonly accepted model of the growth stages, most organisations experience in the use of information technology. The hypothesis that underlies the stages of growth model – sometimes known as the Nolan model – is that organisations go through a learning curve in the use of the technology which parallels the relative budget allocated to its acquisition. It has been argued that this is not a particularly sound premise on which to base a theory of growth, and also there are some weaknesses in the theory (as amply demonstrated by the first paper in this chapter). Nevertheless, a theory of growth provides a useful framework for the consideration of how far an organisation has gone along the road to being a 'mature' information technology user. This also helps in understanding the kind of information systems management issues which are most likely to prevail at the different stages of growth.

Another feature, arising from the introduction of information technology, with which companies have begun to be increasingly familiar, is the fact that the technology itself is capable of having a considerable impact on organisational structures. The second paper in this chapter discusses the organisational impact of the technology in the retail industry and provides us with the timely warning that, as well as having the potential of de-skilling tasks at the operational level (of which most managers are aware), it can also reduce managerial responsibility at the middle management level, thus producing a much 'flatter' organisational hierarchy. Such issues may or may not be seen to be of significance in a particular organisation. Nevertheless, it is important that management is aware of the likely impact of the technology on the organisational structure prior to the introduction of technology, so that this is taken into account at the time when acquisition decisions are being made and undesirable side-effects can be countered.

As a result of the realisation that the technology could – and did – have the capability of changing organisational structures and individual jobs, two different developments occurred. One, the subject of the third paper in this chapter, relates to the need to carefully consider job (re) design in relation to the introduction of information technology. This paper presents a case study on the topic in the use of computerised numerically controlled (CNC) machine tools in an engineering company. Arising from the case study, a set of conclusions and predictions are made regarding the management issues associated with the operation of information technology in manufacturing industries.

The second development, which is the subject of the final paper in this chapter, stresses the necessity of organisational policy to incorporate a consideration of technological trends, with a view to harnessing the potential the technology offers in terms of assisting in the attainment of strategic objectives and, furthermore, in moulding strategy formulation. The central message is that those organisations that really want to take advantage of the opportunities made available by the technology, must develop strategic vision or run the risk of losing the opportunity for competitive advantage – a topic which is dealt with in more detail in chapter IV.

1. EVOLUTION AND ORGANIZATIONAL INFORMATION SYSTEMS: AN ASSESSMENT OF NOLAN'S STAGE MODEL*

John Leslie King and Kenneth L. Kraemer

ABSTRACT: Richard Nolan's stage model is the best known and most widely cited model of computing evolution in organizations. The model's development over a decade demonstrates its own evolution from a simple theory, based on the factoring of change states indicated by changes in computing budgets, to an elaborate account of the characteristics of six stages of computing growth. An analysis of the model's logical and empirical structure reveals a number of problems in its formulation that help to account for the fact that its principal tenets have not been independently validated. The model is shown to be an 'evolutionistic' theory within the theories of evolution in the social sciences, focusing on assumed directions of growth and an implied end state toward which growth proceeds, and suffering from problems inherent in such theories. Further research based on an 'evolutionary' view of computing growth is suggested as a means of improving theories of computing in organizations.

INTRODUCTION

The best known model of evolution related to organizational information systems is the 'stage' model developed by Richard Nolan. This model, which first appeared in print in 1973, has been cited extensively as the major statement about the growth of information systems in organizations. From its beginnings as a tentative hypothesis [26], it has become regarded as an empirically grounded theory [27] and an accepted description of how changes in organizational information systems take place over time [1, 2, 7, 13, 22, 29].

Despite the widespread attention Nolan's model has attracted, it has never been subjected to a careful analytical review in the published literature. Given the

The work reported in this paper is based on two projects, one supported by IBM Corporation and the other one supported by the National Science Foundation. The opinions presented here are the authors' and should not be ascribed to IBM or the National Science Foundation.

* *Reprinted from Communications of the ACM, 27, No 5., May, 1984.*

John L. King holds the Chair of Information & Computer Science at the University of California, Irvine.
Kenneth L. Kraemer is with the Graduate School of Management, Public Policy Research Organisation, University of California, Irvine.

importance of the model in the information systems field, and the interpretations of data and prescriptions for management based upon it, such a review is overdue. This paper reviews the basic structure of the model itself, discusses its use as a theory of evolution within the context of explanations of evolution describing the social sciences, and assesses the model's practical utility as a descriptor of the process of change in organizational information systems over time.

THE NOLAN MODEL

The Nolan model[1] does not appear in the literature as a single model, but rather as a number of versions of the same model developed between 1969 and 1979. The model originated in discussions between Nolan, Neil Churchill, and F. Warren McFarlan between 1969 and 1971 [26], and was subsequently elaborated upon by Gibson and Nolan [9], Nolan [25], and Nolan [27]. Although basic aspects of the model have remained the same over time, sigificant elaborations of the earlier model have appeared in later versions. In this section we examine the development of the model through these versions.

THE 1973 VERSION

The core concept behind the model first appeared in print in Nolan's 1973 paper in *Communications of the ACM* [26]. The model was presented as a hypothesis grounded in observations and discussions with managers in three firms. The experiences of these firms formed the basis of a 'stage theory' of computing growth intended to meet two conditions adopted from Kuznets [19]: identification of distinct and empirically verifiable characteristics of change, and detailed specification of the characteristics of succession whereby one stage moves to the next.

To capture the characteristics of change in computing in organizations, Nolan made the assumption that changes in the amount organizations spend on computing can serve as a surrogate measure for change in a wide array of environmental and technical variables, including changes in industry conditions, corporate sales, organizational strategy, management practices, and uses of computer technology ([26], p. 401). Plotting the changes in budgets for computing in the three firms revealed that budgets seemed to grow according to an S-shaped curve. This led to a second major assumption: The turning points in the budget curve (shown in Figure 1) are transition points between stages of growth. The turning points *A, B* and *C* in Figure 1 break the *S* curve into four stages. From here, Nolan made a third major assumption: These stages 'capture the central tendencies' of the major tasks in the management of computing – planning, organizing and controlling. Working backward, the logic of the model runs as follows: The major activities in the management of computing are identifiable in stages that correspond to periods of stability along the

[1] We use the title 'Nolan Model' for convenience. Nolan himself described the origin of the model and the role others played in it in Nolan [21, 25].

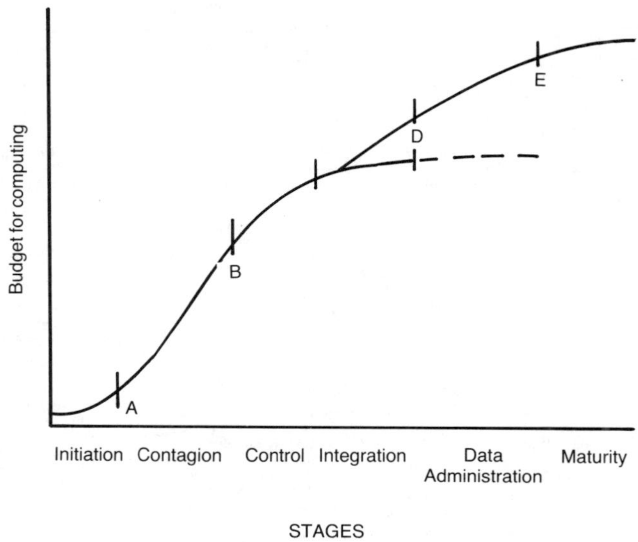

Figure 1. Budget Curve and Nolan's Stage Theory

growth path of computing use, traced by changes in computing budgets which act as a surrogate measure of environmental and technical variables that make up the computing phenomenon in an organization. Management practices related to computing are thus explained as responses to environmental and technical changes. (The complete model based on all versions is shown in Table I.)

Briefly, Nolan's four stages from the 1973 model are:

I. *Initiation*: Introduction of computing into the organization to meet basic needs; slow growth in use; beginning of problems caused by computing's role as a 'change agent'; little management response to these problems; decentralized control; minimal planning.

II. *Contagion*: Rapid growth in computing use due to top management commitment to exploiting computing potential plus high expectations among users; rapid rise in costs; top management search for controls to contain cost growth; beginning of centralization; little increase in planning.

III. *Control*: Cost control measures instituted by top management; planning now a major priority; computing function centralized; DP manager's position raised in the organizational hierarchy; priority setting mandatory; standards established for programming, documentation, and operations; chargeout systems adopted to impose marketlike constraints on use; controls often

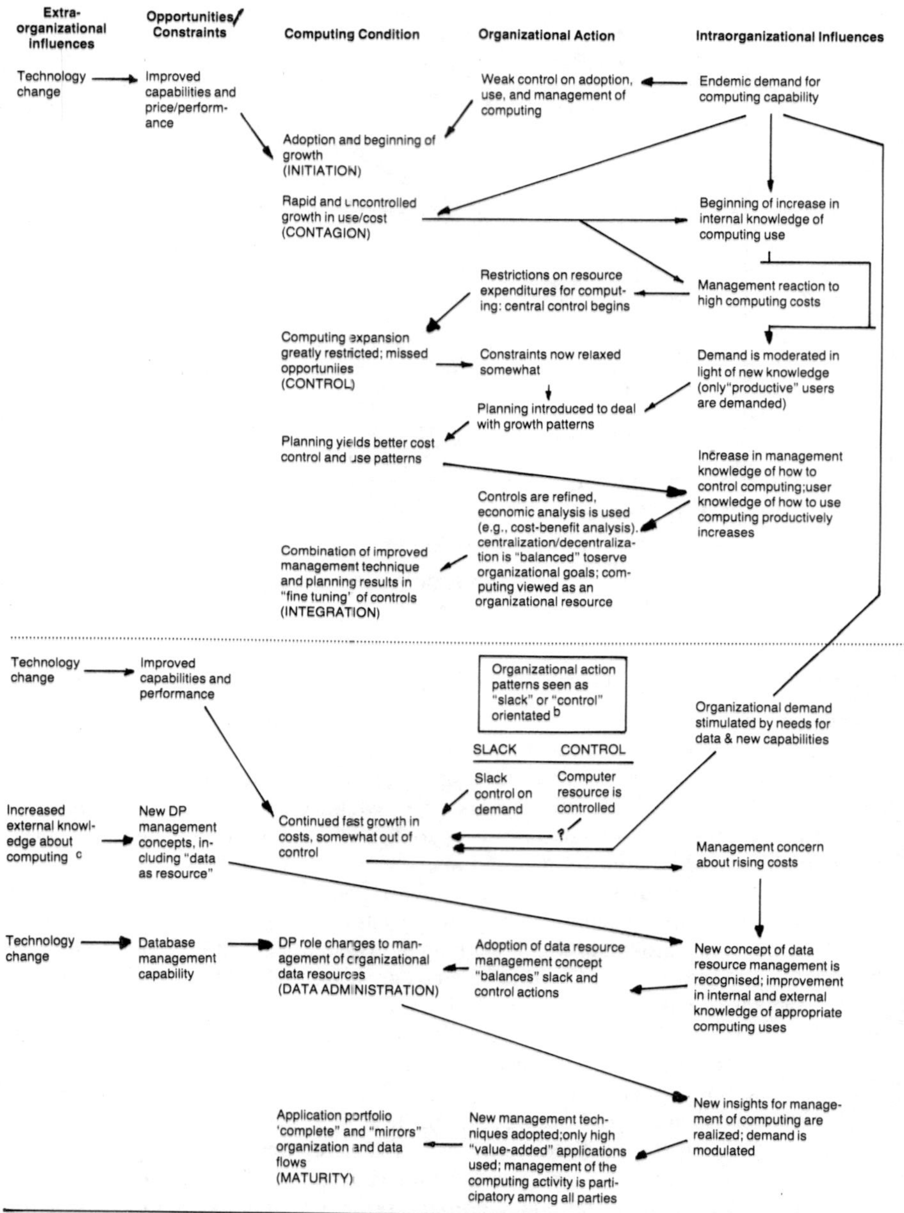

a Titles in brackets are the stages of growth Nolan posits.
b This refined concept of organizational action appears first in Nolan, 1977.
c "Internal" and "external" knowledge is explained in Nolan 1979.
............Indicates demarcation between the 1973/1974 and 1977/1979 models

proving to be too stringent, resulting in failure to exploit the potential of computing or to meet user expectations.

IV. *Integration*: Controls refined to allow exploitation of computing without runaway costs; planning well established: users more knowledgeable and capable in their uses of computing; operations more rational; economic analyses (e.g., cost benefit analysis) used to set priorities for new systems; chargeout systems modified to ease restriction on use; system analysts sometimes decentralized to user departments to encourage improved systems development; centralization/decentralization decisions made in light of organizational and business strategy; growth slowing markedly, but new investments bringing greater marginal benefits.

Nolan claimed, in this paper, that no organizations had reached Stage IV-Integration, but that they would begin to do so soon and growth in computing costs would begin to decline as they did so. Using the assumption that the stages capture the management tasks of control, organization, and planning, Nolan summarized the implications of the model: control is lax in Stages I and II; reactionary and overdone in Stage III; and refined and effective in Stage IV.

THE 1974 VERSION

Although Nolan specifically stated that the model does not assert cause and effect relationships ([26], p. 401), it clearly does so. This was borne out in the 1974 version of the model [9], which translated the descriptive model of the 1973 paper into a prescriptive tool to aid managers in dealing with computing growth. The model was used to explain growth patterns and to predict future growth within the context of changes in intraorganizational and extraorganizational variables, such as the emergence of new technology and increased organizational sophistication in computing use ([9], p. 77). The four stages from the 1973 model were presented anew, with some changes in their names, and were discussed in terms of the management challenges each stage poses. The most important change in this new formulation of the stages was the claim that the fourth stage, formerly called integration, was actually a state of maturity in the use of computing. In this stage, the manager of the computing enterprise would have to balance the need for maintaining stability in computing use with the need to respond flexibly to new opportunities brought by changes in technology.

At the conclusion of the 1974 paper, Gibson and Nolan revised the 1973 observation, claiming that some organizations were already in Stage IV. More importantly, they specifically stated that, the S-shaped curve from which the changes were identified, was driven primarily by changes in computing technology ([9], p. 88). They claimed that most changes up to that time had arisen from advancements in hardware, but that future changes would come from advances in software, particularly database management systems. Such changes were predicted to initiate new S-shaped curves, and the same integrative problems present in the earlier four stages would underlie future S-shaped curves. Thus, technological change was established as the model's basic causal agent, and management reactions to those changes were established as the effects of that cause. Although not noted by Gibson and Nolan, this formulation posits Stage IV-Maturity as an equilibrium stage in which computing growth is brought under control by appropriate management actions, and persisting until new technological changes upset the equilibrium.

THE 1977 VERSION

Nolan subsequently used the stage model in a study of the effectiveness of chargeout policies in 18 firms [25]. In this study, the model was used to describe the firms in terms of their relative positions on the growth continuum. Although no data were presented to support the claim, Nolan stated that the budget growth curve was used to develop an initial stage profile of the companies ([25], p. 30). The detailed data presented suggest that the factoring of the firms by stage was accomplished primarily by comparing variables in individual firms with variables assumed to be associated with each stage as outlined in earlier versions of the model. Four variables were used in this analysis: the state of the firms's applications portfolio (e.g., what computing is being used for); the nature of the DP organization within the firm; the characteristics of management planning and control for computing in the firm; and the level and character of 'user awareness' in the use of computing ([25], p. 22).

Three important changes appeared in the 1977 version of the model. First, management responses for dealing with computing were dichotomized according to Cyert and March's [4] concept of 'control' and 'slack.' A control environment was characterized by the presence of elaborate management systems to ensure efficiency of computing use (e.g., planning, budgeting, performance reviews, chargeout.) A slack environment was characterized by a lack of such controls and a willingness of top management to spend more on computing use than strictly required to do the jobs needed. A control environment would nurture efficiency but constrain innovation; a slack environment would nurture innovation but allow inefficiencies.

A second major change in this formulation of the model was the claim that the S-shaped curve of computing budget changes also represents the organization's 'learning curve' in the quest to control computing effectively ([25], p. 20). This claim, adopted from the work of Estes [8] and Jordan [12], was the turning point in the clarification of Nolan's model as a learning model: Change in technology upsets organizational equilibrium; increased knowledge on the part of organizational actors reestablishes equilibrium.[2]

Most of the remainder of the 1977 book deals with the establishment and use of chargeout systems and steering committees as control tools, and two models of the evolution of such tools are presented ([25], pp. 60 and 128). However, a third basic change in the stage model was presented at the end of the book [25, pp. 153–160]. Here, Nolan claimed that a basic shift was underway in the orientation of management toward the control of computing. Control was shifting away from its focus on

[2] Gibson and Nolan [9] suggest obliquely that the stage model is a learning model, but the claim is not made explicit until the 1977 version.

management of computing as a resource and toward management of organizational data as a resource. Nolan predicted that this shift would be made possible by the advent of the then-new technology of database management systems, and that this shift would initiate two new stages in the model following Stage IV. (See Points *D* and *E* in Figure 1.) He called the final stage 'Maturity.' The new fifth stage was not named in the 1977 book, nor were its implications for the model discussed.

The addition of the new stages is important for understanding the development of the model. First, it fulfilled the prophecy of Gibson and Nolan [9] that changes in technology (database management in this case) would spur changes in the growth rate of computing. In this way, the model was pushed beyond its descriptive role to a clearly predictive one. Second, addition of the new stage reinforced the development of the model as a learning model in which disruptions brought by technical change can be overcome through organizational learning, resulting in the adoption of management policies to integrate the technology with the goals of the organization. This integration would result, in turn, in the equilibrium state of maturity. The fact, that the previously predicted state of integration (maturity) was either not achieved or was short-lived, was not explored in this version.

THE 1979 VERSION

The last formulation of the model appeared in the open literature in 1979 [27]. The ideas presented tentatively in the 1977 book were described in detail in this final paper. The article began with the recognition that a prediction made by the earlier articles [9, 26] did not come to pass: Instead of leveling off as predicted, computing cost continued to grow rapidly. This failure was said to result from changes in both the external and internal environment of organizations, occurring after the previous papers were written. The external changes were the appearance of new technologies and the knowledge of how to use them. Internal changes arose from the acquisition of experience, resulting in internal knowledge. Nolan still used the basic model, but expanded it to include the six stages discussed at the end of the 1977 book. His faith in this expanded model was based on additional studies made after the early model was developed (studies in 35 companies and a 'large number' of IBM customers and other organizations) ([27], p. 11), although no data or references to data from these studies were presented.

The 1979 model formalized the 'control' and 'slack' concept of the 1977 book and reanalyzed the four stages of the 1973 model in light of this concept. The two new stages were included (see Table 1), and the whole model articulated anew. In Stage I, few applications are installed, control is lax, and planning is almost non-existent. In Stage II, development is encouraged (i.e., greater slack), but lack of planning results in systems of poor design quality. In Stage III, the problems from bad design and rising costs create difficulties for users and management, so control becomes tighter. Users almost give up on getting what they want, but with the advent of data communications and user terminals they relax and become tolerant of rising costs they pay through the chargeout system. Top management begins to rethink the management of computing in terms of data resources rather than computer resources. The organization then enters Stage IV, in which costs continue to rise rapidly as computing use increases.[3] Database systems are brought in, which helps the move toward data resource management. In Stage V, the focus of computing management turns completely to Data Administration, in which control of computing resources is tight but slack is maintained in development of systems that bring high, added value. Stage VI, Maturity, is achieved when the applications portfolio is 'complete' (how completion is recognized is not specified), and its "structure 'mirrors' the organization and the information flows in the company" ([27], p. 120).

The 1979 version of the model retained many features of the earlier models. The budget curve was still used as the primary indicator of change, although this measure was modified to be the ratio of computing budget growth to sales growth. Changes in technology still served as fundamental drivers of changes in the stages. An end state (maturity) was still predicted wherein costs rise slowly and benefits rise more rapidly. But the new version of the model differed from the earlier versions in important ways. First, the learning mechanism was fully incorporated. Change was said to be driven by technology, but modulated through internal adoption and application of external and internal knowledge. Second, the 1979 model claimed that a basic shift in organizational goals regarding computing management was taking place, changing from a focus on the management of the computer resource to the management of organizational data resources. Finally, the 1979 model moved beyond the limits of its earlier versions and was described as a tool for evaluating computing in individual firms. In closing the 1979 paper, Nolan made the remarkable claim that 'there is now a generic and empirically supported theory of the evolution of the DP activity – the stage theory' ([27], p. 125).

EVALUATION OF NOLAN'S MODEL

BASIC ASSUMPTIONS OF THE MODEL

Nolan's model rests on a number of important claims and assumptions that invite scrutiny. In this section, we assess these claims and assumptions in terms of their empirical validity and their plausibility.

Empirical Foundations

We question some central empirical assumptions that form the foundation of the model.[4] First, we doubt the validity of the initial hypothesis of the model: That change

[3] A curious puzzle is evident here. A major purpose of chargeout policies was to impose marketlike constraints on users of computing, that would help attenuate uncontrolled growth. Did chargeout fail? The model does not say.

[4] A very useful review of the empirical studies that have addressed aspects of the Nolan model can be found in Benbasat *et al.* [3].

in budgets for computing serve as a surrogate measure for such important and different variables as organizational environment, managerial strategies for growth of computing, and the organization's learning curve in dealing with computing. Is it reasonable to assume that a single variable serves as a suitable surrogate for so much? We think not. It is logically possible that this one variable tracks the changes in others, but it seems unlikely and Nolan does not provide any explanation of the probable linkages that would make the claim plausible.[5]

Beyond this, we question the derivation of such a complex set of stages from the turning points in the curve tracing budget changes (see Figure 1). Finally, there is little evidence in any of the versions of the model to suggest that budgets do follow this curve. Even assuming that Nolan's budgetary data for all the firms he investigated yield S-shaped curves in conformance with his claims (the data presented are not sufficient to tell), there is evidence that many organizations' computing budgets do not show such behavior.

For example, Lucas and Sutton's study [20] of computing budgets in California local governments showed that growth in computing expenditures tended to be linear rather than curvilinear (a phenomenon noted by Nolan in the 1979 paper), and that factors more powerful than Nolan's stage theory would account for this pattern. These findings do not destroy Nolan's initial empirical assumption; they merely weaken its generalizability. We cannot test directly the correspondence between budget growth and changes in other variables without data on the firms he investigated.

Second, the very classification scheme Nolan [27] developed for benchmarking the stages of growth is questioned by Drury's findings [6] in his study of computing in 144 firms. The six benchmarks provided by Nolan do not classify Drury's firms according to the stage model, although a precedence ordering of growth can be seen within each of the six benchmarks. Drury further found that the important 'learning' variable of user awareness of data processing did not correlate with a reduction in problems with computing, as the model suggests.

Third, empirical tests of the model's predictions do not support it. The most obvious failure of prediction Nolan himself acknowledges: the failure of the slow-growth stage of integration ('Maturity' in the 1974 paper) to appear according to prediction. Nolan explains this failure by extending the model to incorporate major contextual changes, in particular the shift in organizational emphasis to management of data resources and the emergence of database management technology. But this is merely a rewrite of the premises to accommodate a change in the conclusions. If post-hoc analyses reveal flaws in the basic assumptions of the model, the predictive power of the model must be questioned. Nevertheless, the model in its later versions is used to make predictions. For example, in the 1979 version ([27], p. 121), Nolan predicts that the major new growth in computing budgets, resulting from adoption of Data

[5] There is an implicit danger of circularity in this kind of model. The shape of the cost growth curve is due, in large part, to the influences of the major variables of environment, technology, etc. Yet the curve is used to demonstrate what changes in these variables take place. The model is too loosely specified to see whether this danger is serious. It could be, that the behavior of the cost curve is not significantly caused by the changes in these other variables, but merely correlates with them. In this case, there would be no circularity, but the claim that the cost curve does capture the behavior of the other variables would be correspondingly weaker without empirical evidence to back it up (*cf.*, [34]. pp. 27–30, pp. 112–114).

Administration, will decline as adoption becomes complete in 2–5 years. (From 1979, this means 1981–1984.) Whether this will happen remains to be seen.*

Two recent empirical studies also raised questions about the soundness of the model's predictions. Goldstein and McCririk's 1981 study of 273 organizations [11] tested the model's prediction that data administration would be more formalized in 'mature' data processing departments and failed to confirm the model's prediction. Our own study of computing in 56 cities in 10 countries [18] collected extensive data on the variables that the budget curve in Nolan's model is said to capture (e.g., environmental variables, computing management policies, outcomes of computing use). Our data did permit the grouping of the organizations into categories according to a simple set of computing development stages. But the study also found that those organizations using the more 'mature' policies for computing management, as articulated by the more prescriptive versions of the model, suffered from the highest levels of problems with computing. Either these organizations had adopted mature policies for computing management but had not refined them sufficiently to make them work right, or the whole concept of organizational learning in dealing with computing is somewhat optimistic.[6] In any case, the primary claims of empirical support for the predictions of the model come from Nolan himself and have not been corroborated by others.

These problems with the empirical bases of Nolan's model challenge its acceptance as a validated theory in the scientific sense of that term. The question remains, is the theory intuitively powerful and practically useful? By examining the remaining assumptions behind the model, we can identify several serious problems that weaken the intellectual base of the model and that might account for the lack of empirical evidence in support of its validity.

Technological Change

The model holds that technological change is the primary driving force behind the growth of computing through the stages ([9], p. 88; [25], p. 20; [27], p. 116). This probably overstates the dominance of this variable. Technological change certainly plays a role in the complex of factors that drive change, but there are additional factors that should be considered. Most important are the 'demand-side' factors that create a ripe environment for technological changes to be considered and adopted.[7] At least three such forces seem appropriate for consideration. One is the 'institutionalized demand' created by the extant presence of computing in organizations [16, 31]. Once routinized, computing applications must be maintained and upgraded over time. Such changes add to the cost of computing and to the need for even further changes (e.g., hardware upgrades, more disk storage), irrespective of changes in technology. Another is demand among users for computer services arising from powerful but often

* *In fact, such a decline in computing budgets did not occur. (Ed)*

[6] As with the Lucas and Sutton study [20], our research was conducted in local governments. An argument can be made that our findings are explained entirely by differences between corporations of the kind Nolan studied, the counties Lucas and Sutton studied, and the cities we studied; however, we doubt it.

[7] The concept of 'supply push' and 'demand pull' in the process of innovation diffusion is extensively explored in Roessner [30]. See also Tornatzky *et al.* [33].

overlooked aspects of computing as a political resource [5, 14, 18, 21]. Computing brings capabilities that are more desirable for some users than for others, and the use of computing provides departments with opportunities to justify additional capital, personnel and space demands. Finally, computing is appealing to many people on purely affective grounds as an entertaining and status-increasing technology [14]. These demand-pull drivers of change can and often do take precedence over the supply-push factors of technological change.

Clarity of Organizational Goals

The model assumes that there are clear-cut organizational goals to be realized through application of the technology ([26], p. 399; [9], p. 88; [25], p. 3; [27], p. 116). This assumption might apply to some organizations, but not to all, and possibly not to many. The question of whether organizational goals are uniform and consistent guides for the behavior of organizational actors, as opposed to dynamic and changing targets that result from competition and conflict among organizational actors, has received considerable attention in the literature on computing [5, 13–16, 28]. This research suggests that the setting and maintenance of organizational goals is a dynamic process in which internal disagreements on strategy are only resolved temporarily through goal-clarifying processes, and that organizational norms that result are often temporary.[8] If the organizational goals for the application of computing are themselves undergoing change, there can be no lasting consensus on how 'best' to manage computing activity, and no reasonable expectation that management will know what it is searching for in its effort to master the technology. Very general goals of the organization might be agreed on (e.g., making a profit, organizational survival, sustained growth), but the linkage between use of computing and the achievement of these broad goals requires specification of much more detailed subgoals directed specifically at the application of the technology to particular tasks and needs. Given the array of possible demand-pull factors on the growth of computing mentioned above, agreement on subgoals cannot be assumed *a priori*, and that the different goals of organizational actors will have unitary correspondence with agreed-on organizational goals, cannot be assumed at all.

Knowledge

The model assumes that increased external and internal knowledge will eventually lead to effective and efficient control over computing ([25], p. 20; [27], p. 116). This assumption poses difficulties because it implies the further assumption, that the 'right' knowledge is available and the organizational actors will acquire and act appropriately on this knowledge. External knowledge, which in the Nolan model enters the organization in the form of new technologies and information about how to exploit them, varies greatly in its utility. There are many competing theories about how best

[8] Among the versions of the Nolan model, Gibson and Nolan [9] and Nolan [25] come closest to acknowledging conflicts in goal-setting. In neither case is such conflict explored as important for the assumptions of the model.

to exploit computing, and there are no proven tests by which a manager can tell which theories are correct and appropriate for the organization in question. Internal knowledge, which is based on organizational experience, also varies greatly from one organization to the next. Some organizations have been successful in routinizing sophisticated computing applications, others have not. According to Nolan's model, successful organizations are those that have learned how to cope with the technology, while unsuccessful organizations have not. But what accounts for these differences in learning? The model does not answer this question. The processes by which knowledge is brought to bear on problems are not explained in the model, and there is no specification for how the appropriate policies, leading to Integration, Data Administration and Maturity, are found and applied.

Control Versus Slack

The model assumes that the task of effective management of computing is to strike a balance between 'control' and 'slack' ([25], p. 22; [27], p. 116). This implies that top management, which has the prerogative to implement control or slack policies, can know when either course is appropriate for each of the policies they promulgate. Policies must be chosen from some point on the 'control' to 'slack' continuum, but from where should they be chosen in any given instance? If policies are to be proactive, management must be able to anticipate when policies embodying greater control or greater slack will achieve desired ends. This implies, that managers will know which way their organization is headed in its use of computing. In fact, most policies for computing management are probably reactive, developed in response to problems experienced with computing. Control and slack might be good general descriptors of the characteristics of policies managers *can* follow, but simply categorizing policies this way does not indicate what policies managers *should* follow.

Continuous Change

The model assumes that change in organizational information systems is a 'continuous' process.[9] Our observations of the processes of change in organizations lead us to doubt this assumption. The S-shaped curve implies continuous change, but does not accommodate the cyclical or recursive behaviors so often encountered in the development and refinement of organizational policies. As noted by Moore ([23], p. 259), most organizations exhibit cyclical behavior in resolving basic policy dilemmas, such as, whether to centralize or decentralize functions. The adoption of a function, such as the smooth S-shaped curve, might be appropriate for characterizing the ideal theoretical behavior of a single organization or for summarizing the aggregate behaviors of a populations of organizations, but it does not fit well the often erratic behavior exhibited by individual organizations.

These problems with Nolan's model do not disprove the model's assertions.

[9] 'Continuous change' is used here to mean a change occurring in a logical gradation of steps within a single series, not in a sense of constant or omnipresent change. Nisbet ([24], p. 174) provides an explanation of this use.

However, they do raise important questions about the empirical validity of the model and its utility for describing the process of change in specific organizations. In the next section we assess the model's performance as a theory of evolution of the growth of computing across organizations.

The Model as an Evolution Theory

Nolan describes his model as a theory of the evolution of the DP activity in organizations ([27], p. 125). In this section, we evaluate the model within the context of theories of evolution in the social sciences, to determine the extent to which this description is correct.[10]

In its simplest conception, 'evolution' refers to any succession of changes that affect an entity (e.g., a species, an industry, a society). Within this concept are the ideas, 'evolutionist' and 'evolutionary.' These terms are used interchangably and imprecisely much of the time. A distinction must be made between models that characterize successions of change by the *direction* the change is taking, and those that characterize such successions of change by their *mechanisms* ([34], p. 51). Models that describe change in terms of direction can be called 'evolutionist' models and are distinct from 'evolutionary' models that describe change in terms of mechanisms.

The evolutionist perspective assesses history as a developmental, progressive and directional set of changes that increase in their complexity or perfection with the passage of time. Such theories embody a clear concept of the direction of change and the destination of change. Evolutionist models explain the *logic* of development, typically in the form of stages that follow one another, and in which each stage is a precursor for the next one. More elaborate evolutionist theories extend to the description of the dynamics of development, in which successions of stages correspond to a path along which entities are inexorably compelled toward their appointed 'end state'.

Evolutionary models, by contrast, are agnostic about either the direction of change or the likely end state to which change is headed. Evolutionary models focus on the mechanisms by which changes occur and new features of entities come into being. Evolutionary mechanisms are mechanisms of local optimization, in which features of an entity change (either through genetic mutation or adoption of new behaviors) and in which the new features are preferable to the old features in aiding survival of the entity or improving its chances of satisfaction. If the new state is 'adequate' for the entity (that is, it can survive and reproduce, or it is satisfied), current features are stabilized, resulting in a new state of equilibrium. The consequences of 'selections' made by these mechanisms feed back and influence the process of change toward a new state of locally optimized equilibrium.

An initial reading of the model, particularly in its earlier versions, suggests that it is an evolutionist theory. The persistence of change in information systems is noted, and the model attempts to explain the course of change in terms of its direction (growth) and its 'end state' (Integration or Maturity). This formulation, as with many

[10] This brief discussion of evolution concepts in the social sciences is informed by several sources, particularly van Parijs ([34], especially Ch. 2), Moore [23], and Nisbet [24].

evolutionist theories, bears a striking resemblance to 'life cycle' models that parallel the process of change in living organisms (birth, growth, maturation), although there is no expectation of a final state of demise (death). The model stops at Maturity.

The other evolutionist characteristic of the model is its focus on the logic of what happens, rather than on the mechanisms by which particular changes take place. Although discussions of the model embody preditions about further changes, these predictions are based mainly on the trends in past change. The model concentrates more on these trends in change than on the persistent features of the entities (organizations that use information systems) and why they are there. The explanations of the presence of features are functionalist, in that they account for the purpose of the features, but generally within a rationalistic framework in which organizational actors learn what to do and then do it. While the primary incentive for change comes from without in the form of changes in technology and external knowledge, the reaction to this change is purposeful on the part of the organization's leadership. As with many of the better known theories of social evolution, especially those based on Hegelian dialectic, a constant tension between change in environment and organizational reaction to change is the primary structural feature of the model.[11] The evolutionistic twist here, in these social theories and in Nolan's model, is the belief that an end state is somehow eventually achieved.

To the extent that Nolan's model is an evolutionist theory, it exhibits the same strengths and weaknesses of other evolutionist theories. The primary strength of such models is their attention to the logic of past development, which can be assessed empirically, as long as correct historical accounts of change are available. In this sense, the Nolan model does ring true. Many of its characterizations of the history of organizational information systems are insightful. In the end, the predictions made using such models might very well turn out to be correct. If a model truly captures the basic driving forces behind change and accurately specifies the relationships between these forces, and assuming that larger contextual features of the 'change space' do not themselves change, there is nothing to prevent evolutionist theories from being powerful predictors. However, the primary weaknesses of evolutionist theories rest precisely in the generality of their perceptions of reality and the resulting difficulty in assessing their factual correctness. Such theories are concerned with the broad picture of change, not with the actual experiences of change in individual cases. The lack of mechanistic explanation in these theories makes them difficult to test empirically at the level of individual instances of change. Rather, they can be empirically tested only by examining the correctness of their historical accounts or by waiting to see whether the predictions made using them turn out to be correct. Evolutionist theories are therefore useful for organizing frameworks that might prove to have been insightful and correct, once enough time has passed to see whether their predictions have come to pass. But they do not explain why changes happen the way they do. This limits their utility in explaining changes or predicting the future of change in specific instances.

There are elements of evolutionary explanation in the Nolan model, too, and these are worth noting, Gibson and Nolan [9] first suggest the possibility that the end state of maturity is not, in fact, an end state, but rather an equilibrium state. This

[11] See Nisbet ([24]. Ch. 5) for an extensive discussion of this matter.

allows an interpretation of the model in terms of locally optimized equilibrium states common to evolutionary theories. Under this construction, there are forces of environmental change (e.g. technological change, new external knowledge) that affect the current state of an entity (the organization) that is capable of recognizing that the changes have altered its chances of satisfaction under the current state. The entity is also capable of recognizing (through internal learning) that local alternative states are comparatively attractive. A mechanism, used in evolutionary explanations in social sciences, called 'reinforcement', causes the entity to alter its persistent features (behaviors) to correspond to those alternatives.[12] If adoption of the alternative features provides sufficient improvement in satisfaction to accommodate the environmental change, and no other locally available states appear more attractive, the entity has evolved to a new state of locally optimal equilibrium.

In this interpretation, the selection choices available to the entity in its search for satisfaction are limited to policy options that range from 'slack' to 'control' along one dimension. There can be a number of different policies adopted, and each policy falls somewhere along the slack/control continuum. The earlier versions of the model portrayed policy as a monolithic variable: The sought-after state was a simple balance between slack and control (although these terms were not used). In later versions, the model was modified to accept greater control in some variables and greater slack in others. The preferred state results from balance between slack and control for each major policy variable.

In an effort to improve its recognition of what policies are appropriate, the organization evolves toward a state of improved planning; that is, an intensified effort to anticipate the future and develop appropriate controls for the present to improve chances of future satisfaction. But in this, the Nolan model departs somewhat from a truly evolutionary theory. Planning implies the anticipation of consequences, and in its ultimate formulation, the presence of an omniscient actor capable of seeing the future. The presence of such an omniscient actor would remove all aspects of evolutionary explanation and substitute instead a purely 'actional' explanation.[13] Since we cannot assume omniscience, the goal of planning is less to provide foresight than to anticipate a bounded set of *likely* characteristics of the future and to assess options that might improve satisfaction under each anticipated case. The reinforcement mechanism in this case continues to operate through consequence feedback, and planning remains limited to educated guesswork.

CONCLUSION

On close examination, the Nolan model reveals several shortcomings. The empirical bases of the model are questionable, and some evidence is available that they are

[12] A thorough discussion of reinforcement as an evolutionary mechanism, and particularly its dissimilarity to the more commonly cited natural selection mechanism, is found in van Parijs ([34]. Ch. 4). The natural selection mechanism has been applied to the analysis of computing growth by Swanson (1982).

[13] The actional view refers to the deliberate actions of entities, given correct anticipation of the consequences of action ([34]. pp. 18–20, 51–53).

factually mistaken. Many of the other structural assumptions of the model are too simplistic to be useful, or are simply implausible. The Nolan model has had a powerful influence on the information systems field. Its popularity is probably due to its bold approach to dealing with a phenomenon of great complexity in a straightforward and clever manner. Nolan was the first researcher to introduce a structured scheme for explaining the growth of computing in organizations. Aspects of the model ring true to practitioners and researchers alike. But it is incomplete in its attempt to capture the larger organizational context within which computing occurs, and it is not accurate in the accounting of the relationships between the various components in this context.

As a 'grounded theory' [10], the model fails. However, the model makes two significant theoretical contributions. First, it makes explicit the notion that the growth of computing must be due to the influence of forces both inside and outside the organization. To many, this seems trivially true. But the interplay between external and internal forces in shaping computing is noticeably absent in much of the research on this subject. Second, it introduces an intellectually powerful construct of dialectical interplay between freedom and constraint in the control of computing that yields periodic states of equilibrium. Both of these are embodied in the specific features of the model, but they are fully explained in terms of their mechanisms of consequences. From the standpoint of the creation of sound descriptions of computing evolution, the primary contribution of the Nolan model has been the provision of interesting and testable hypotheses for researchers to explore. The goal of future research must be the creation of improved models that avoid the problems evident in the Nolan model.

REFERENCES

1. N. Ahituv and S. Neumann, *Principles of Information Systems for Management*. W. C. Brown, Dubuque, Iowa, 1982.
2. S. Alter, *Decision Support Systems: Current Practices and Continuing Challenges*. Addison-Wesley, Reading. Mass, 1980.
3. I. Benbasat, A. S. Dexter, D. H. Drury and R. C. Goldstein, *A critique of the stage hypothesis: Theory and empirical evidence*. Working paper 194, Faculty of Commerce and Business Administration, University of British Columbia, B. C. Vancouver, Canada, 1983.
4. R. M. Cyert and J. G. March, *Organizational factors in the theory of oligopoly. J. Quart Economics* (Feb. 1956). 44.
5. J. N. Danziger, W. H. Dutton, R. Kling and K. L. Kraemer, *Computers and Politics*. Columbia Univ. Press, New York, 1982.
6. D. H. Drury, *An empirical assessment of the stages of DP growth. MIS Quart.* (June, 1983), 59–70.
7. P. Ein-Dor, and E. Segev, *Managing Management Information Systems*. Lexington Books, Lexington, Mass., 1978.
8. W. E. Estes, *Toward a statistical theory of learning*, *Psych. Rev.* 57 (1950), 94–107.
9. C. F. Gibson and R. L. Nolan, *Managing the four stages of EDP growth. Harvard Business Rev.* (Jan./Feb. (1974), 76–88.

10. B. Glaser and A. Strauss, *The Discovery of Grounded Theory*. Aldine, Chicago, Ill., 1967.
11. R. Goldstein and I. McCririk, *The stage hypothesis and data administration*. In C. Ross (Ed). Proc. 2nd Int. Conf. Information Systems. Society for Management Information Systems, Cambridge, Mass., pp. 309–324.
12. R. Jordan, *How to Use the Learning Curve*. Materials Management Institute, Boston, Mass., 1965.
13. P. W. G. Keen and M. S. Scott Morton, *Decision Support Systems: An Organizational Perspective*. Addison-Wesley. Reading. Mass., 1978.
14. J. L. King, *Centralization versus decentralization of computing: Organizational considerations and management options*. Dept. Information and Computer Science. Univ. California, Irvine, 1983.
15. Kling, R. Social analyses of computing: Theoretical perspectives in recent empirical research. *Comput. Surv. 12*, 1, (1980), 61–110.
16. Kling, R. and Scacchi, W. The Web of Computing. In *Advances in Computers*, vol. 20. Academic Press, New York, 1982.
17. Kraemer, K. L. Computers, information and power in local governments: A stage theory. In A. Mowshowitz (Ed), *Human Choice and Computers*, No. 2. North Holland, New York, 1980.
18. Kraemer, K. L. and King, J. L. Computing policies and problems: A stage theory approach. *Telecommun. Policy 5*, 3, (1981), 198–215.
19. Kuznets, S., *Economic Growth and Structure*: *Selected Essays*. W. W. Norton, New York, 1965.
20. Lucas, H. C. and Sutton, J. A. The stage hypothesis S-curve: Some contradictory evidence. *Commun. ACM 20*, 4, (1977), 254–259.
21. Markus, M. L. Implementation politics: top management support and user involvement. *Systems*, *Objectives*, *Solutions 1*, 4, (1981), 203–215.
22. McKenney, J. L. and McFarlan, W. Merging the islands of information service. In C. Ross (Ed), Proc. and Int. Conf. Information System. Society for Management Information Systems, Cambridge, Mass., pp. 331–350.
23. Moore, W. E. *Order and Change*: *Essays in Contemporary Sociology*. Wiley, New York, 1967.
24. Nisbet, R. *Social Change and History*. Oxford Univ. Press, New York, 1969.
25. Nolan, R. L. *Management Accounting and Control of Data Processing*. National Association of Accountants, New York, 1977.
26. Nolan, R. L. Managing the computer resource: A stage hypothesis. *Commun. ACM 16*, 7 (1973), 399–405.
27. Nolan, R. L. Managing the crisis in data processing. *Harvard Business Rev.* (March/April 1979), 115–26.
28. Pfeffer, J. *Power in Organizations*. Pitman, Boston, Mass., 1978.
29. Rockhart, J. F. and Flannery, L. S. The management of end user computting. In C. Ross (Ed). Proc. 2nd Int. Conf. Information Systems. *Society for Management Information Systems*, Cambridge, Mass., pp. 351–364.
30. Roessner, J. D. Federal technology policy: Innovation and problem solving in state and local governments. *Policy Analysis 5*, (1979), 181–200.
31. Scacchi, W. S. The process of innovation in computing: A study of the social dynamics of computing. Unpublished Ph.D. Dissertation, Dept. Information and Computer Science, Univ. California, Irvine, 1981.
32. Swanson, E. B. A view of information systems evolution. In J. Hawgood (Ed), *Evolutionary Information Systems*. North Holland, New York, pp. 55–62.

33. Tornatzky, L. G. Roitman, D., Boylan, M., Carpenter, J., Eveland, J. D., Hetzner, W. A., Lucas, B. G. and Schneider, J. Innovation processes and their management: A conceptual, empirical and policy review of innovation process research. National Science Foundation, Washington, D. C., 1980.
34. van Parijs, P. *Evolutionary Explanations in the Social Sciences*. Rowman and Littlefield, Totowa. N. J., 1981.

2. HOW TO MANAGE IT*

Nigel Piercy

ABSTRACT: New technology raises issues beyond operating efficiency; a long-term strategic response is called for.

If Rip van Winkle had found himself a business manager in the early 1980s, he might just have remained unaware of the microelectronics revolution and its crop of electronic information handling products. For anyone who had been awake, that would be entirely impossible. Managers have been positively besieged by computing equipment manufacturers, software producers, systems analysts and consultants proposing novel areas of application for new information technology.

From the word-processor in the office to the mini or microcomputer for the manager, to the remote computer terminal in the salesman's hand, to the robot or automatically controlled machine in the factory or warehouse, or to the fully automated production line, the wonders of technology apparently never cease.

However, it is becoming increasingly evident that the new information processing abilities and capacities are themselves producing a different and constantly changing environment within which managers have to act. As a result, coming to terms with the technology means far more than simply adding a new piece of equipment to the office or factory, like an electronic typewriter, say, or a more modern lathe.

The changes wrought by new information technology relate to fundamentals, such as the way in which organizations are structured; the content and pattern of jobs and the quality of employees' working lives; relationships with suppliers and customers; and the nature of the management task itself.

Take something as apparently straight-forward as the introduction of electronic check-outs in supermarkets and other retail stores. On the face of it, this involves no more than replacing an existing human-mechanical process with a human-electronic one – or ultimately, perhaps, with a wholly electronic process, having no check-out operator at all. But the real impact is elsewhere. The collection of sales and revenue data through electronic tills has dramatic implications for fundamental change throughout the whole retail world.

For example: the potential for instantaneous and almost costless sales analysis and product-testing is altering relationships with suppliers even further in favour of retailers, even though the full implications have yet to work through the distributive system. Internally, the improved quality of sales analysis over a group of stores facilitates centralization and automation of stock reordering, cash management and merchandising decisions – which must further erode the store manager's and shop assistant's responsibility for information and control.

* *Reprinted from Management Today, March 1984.*

N. Piercy is senior lecturer in the department of Business Administration and Accountancy in UWIST.

The 'networking' effect of making store-level information instantly available at the centre, together with greater ability to process that information, may lead to the removal of a whole tier of middle management which now stands between the stores and head office, as well as reducing the management role in the store itself. The check-out operator's job is effectively de-skilled into a 'slave' role of feeding barcoded products through a laser scanner, accepting the customer's money and providing the change indicated by the till. Relationships with customers could also change as the 'human element' is thus reduced.

In short, what started as a partial automation of a basic process for reasons of operational efficiency has far-reaching effects on the whole business: its staff, its suppliers and its customers. For this reason, the focal point is not specific technological innovation, but the managerial and organizational issues raised by the technology in action.

The argument is that, to cope with the full impact of new information on the company system, it is not enough to adopt new processes and facilities on an *ad hoc* or piecemeal basis. What is needed – in some cases urgently – is a long-term strategic

OUTLINE FOR AN IT STRATEGY

1. Technological Scenario Forecasting
In what areas of the operations, administrative systems, and management information system, could new technology be applied now, and what is the significant potential in the medium and long term?
Who will be responsible for producing and integrating a corporate scenario, and what interests will be represented in it?

2. Organizational Effects
In each of the areas of potential technological change, what effects are possible and which are likely, regarding performance; employees; managers; management style; organizational structure and relationships? Which of these are desirable and which undesirable? How can the organization cope with the effects? How will it cope with unanticipated side-effects if they occur?
Are we at the stage of automating certain processes within the existing organization, modifying the organization to implement technology, or redesigning the organization around the technology? If the company is at an early stage, when will it reach the later ones?

3. Market Effects
In each of the areas of potential technological change, what effects are possible and which are likely regarding: customers; suppliers; competitors? Which of these are desirable and which undesirable? How can the organization cope with the effects? How will it cope with unanticipated side-effects if they occur?

4. Company Needs and Resources
Which possible technological developments meet existing or emerging company needs, e.g. for better stock control, more efficient administration, better information systems, etc? How will company needs change – can the scenario be described for the medium term? Which innovations can be adequately resourced and to what time-scale?

5. Implementation Planning
When and how will the technology be implemented? What implementation strategy can be formulated? How will it be organized and controlled, and how will it cope with resistance to change?

6. Control
At what points and how will management evaluate progress in achievement and cost, against the goals set for technological innovation?

response from corporate management; in fact, a whole strategy for information technology, which, as an integral part of the long-term planning process, would recognize the implications for management and cope with the far-reaching effects of technology as systematically as possible.

The most obvious face of new information technology is the flood of consumer electronic products – that is, those incorporating micro-electronic control and information-processing components. Underlying the ever-increasing stream are changes which in themselves have major competitive significance – such as IBM's launch into High Street trading, or the sale of micros in Tesco supermarkets, or the use by IBM of Ford-style 'box-selling' to enable distributors to market a range based on a standardized set of component products. But this is a change in degree, not in kind, and is far from being the most significant transformation in managerial terms.

The issue at stake here is the impact of new technology on the business organization itself and on its strategic objectives and management. Consider the following examples. In operations and manufacturing, there are now many examples of automated production lines where mini-computers have replaced human control, and robots have taken over tasks previously carried out by human labour. Factory automation has so far been associated mainly with reductions in the size of the labour force, but it should be remembered that automation also modifies the role of management at different levels – for instance, by pushing operational decision-making upwards from lower to middle management, and control from middle to senior management.

In marketing, many of the early IT applications have seemed trivial – using word-processing to personalize sales letters and to change price lists more easily, for example. But the development of information networks between buyers, distributors and suppliers suggests far more. Imagine a network where consumers supply data through interactive television sets and electronic questionnaires and are selectively exposed to advertising and promotion through cable television, or are computer-selected for direct mail shots. Retailers, meanwhile, instantaneously monitor purchasing through laser scanning of bar-coded products and accumulate the disaggregated data; suppliers share their plans and intelligence through the electronic system; and a central market database exists, to be accessed remotely by terminals.

The potential for improving advertising and promotion efficiency, product launch success and pricing, is clear – and consequently, also the potential exists for reducing total marketing and distribution costs. Equally clear, however, is the potential increase in power through information control by the distributor, and through the reliance on information sharing. Such potentials represent a major environmental change affecting relationships between firms, and call for more than a short-term tactical response.

In the field of personnel management and industrial relations, the issues raised include the potential for storing and instantly accessing personnel records. These could include the implications of sharing corporate information with trade unions; and the results of deskilling jobs, with the threat of substantial adverse effects on performance.

In management information systems, there will obviously be a greatly enhanced ability to monitor and report on performance, and to provide an easily accessible data store for management decision-making at all levels. The 'intelligent' machine, using languages developed in artificial intelligence research, may be able not only to answer factual or 'what if' questions (soon even replying to speech), but also to place priorities on problems, to reason, and to recommend/decide what action is to be taken.

The fact that there is a potential for change does not mean that the changes necessarily have to be allowed – choices exist, and should be made clear and explicit. However, even a limited listing such as the one above demonstrates the point: new information technology is changing the ground rules for management. Some companies have begun to recognize this fact. Xerox Corporation, for example, has published details of its long-range planning scenario for IT up to the 1990s. The goal in this case was to forecast the internal use of information systems by 1990 (based on assumptions about the development of the technology) to help in formulating policy guidelines for managers.

This kind of exercise provides a starting point in formulating a strategic response to technological change. However, formal change in information systems is only one dimension of the problem. What about the implications for management control, for managing people, and for the organizational structure itself? Perhaps the most immediately obvious implication of new information technology is its ability to increase central control of people's working activities. Thus, where many managers have been brought up on the principle of a limited 'span of control' – i.e., no manager should attempt to supervise more than five or six people with related work – new technology, by processing, summarizing and communicating faster, increases the span, potentially flattening the traditional pyramid shape of an organization.

Certainly, whether it is a question of operatives and supervisors in the factory, salesmen and marketing people in the field, or administrative personnel of whatever type, new technology can be used to remove certain areas of discretion and to maintain a far closer watch on work effort and output – ranging from counting the key strokes of a computer operator to the daily viewdata reports from salesmen.

On the face of it, this seems quite reasonable. Management has always been about planning and control, so surely all new technology does is to improve the ability to manage? There are two sides to the issue, though. First is the central control of matters hitherto managed lower in the organization; second is the exercise of control over areas where previously it was impossible.

On the first aspect, the retailing example provides a prime instance of lower levels of management losing control over areas like pricing, product choice, stockholding and re-ordering, and so on, which were all previously their responsibility. Maybe these decisions, having been modelled at the centre, will now essentially be 'made' by the machine, with only exceptions drawn to senior management's attention.

The crucial point is that, while it is possible to centralize decision-making (for economies of scale, for tighter integration, and so on), this can only be done at the cost of de-skilling the decentralized jobs. The recognition of the choice involved – say, in the retail setting – implies the need to balance the attractions of centralized control against the possible disadvantages of the organizational change. Will store managers still be motivated? Where will potential middle and senior managers now be trained? How will customer and market diversity be allowed for? Will centralization reduce the ability to be flexible and respond to market changes?

The impact on senior management has to be allowed for, too. To the extent that control is based on the new technology, there is the question of who controls that technology. The increased power – and managerial discretion – of those who program and operate the new systems cannot be ignored.

On the second aspect of control (its extension to areas previously outside its scope), new technology makes it possible to monitor people's performance and plot deviations from plan far more systematically than before. This, in turn, raises a number of significant questions for managers. How should control measurements be used, for example? To enforce targets and penalize sub-optimal performance, or as a guide to the individual to improve his own performance? How much control is desirable before senior managers become mere 'bean-counters', more concerned with keeping to budget than taking risks and attacking new opportunities? How much control is tolerated before people become demotivated and alienated from their work? The history of earlier changes suggests that tight control may be resisted, with consequent harm to the organization. In any case, the new technology demands a decision on which management style and organizational climate to adopt.

Clearly, one side-effect of new technology may be to increase what has been called 'social control' over employees. At the same time, it may reduce the quality of the individual's working life in ways that have considerable practical significance for the business. The almost inevitable process of de-skilling in many jobs, with decisions made by machines and systems rather than humans, coupled with closer management control, may produce 'slave' jobs, like that of the retail check-out operator. According to a research project sponsored by the EEC, elements of 'social control' could also be involved in the new ability to measure the performance of individuals, to restrict how people do their work, to collate information about employees without their knowledge. The effect on promotion prospects of people's ability to 'cope' with new technology is yet another factor.

Evidently, the human resource in a business is faced with a potentially radical change. Managers face quite explicit decisions about how new technology is to be used, and in particular the degree to which the human factor should be regarded as a constraint on policy. In general, trade unions have not been particularly effective in influencing how new technology is adopted and used; nevertheless, the potential damage to satisfaction, commitment, attitudes and working behaviour of employees is great.

Others have suggested, with equal vehemence, that new technology may be highly beneficial for employees. Engineers frequently claim that easy-to-automate jobs and tasks are (before automation) almost by definition the most boring, repetitive and degrading; that information sharing and 'networking' may allow better-informed employees to communicate more rapidly with management; that shared databases will provide a trusted joint foundation for management/union negotiation; and that the reverse side of the de-skilling of some jobs is the upgrading of others in terms of both the skills and the training required, with a subsequent strengthening of the commitment of the individual. Examples might include the toolmaker placed in charge of an expensive computer-based machine set-up, or the typist who now controls a word processor/mini-computer information-handling package.

These human aspects of new information technology are possibly the most serious in their effects on the business operation, as well as the most easily obscured. The fact is that the choices made now will have persistent long-term effects on the satisfaction and performance of employees. Perhaps IT's greatest potential for disruptive change lies in the structure of an organization and the working of its management information system.

One well-documented case involves a branch of the US Army supply service in West Germany. Here, units requiring supplies (or information about availability) contacted a clerk at the supply depot, who passed the enquiry upwards through the hierarchy until the right decision level was reached. The decision was then passed down to a clerk, who either transmitted it to the requisitioning unit, or else telephoned/telexed around to get the information and pass it on. While this sounds clumsy and bureaucratic, it is just the sort of manual system which is developed to ensure proper authorization and to handle important contingencies – such as the substitution of one material for another for certain uses, or spreading knowledge about material specification changes, and so on.

The computerization of this system involved establishing an on-line database of information about stocks. In response to enquiries, this could be accessed by the clerk through a desktop visual display unit. In technology terms, of course, there was no reason why others should not also have access to the information through remote terminals. On the surface, the scheme seemed wholly rational and straightforward. But its hidden consequences were substantial, in effect altering the structure of the organization from a strict hierarchy to a much flatter shape. Now, low-level people communicated directly with the database and each other; while their seniors no longer collated or co-ordinated information for decision-making – and so could not influence decisions by changing the content of messages. In short, as the shape of the structure was flattened, the role of middle management was substantially reduced.

This loss of authority for managers might be thought unavoidable, and perhaps even overdue. On the other hand, note what actually happened. When the impact was felt, the managers insisted that the new system was not yet reliable enough to trust, so the old manual system had to be maintained. Because it was clear that the manual system was still being used, the computer database was not properly maintained; with the result that the new system *did* become unreliable and therefore fell into disuse, thus neatly self-fulfilling the managers' prophecy.

This case sharply illustrates many of the hidden organizational effects of new information technology. The integrated information-communication system first opens up new channels – or networks – of communication which may be quite different from earlier channels, either formal or informal. These information flows directly influence structures. Information in organizations is never neutral – it gives influence, status, and even power – so new technology is unavoidably mixed up with organizational politics. In the subsequent confusion, as the case shows, managers can be extremely effective at fighting back against changes which they see as disadvantageous.

Indeed, researchers at the Massachusetts Institute of Technology have described the efforts of middle managers to divert resources, delay change in information systems and deflect goals, as 'counter-implementation strategies'. The MIT conclusion is that a strategy for successful information change should include actions designed specifically to counter resistance to change. The leader of the change project should be a politician able to head off political resistance; where resisters rely on organizational inertia and practice to maintain the *status quo*, the change strategist looks for a public commitment to change in a given period; where committees may be manipulated by political action, the change strategy needs top management's support; and so on.

Over and above the hidden organizational issues, it is true that identifying real management information needs remains difficult in many cases and near-impossible in some. Computerizing operating and managerial control systems may be comparatively straightforward. But as the computer is brought in at the level of strategic decision-making, it is increasingly hard to decide what information helps and what gets in the way.

When managers are asked what information they need, answers vary from 'don't know' to 'everything' to 'what we get now'. This is because information needs emerge from modelling decisions; some decisions cannot be modelled and some information needs cannot easily be predicted. Some progress has been made in systems towards identifying 'critical success factors' for top managers, but the fact remains that much at this level remains in the realm of 'soft' data and informal channels of communication, regardless of the technological sophistication of the information system.

The largest companies are beginning to recognize that there is an urgent need to formulate a strategy for adopting new information technology and for coping with the full range of changes involved. However, the stage has been reached where new information technology is affecting all sizes of company, not simply major multinationals; and the plan involves much more than simply a time schedule for automation.

Three points must be emphasized. First, the changes faced are strategic rather than tactical, since they affect not just competitive advantage and day-to-day operations, but the way in which the business is controlled, the style with which it is managed, the directions in which organization structure will have to change, and relationships with suppliers, customers and competitors. Second, the issues are long-term, because they tie a company to new ways of operating and continued technological innovation. Third, the level at which the issue has to be approached is that of corporate and strategic planning, where the concern is with integrated development of all parts of the business. The effects of the new methods and machines demand nothing less.

3. INFORMATION TECHNOLOGY AND JOB DESIGN: a case study on CNC machine tool working*

Nigel J. Kemp
and
Chris W. Clegg

INTRODUCTION

The progressive introduction of Information Technology (IT) onto the shopfloor of manufacturing industry has brought with it renewed interest in the nature and distribution of skills and, more generally, in the subject of job design.

Unanimity exists amongst analysts that IT has the capability to influence the content of people's jobs but thereafter there is some disagreement. Two principal schools of thought exist. The first considers IT historically and interprets the development and use of advanced manufacturing technology as a further evolutionary step in the progressive mechanization of work, the net result of which is deskilling. This is manifest in a polarisation between a controlling expert class of managers and specialists, and a group of relatively unskilled shopfloor operators. Indeed, the popularity of computer-aided technology in industry is due, in part, to its potential for control over the production process.

Other investigators recognise that this can and does happen, but point to the availability of choices within organisations. In this view the deskilling of operators is not inevitable and some work has recently been undertaken examining the choices open to organisations as to how they manage and operate technology, along with the contingency factors which guide these choices.

Unfortunately there exist only a few detailed empirical studies which consider these issues and which relate their findings to theory. This paper attempts to contribute to this debate by presenting a case study of Computerised Numerically Controlled (CNC) machine tool working in an engineering factory in the UK. It examines three major questions:

* Working paper to be published in *Behaviour and Information Technology* (Taylor & Francis, London)

N. J. Kemp, Thorn–EMI Home Electronics, Development Centre, Sigma, Windmill Hill, Swindon SN5 9YY.

C. W. Clegg, MRC/ESRC Social & Applied Psychology Unit, Department of Psychology, University of Sheffield, Sheffield, S10 2TN.

i) What choices has the firm made regarding the management and operation of its CNC machines?
ii) What is the impact of these choices on the firm and its employees?
iii) Why have these choices been made, and what are the prospects for the future?

In an attempt to answer these questions in a way that is generalizable to other situations, we analyse and interpret this study using a version of a conceptual framework of job design, whose objective is to explain why some jobs are more complex and involve more skills than others. This model enables us to close the paper with a set of conclusions and predictions regarding the management and operation of Information Technology in manufacturing settings.

The major features of the model can be described in four parts.

First, a job, whether in the context of new or old technology, can be complex or simple. In the extreme, a complex job is skilled and enriched, whereas a simple one is unskilled and impoverished. In part this is because of the tasks that the person does and in part because of the work roles undertaken. The physical tasks performed are largely determined by the technology, but the work roles are not. The technology used by a machinist for example, influences the kinds of operating skills needed and hence contributes to the overall complexity or simplicity of the job.

Second, major influences over the work roles undertaken by an operator are the chosen patterns of local control and the division of local responsibilities. Work roles are concerned with decision-making rights; for example, in addition to machine operation, an employee may order materials, undertake routine maintenance, decide on the order in which to do the work, and liaise with co-workers. Alternatively, these roles can be performed by specialists in support functions (e.g. materials control, maintenance engineering, production control), or by local supervision. The critical point is that an organization has a choice over how to allocate these responsibilities and who controls the operational aspects of work. These choices can be made almost independently of the technology and the resulting work roles contribute to the overall complexity or simplicity of the job.

Third, the choices are a function of a number of contingencies internal and external to the firm. Internal influences arise, for example, from the quality and complexity of the product, the product batch size, and the values of influential members within the organization. External influences include the competitiveness and stability of the market, and the availability of skilled manpower.

Finally, a useful explanatory concept is the notion of uncertainty. In this view the organization is seen as an information processing system which adapts to cope with prevailing uncertainties. These uncertainties arise from the market place and from the nature of the production process within the firm. Organisations have to choose a structure which enables them to handle these uncertainties. For example, organizations working in uncertain environments characterised by market competition, small batches, high product quality and complexity, may choose to give operators local control over key work roles in order to promote effective working. The logic here is that uncertainty (or variance) is best handled at source. In contrast, organizations which operate in relatively certain environments characterised by predictable and stable markets, large batches and products with less emphasis on quality, are less likely to locate operational control at shopfloor level. Thus, more complex jobs are more likely to exist in conditions of uncertainty whereas simplified work roles will be found in relatively certain environments.

The above framework is presented as an analytical tool which we have found useful in understanding the job designs resulting from the use of both traditional and new technologies. It is not presumed to be a total explanation of the impact of technology on shopfloor jobs. In the remainder of the paper we describe the case study using the framework as a guide. First, however, we briefly describe CNC machine tool working.

CNC MACHINE TOOLS

A traditional manual machine tool is a mechanised tool for cutting or shaping metal. It requires three principal activities (excluding loading and unloading). Thus, it must have the correct tool fitted to cut the metal (called tool-setting). The workpiece to be cut must be secured in the correct place so that it will be cut properly (machine-setting). Finally, the machine needs operating at the appropriate speeds and feeds (which will vary with the tools and materials in use). A CNC machine tool is similar, except that it is controlled by a computer program, usually in the form of a tape. Thus, in addition to tool-setting and machine-setting, it requires programming. Since these programs in practice almost always require correction or improvement, they need checking (or proving-out) and then editing. To the traditional machining activities then must be added new ones of programming, proving-out and editing.

The advantages claimed for CNC working over manual machine tools are threefold. First, they can provide for savings in direct machining costs (e.g. a reduction in machining and setting times). Second, there are potential cost savings resulting from reduced work in progress, scrap rework and inspection. And third, there is the possibility of increased flexibility through, for example, faster introduction of design changes and the ability to machine complex components. However, CNC machine tools are expensive and have costs associated with programming and maintenance activities. Technically, the advantages of CNC working are such that, in some markets, only firms using CNC are allowed to tender to make some high precision components. Overall, CNC machine tools are particularly suited to making small batches of complex engineering parts to a high degree of accuracy and repeatability.

The adoption rate of CNCs, since their emergence in the early 1970s, has been dramatic. In 1981, CNC accounted, by value, for one third of all machine tool sales in the UK. Indeed, an estimated one quarter of engineering establishments has some form of numerical control, although the total number of CNC machine tools represents only about 5 per cent of the machine tool population in Britain. Sales are high in the aerospace industry. Indeed, CNC machine tools are the most widespread form of applied IT in manufacturing industry throughout the world. Accordingly, they provide the ideal focus for those with an interest in how such advanced systems are managed and operated. The case study below describes an organisation which has invested heavily in CNC technology.

THE CASE STUDY

ORGANIZATIONAL SETTING

The study is set within a small, non-unionised precision engineering firm which is part of a large multi-national corporation. Originally, it was a family owned tool making firm which was bought-out in the late 1970s after being taken into receivership. It is located in the UK and employs approximately 150 people.

The firm, Precision Engineering Ltd (PEL), operates as a contract jobbing shop making complex parts in small batches (typically from 5–10 items) for firms in the aerospace business and in other specialized markets. Almost all the work involves precision engineering and includes special 'one-off' jobs. Some of the orders are repeated periodically. The market within which PEL operates is very competitive and uncertain due to the specialized batches. Direct competitors chase tenders which are most often contracted-out by large manufacturers who control the market. PEL's major advantage over some of its rivals results from the quality of its products. This is due primarily to the skills of its workforce and to its investment in capital equipment. A skilled workforce is available in the locality.

TECHNOLOGY AND STRUCTURE

Over the past 8–10 years PEL has invested heavily in CNC machines, to the extent that there are 40 such machines working alongside over 100 manual machines. The latest CNC machines in particular are large machining centres with 3 or 5 axis control, and each represents a major capital investment of up to £800,000. For financial and operational reasons, these machines are loaded heavily, the aim being to achieve continuous utilization. The primary reason for purchasing CNC technology was in order to succeed in the market place by machining highly complex parts to a high quality and with good repeatability. The CNCs were introduced for strategic and operational rather than control (or labour displacement) reasons.

PEL is a small company and, although it has its functional specialisms (manufacturing, planning and programming, quality, sales and finance), it is organic in structure, and is organised around the personal relationships of managers rather than being highly bureaucratic in form. The vertical authority structure is relatively flat and operates through mutual adjustment, that is, by openness, approachability and co-operation rather than by close control or the use of power.

JOB DESIGN AND THE ORGANIZATION OF WORK

To cope with the uncertainties of the production process, PEL management has chosen to staff machines with skilled men and to give them day-to-day operational control of both the manual and CNC machines. Thus, on all the machines, the operators do the bulk of their own tool setting and always set-up their own machines.

On the CNCs, the men also prove-out new tapes using polystyrene moulds as test pieces, undertake some straightforward programming in machine code (except for 5 axes), and edit their own tapes either for correction or to improve the working methods. In the case of 5 axes programs, they work alongside the programmer who comes onto the shopfloor to validate and edit these tapes. The emphasis is very much on collaboration and the sharing of skills and experiences between programmer and operator.

In general, CNC operators are able to use most of the CNC and manual machines although, in practice, they tend to specialise. Operators are flexible and multi-skilled, their tasks are complex, and they have roles within PEL covering many operating areas, incorporating wide decision-making rights. Indeed, this arrangement is supported by the local system of supervision. Here, chargehands are technical experts, rather than man–managers, and assist both in solving technical problems and ensuring that batches are moving through the system. Moreover, the indirect functions (for example, stores, planning and programming) are seen as supports to production. It is their role to provide the necessary information and materials for the job.

FINDINGS

Findings from questionnaires and interviews illustrate and confirm the positive and negative effects associated with this method of organizing for CNC working. Our presentation is in terms of the data gathered from 23 CNC operators. Comparisons with 27 manual machinists revealed few statistically significant differences in descriptions of their jobs or the company. In this general sense, the CNC operators were not disadvantaged in comparison with their manual co-workers, a finding contrary to the deskilling hypothesis.

Two particular sets of findings are considered. The first concerns the tasks and roles of the CNC operators and their reactions to their jobs. The second set relates to the integration of work and focuses on the indirect, support functions and the organization of work around the CNC machines.

Tasks and roles

The CNC operators report that their jobs are complex and contain many of the features considered necessary to motivate people at work. Thus, for example, ninety-one per cent of operators report 'a great deal', 'quite a lot', or 'a moderate amount' both of responsibility in their work and of task significance (i.e. doing a worthwhile job). Similarly most of them report that they have many opportunities to use their skills and abilities, that their jobs involve variety, feedback and identity (i.e. doing a whole and complete piece of work), and many report that they have some freedom to choose their own work methods. However, relatively few operators perceive that attention is paid to their suggestions, and almost none believe that they receive recognition for good work or have prospects for promotion.

In general, CNC operators report that they need all the basic engineering skills that they did when operating manual machines, for example, concerned with setting up machines and tools, and with reading complex drawings, although some manual skills (e.g. labouring) are less frequently used. In addition, they have acquired and developed some new computer based skills, including editing and programming. Moreover, most report that they have fairly complex work roles related to controlling their own work, solving local problems and checking the quality of their work. However, for most, these discretionary rights do not extend to supervisory activities such as planning the work of other people, deciding on work priorities, or organizing breaks.

Overall, the CNC operators consider their jobs to be complex with respect both to the constituent tasks and roles. In addition, they are highly motivated (a mean score of 38 out of a maximum score of 42, compared with a national norm of 36) and are satisfied with the intrinsic aspects of their work. For example, the proportion of operators reporting satisfaction ('extremely satisfied', 'very satisfied', or 'moderately satisfied') with the 'opportunity to use their abilities' was 78%; 74% were satisfied with the amount of variety in their work; and 61% and 52% respectively were satisfied with the 'amount of responsibility in their work' and 'the freedom to choose their own work methods'. In contrast, only 35% were satisfied with the attention paid to suggestions they make, and only 17% reported satisfaction with the recognition they receive for good work. Finally, 'taking everything into consideration', some 70% of CNC operators were satisfied with their work as a whole.

In summary, CNC operators at PEL take an obvious pride in their work and in their skills, and their commitment to high quality engineering was evident to us. They report that they enjoy the challenge of making complex parts and are keen to demonstrate that they can improve the working methods. They see the task as worthwhile and report satisfaction in completing a whole, identifiable component. It was also clear that their operational control of the production process is a source of great satisfaction to them and something they are anxious to protect.

Comments from the questionnaire serve to illustrate and broaden these conclusions. The comments were remarkably consistent across all CNC employees. Thus, in response to the question 'What are the best parts of your job?', typical replies were as follows:

> 'Working with modern technology as opposed to working on a dated manual machine. A wide scope of work is also a plus. Working with different materials. Being able to edit and write programs. Also having good workmates who can do their job.'
>
> '. . . the best parts of my job are when I get interesting 'one-off' components to manufacture, as I seem to get very bored with mass production work, but give me an intricate and challenging 'one-off' job, and I get so much satisfaction out of doing that job than anything (sic).'
>
> 'Working on what must be one of the finest machines in the country and turning out on occasions the finest work.'
>
> 'Independence, you are allowed to work with your own initiative, appraised occasionally, but allowed to get on with the job and trusted to do so.'

Integration of Work

In contrast to the positive work experiences identified above, the CNC operators report dissatisfactions with certain extrinsic aspects of their work and, in particular, negative comments were voiced concerning the levels of integration and co-operation between functions. The following responses were recorded for specific work factors such as the 'supervision/management you receive' (only 39% extremely, very or moderately satisfied); 'the amount of training you receive' (35%); 'industrial relations' (26%); 'communications in the factory' (22%) 'your rate of pay' (17%); 'the way your firm is managed' (4%); and 'the maintenance of machinery' (4%).

Comments taken from the questionnaire focus particularly on the problems associated with the lateral integration of work at PEL. Essentially, these comments are addressed to work-in-progress, that is, getting the right drawings, plans, programs, tools and materials to the right place at the right time. Typical responses to questions on job difficulties, the worst parts of the job and suggestions for improvements, are as follows:

> 'In my opinion the main things that make some jobs difficult is the lack of liaison between management, programming etc. when new jobs come in. We have been told that the policy now is to have all fixtures, tools etc. ready when jobs come into the factory, but 9 times out of 10 a lot of time and effort is spent sorting these things out for ourselves.'

> 'Jobs planned badly. Jobs programmed badly. Badly designed jigs and fixtures. Waiting for jobs (especially first-offs) to be inspected. Chasing round for tooling...'

> 'Too little information. Inaccurate information. Lack of necessary equipment.'

Indeed, employees were concerned that:

> '... a lot of time is wasted because of non-liaison between departments ... I feel that a lot of jobs could be done a lot quicker and efficiently if they went straight down to the shopfloor.'

that is PEL should:

> 'involve shopfloor workers more in the day-to-day running of the factory.'

perhaps by:

> 'transfer(ring) experienced CNC machinists into planning and programming to benefit from their experience and skills. Treat the shopfloor as intelligent people in their own field ... and listen to the suggestions they put forward and act on them.'

Overall then, the major points here concern a perceived lack of support and coordination. These complement earlier findings, where it was shown that there was a perception that management do not fully recognise the expertise nor the potential of shopfloor personnel. Indeed, many comments arising from the questionnaire concerned a need for greater participation in operational decision-making in order to use and capitalise upon the skills and experience of the CNC operators in planning and coordinating work.

ANALYSIS

In this section we analyse the case study in the light of the three questions posed earlier. Conclusions and predictions concerning more general use of Information Technology in manufacturing industry, will be presented in the final part of the paper.

WHAT CHOICES HAS THE FIRM MADE REGARDING THE MANAGEMENT AND OPERATION OF ITS CNC MACHINES?

As we have seen, management chose to invest in the purchase of CNC machine tools, principally in order to produce high quality goods in small batches for a particular market. To accommodate this technological decision, management chose to staff these machines with skilled operators and to delegate operational control to the shopfloor. The indirect functions act as supports to production; their role is an enabling one which, through the provision of services and materials, ensures that production meets customer deadlines and requirements.

The staffing of advanced manufacturing technology with skilled employees runs counter to the deskilling hypothesis described at the start of this paper. Indeed, the manning and operating of CNC machine tools by skilled operators has been found in a number of other studies. This may be so even though deskilling, through automation of the production process, was a stated intention in some instances.

WHAT IS THE IMPACT OF THESE CHOICES ON THE FIRM AND ITS EMPLOYEES?

One major outcome of these choices is that the company has been able to succeed in the market place. To withstand competition and to operate effectively in an unstable environment, the company needed to be flexible in its working arrangements and to consistently produce very high quality goods. To guarantee flexibility and product quality, it invested both in advanced manufacturing technology and in human resources. Together, these factors have promoted the economic viability of the firm.

Within the firm, the choices management has made over the working arrangements and the pattern of local control have resulted in shop-floor employees controlling large amounts of day-to-day operational decisions. The CNC operators are clearly satisfied with these arrangements, as they are with the content of their jobs, and they are motivated to produce good quality work. Indeed, management state that they are conscious of, and reward, this high level of skill and the ethos of self-control, although this contrasts with the perceptions of CNC employees themselves. The production manager, for example, told us 'We've got good blokes here – they're very skilled' and, on being asked if he completely specified machine speeds and feeds, a planner retorted, 'We wouldn't insult their intelligence.'

It is widely accepted within the company that problems arise, are recognised and corrected on the shopfloor and that operators need to have the levels of skill and the degree of control necessary to take action. Management's view is that paying 50 pence per hour more for a highly skilled machinist is a marginal cost, bearing in mind the value of the part being worked on (often £4,000–£6,000) and the cost of the capital equipment. Additional benefits of this method of organizing work include the speedy resolution of problems and better utilisation of equipment, since external specialists are relatively rarely called in.

There are also, of course, disadvantages. One, in particular, concerns the relationships between the indirect functions and production. Clearly, if indirect staff (such as programmers) are used as 'supports' rather than 'experts', then they may become dissatisfied with the working arrangements.

In addition, the choice to make a 'relative investment' in direct employees (rather than in indirect functions) can produce problems of coordination between functions and a perceived lack of adequate support. For example, without large numbers of support staff in stores, programming and maintenance, occasions arise when materials and tapes are not available and when corrections for machine faults are not speedily undertaken. Earlier, we described the dissatisfactions expressed by the CNC operators over the lateral work arrangements. Interestingly, the nature of their work has promoted a paradoxical duality of response. Thus, the CNC operators, whilst gaining much satisfaction from solving problems, also express frustration and dissatisfaction with the arrangements which allow them the freedom for such control. It is also clear, that the skilled CNC men are a powerful, largely self-controlling group and that their managers currently have little direct control of the production process.

The emergence of problems associated with the integration of work activities is not, of course, confined to this case study. Where control of the production process is in the hands of management and there is a relative investment in the indirect functions, major integration and coordination problems may also occur. These can be accentuated by the proliferation of experts across a range of departments, who may work with different priorities and goals from each other and from production. The establishment of integrative mechanisms is probably necessary for both types of work organization.

WHY HAVE THE CHOICES BEEN MADE, AND WHAT ARE THE PROSPECTS FOR THE FUTURE?

According to the conceptual framework described earlier, it is appropriate to view these choices as a function of a set of external and internal contingencies. Externally, the company works in a highly competitive market, characterised by small batch, high quality, complex precision engineering products. Internal contingencies are to be found in the unpredictability of work flows, and managerial values which favour self-control and the delegation of responsibility. The result of these contingencies is that management has chosen to locate control for operational decision-making at the level of the shopfloor, that employee tasks are skilled, roles are complex, and the indirect functions act as supports to production. This form of job design is equivalent to the socio-technical perspective, that variances are best handled at source – that is, it is consistent with the logic which considers people on the ground to have the appropriate knowledge, expertise and experience to control the operation.

The importance of these choices should not be underestimated, either for the success of the company or the satisfactions and well-being of its employees. Indeed, recent developments within the firm highlight how dynamic these processes may be. On a return visit to the site following the completion of the study, we discussed the future of the firm with senior management and three major changes were identified. The first involved the hiring of a new manufacturing manager whose values and experience conflict with the ethos of the company. Thus, he is attempting to gain control over the production process, in particular, by exerting direct control over the throughput of batches – 'getting metal out of the door' – and by changing shift working and overtime practices. The workforce are understandably concerned over this issue. This development, however, is part of a more general move towards improving efficiency and productivity by, for example, reducing cutting times. It is also directly linked with the other two changes.

The second change involves the implementation of a computerised information system which will gather data from the shopfloor to be used primarily for production control. This move is seen as an attempt to relocate operational control with management, away from the shopfloor. Thus, the roles undertaken by CNC operators will change, and overall job complexity will be reduced. This may have a major impact on employee satisfaction, commitment and the motivation to produce high quality goods. In addition, the indirect functions may no longer operate as support services but may become more powerful as a result of the information they hold. In a more general sense, the move is an attempt to centralize information and control and to break away from a decentralized structure.

Finally, the marketing strategy of the company is changing. There is a growing feeling and recognition amongst senior managers that the long-term future of 'one-off' specialised products is uncertain and that the company should move towards more standardised batch work for a more secure future (for example, larger batch defence work in home and overseas markets). Management are currently wrestling with the problem of implementing long runs of standardised batches, without changing dramatically the motivation and commitment of the workforce. The arrangements in the firm are changing, therefore, through decisions taken largely for commercial reasons, and they conflict with the present job designs and the values that have been held by management. Although they have stated that they do not want to deskill the production process, the workforce is less sure and has already voiced concerns. Principal themes to emerge are those concerned with a loss of pride in their own engineering skills and the loss of personal control of the operational aspects of work. Some employees have already labelled bigger batch work as 'rubbish', and three of the most skilled and respected CNC operators have voted with their feet and left the company.

CONCLUSIONS AND IMPLICATIONS

We conclude that this firm has chosen to manage and operate its Information Technology by placing reliance and emphasis on the skills of the operators. The investment is in shopfloor skills and abilities in pursuit of high quality, small batch, precision engineering products in order to meet the demands of a particular niche in the market. The impact has been positive, so far as the job designs of the shopfloor operators are concerned, though this strategy is not without its problems, particularly with regard to the firm's ability to integrate the efforts of the different departments. In our view these choices have been made for a combination of external and internal reasons, including an emphasis on product quality, the level of competition in the market place, the small batch nature of the business, the prevailing managerial values and the general ethos of local skills and control. It is clear, however, that these choices may be somewhat 'fragile'. A new, influential manager, emphasising 'metal out of the door' and tighter control, arriving at the very time that the marketing strategy is under review and may be changing from small to bigger batch work, also puts choices about the management and operation of the technology under review (or 'under threat' depending on your viewpoint).

So what does this mean? First, it is clear that the overall deskilling thesis has not been substantiated in this organisation. The operators are a most impressive group of people, deriving evident satisfaction from the exercise of self control and of their engineering skills.

Second, it seems likely that the emergent choices are determined by a set of complex, dynamic external and internal factors which are not 'set in concrete'. Certainly, the operators themselves see their working arrangements as relatively fragile. One might speculate, that it is easier for organisations to move from a skilled operation towards deskilling, rather than vice versa. For example, we have seen instances where the deskilling approach has become self-perpetuating in organisations, as a result of people's responses to impoverished work.

Third, if we are correct about the reasons why these organisational choices have been made, then we can predict that those organisations facing similar levels of market and/or production uncertainty, may make similar choices towards skilling up the production process.

Fourth, we speculate that new information based technologies will more and more be applied to small batch production environments, which are characterised by market, as well as production uncertainties. Indeed, Information Technology provides the means for enabling increased levels of automation in this, one of the largest and most important industrial sectors. But some commentators argue that such new technologies increase the level of uncertainty in the production system because they are so complex, and that such advanced systems will inevitably be imperfect under conditions of uncertainty, and will require skilled human support no matter how automated they are in principle.

And fifth, given the above, we speculate that the future of Information Technology in such industrial sectors promises the opportunity to skill up the production process and indeed may demand it for effective performance, quite the opposite of the deskilling hypothesis. We propose, that such a strategy will be optimal both for the individuals concerned and for the overall effectiveness of the system. This logic stresses the opportunities for synergy between the technical and the human systems. In this view, the technical system may offer benefits in terms of speed, reliability and repeatability, but a human system, designed to promote local operator skills, adds the complementary benefits of motivation, flexibility and responsiveness. Such logic, it must be stressed, has not been proven, but we believe it is based on reasoned speculation. Furthermore, there is evidence that some companies are beginning to manage and operate their advanced technologies in this way.

4. STRATEGIC VISION*

Charles Wiseman

ABSTRACT: Some companies realize that the conventional use of information system is not good enough. They need strategic union.

The reigning dogma on the organizational uses of information systems won't do. The company that fails to rethink its use of computer technology may find itself at risk.

Since the advent of data processing in the 1950s, one viewpoint has exclusively dominated the thinking about information system opportunities. It holds, that the organizational purpose served by computer applications is either to automate a basic process (subprocess or task) or to provide information for decision making.

This view is concerned primarily with information flows, data bases and the production of reports related to the organization's planning and control operations. I call this the conventional perspective on information systems.

A data processing professional exemplified this view in the early '70s when he advocated a new approach for information systems planning, a top-down method 'to focus on the critical tasks and decisions made within an organization and to provide the kind of information that the manager needs to perform those tasks and make those decisions'.

The author of a recent book on the health care industry reflects this view when he asserts that 'the only computer services that a hospital really needs – the basic financial, billing and accounting operations – could be purchased relatively inexpensively from any service company'.

When adherents of the conventional perspective search for information system opportunities, they look for two varieties; management information systems (MIS) and management support systems (MSS). (MSS includes as its two main species decision support systems and executive information systems.) These varieties are intended to serve organizational purposes associated with the conventional perspective, that is, automating basic processes (the domain of MIS) and satisfying the information needs of managers and professionals, needs often closely connected with planning and control decisions (the domain of MSS).

But the conventional perspective, important as it is for identifying and illuminating the significance of these two varieties, offers too limited a view of the world of information systems.

The word 'nation' in the text refers to the United States of America. (Ed)

CLINICAL LABORATORY

Consider, for example, how Metpath, Inc. uses systems to compete in the tough, fragmented clinical laboratory industry, where low differentiation of service has led to a lack of customer loyalty and frequent price discounting. Doctors send specimens to the lab for processing and, in return, expect timely, accurate analyses. Metpath enhanced its customer service by installing computer terminals in doctors' offices and linking them to its lab computers. For a small monthly fee, physicians receive test results as soon as they are determined.

From the conventional vantage point, the system might be seen as a transaction processing, on-line data base application providing critical diagnostic information to physicians. But this description captures neither its competitive importance nor its innovative character. By changing conceptual lenses and viewing it from a strategic perspective, we see it as an attempt by Metpath to use its information system as a double-edged sword.

First, it builds barriers against new and existing rivals by raising the information systems ante. Second, it enables Metpath to gain an edge over other labs by differentiating an otherwise commodity service. Metpath keeps historical records of patient data on file and offers its customers computerized processing services for billing and accounts payable operations, as well as easy access to stock market quotations from the Dow Jones network.

Finally, the system can expand the services it offers into such areas as diagnosis (when expert systems become available) and drug interaction testing. Referring to the latter, the vice-president for scientific affairs of the American Pharmaceutical Association said: 'If there is such a thing as the wave of the future, this is it.'

Primed, as it is, to store patient profile data on such items as drug and food allergies, chronic illnesses and medications taken, the Metpath system will permit physicians to conduct drug interaction tests prior to writing prescriptions. Each of these information system-based hooks serves to differentiate a commodity service and thereby secures the loyalty of the estimated one in five doctors who switch annually from lab to lab in search of lower prices.

COMPETITIVE WEAPONS

The conventional perspective on information systems supplies scant guidance to those who wish to discover such application opportunities or explain their strategic impact. Nor is it of much help in accounting for the extended uses made by American Airlines and United Airlines of their computerized reservation systems, Sabre and Apollo, respectively. Built in the 1970s at a cost of more than $250 million each, these information systems are no longer employed merely as neutral scheduling mechanisms to automate the seat reservation process. Rather, they are being used increasingly as weapons in the struggle for industry domination.

Sabre and Apollo give priority listing to American and United flights when travel agents request information on their computer terminals. An agent, who uses the Sabre system and requests a listing of flights from New York to Los Angeles with stops in between, knows that the first few items to appear on the screen may not show the most direct way, nor the least expensive way, but for sure they'll show the American way.

American and United have used their reservation systems to pre-empt the major channel of distribution. In the computerized travel agency market, the two form a powerful duopoly with shares of 41% and 39%, respectively. The crumbs (the remaining 20%) have been left to the competition. While Delta, Eastern and TWA have developed smaller systems, the other carriers are at risk. As one of the less fortunate put it: 'We clearly didn't pay enough attention, and now it's a direct threat.'*

More than 80% of the nation's 20,000 travel agencies, accounting for 90% of airline ticket sales, are computerized. In regions where the airline with the reservation system has numerous flights, the prioritization procedure can lead to as much as 20% more revenue.

In addition, Sabre and Apollo have become vehicles of diversification and growth, propelling American and United into new lines of business. According to the president of American, 'This industry needs every cent it can generate. We've got to be creative about using our huge asset base to develop new revenues. We're looking at businesses we can be in at low costs because some of the links are already in place.' These links form, in American's words, 'the world's most powerful nonmilitary computer system.'

According to the vice-president of marketing and automation systems at American, 65,000 devices hang off the network, which runs 23 hours a day, 365 days a year and keeps track of 6.5 million domestic and international airfare combinations, more than 10,000 daily fare changes and the schedules of about 650 airlines around the world. In 1983, for example, it handled more than 55 million calls at its four reservation centers.

To exploit excess capacity on Sabre, the carrier recently formed American Airlines Telemarketing Services, which performs services such as conducting marketing surveys and taking pledges generated by telethons. American expects that the fee income from these operations will be supplemented in the future when it uses its network to offer consumer products to home computer users.

NEW VARIETY

The two cases just described are instances of strategic information systems, information systems used to support or shape the competitive strategy of the organization. Strategic information systems represent a new information system variety, radically different in organizational use from those countenanced by the conventional perspective.

The conventional perspective is unsuited for guiding the systematic search for strategic information systems opportunities and is incapable of explaining the strategic

* A detailed description of the famous airline reservation system case is presented in the next chapter by J.I. Cash, Jr. (Ed.)

significance of applications. Believers in the conventional gospel on information systems are unable to discern most strategic information systems opportunities. Lying still further beyond the conventional field of vision, the entire spectrum of strategic alliances supported or shaped by information systems also goes undetected.

Paine Webber, for instance, seized an alliance opportunity in 1984 that no other brokerage house had previously been able to capture. It negotiated a pact with the State Street Bank and Trust Co. of Boston, enabling it to participate in Masterteller, the nationwide automated teller network run for banks by Mastercard International, a credit card and traveler's check organization, owned by 24,000 banks and other institutions. The Masterteller network lets cardholders withdraw cash from more than 1,500 automated teller machines throughout the U.S.

Up to this time, banks had been very careful to exclude rivals offering competitive financial services from entry to their networks. Indeed, two of the largest bank-owned nationwide networks, the Plus and Cirrus systems, rejected requests from Merrill Lynch and the Fidelity Group, a Boston-based mutual fund company, to establish similar arrangements.

Now Paine Webber customers can use credit cards issued by State Street to get the same 24-hour access to cash that bank cardholders enjoy. Because of this alliance, a cardholder with a Paine Webber account can withdraw money at automatic teller machines across the country. The story of how Paine Webber will use this new alliance in packaging its products has yet to unfold. In any case, the deal illustrates how the broker capitalized on information systems assets developed by others, to serve its own strategic ends.

JOINT VENTURE

Another form of strategic alliance involving information systems is illustrated by a recent joint venture. IBM and Merrill Lynch announced in 1984 the formation of International Marketnet, a new information service intended to provide users of IBM Personal Computers with stock quotations, investment data, analytical processing, financial software and so on. The service will enable end users to communicate via satellite links with Merrill Lynch's host computers. Monchik-Weber Corp., a software house specializing in the securities industry and acquired by McGraw-Hill, Inc. after International Marketnet opened its doors, won the contract to develop the systems that will run the service.

International Marketnet is a 50–50 joint venture of IBM and Merrill Lynch. The venture's customers will be drawn from Merrill's 10,000 account representatives, other brokerage houses, commercial banks, money managers and clients of these firms. For IBM, the alliance supports its strategy of market expansion; for Merrill, the venture supports plans to diversify into the information services industry and to reduce and eventually eliminate the fees it now pays to Quotron Systems, Inc. for the use of its stock-quotation system.

These alliances, as well as the examples detailed earlier, exemplify the strategic use of information systems. Representing instances in which competitive strategy is supported or shaped by the application of computer technology, they mark a dramatic turning in the brief evolutionary history of information systems. But to appreciate more deeply this break with the past – this movement from the conventional to the strategic – requires something more than the trotting out of strategic information systems cases. What we need to show, are examples of firms that have developed a vision of information systems to guide their strategic course.

STRATEGIC VISION

To see that an information system application is a strategic information system, we need to understand how information systems are used to support or shape the firm's competitive strategy. This ability to see and understand, I call strategic information systems vision.

A firm with a powerful strategic information systems vision zealously encourages the search for opportunities to use information systems to gain a competitive edge. And when they are discovered, it marshals the proper resources to support them. In some cases, strategic information systems vision develops into an image of the future, that top management uses to navigate the firm's strategic path.

How can we determine whether a firm possesses this vision? The best test is to examine what the firm says and does. If it purports to appreciate the strategic significance of information systems and if it launches thrusts supported or shaped by systems, we are justified in believing that strategic information systems vision is operating.

It would be preferable, to be sure, to explore from within, to observe in detail the strategic decision-making process and how information systems are woven into the fabric of strategic programs, before making a judgement.

DUN & BRADSTREET

The Dun & Bradstreet Corp. traces its origin back to 1841 when Louis Tappan, a New York dry-goods jobber, founded the Mercantile Agency, the first credit-reporting firm in the U.S. Within a decade, the Bradstreet Agency became the second company to enter the field. By 1890, Mercantile (now run by R. G. Dun) had established 69 branch offices in major business centers.

Being the first two firms to create nationwide networks, Bradstreet and Dun dominated the credit-reporting business. In the 1870s, Dun employed more than 10,000 reporters or investigators and received some 5,000 requests a day for information. In 1930, the two firms merged to form Dun & Bradstreet.

By 1978, Dun & Bradstreet had become a $763 million diversified information services company with four major divisions: Businesses Information Services, Publishing, Marketing Services and Broadcasting. Business Information Services contributed 38% of the revenues and 27% of the operating income.

In 1979, Dun & Bradstreet recorded its best year ever and made two significant strategic moves. It purchased for $164 million National CSS, Inc. (NCSS), a leading computer service company with a nationwide, 80,000-mile time-sharing network, and agreed to acquire its sixth television station together with half-a-dozen small cable systems. This move gave Dun & Bradstreet its first hands-on experience in the growing cable industry. The NCSS acquisition became part of Dun & Bradstreet's Business Information Service Division, while the television station and cable systems were to become part of the broadcasting group.

In its annual report, Dun & Bradstreet explained how it saw these moves as consistent with its strategic vision: 'There are three principal resources that are central to the continued success of the Dun & Bradstreet Corporation: our ability to collect timely and relevant information for the decision-making use of our various customer groups; our capacity for applying technology effectively to maximize information delivery and utility; and the management to anticipate the needs of our customers and, in partnership with our highly skilled people, to provide quality products and services worldwide.'

INFORMATION SERVICES GIANT

At the close of 1983, Dun & Bradstreet has become a $1.5 billion information services giant. The contribution of the Business Information Services Division had risen in four years to 45% of total revenue and 34% of operating income. During the year, Dun & Bradstreet made two significant strategic moves. It acquired McCormack & Dodge Corp. (M&D), a major software company specializing in finanical and human resources packages, and departed from the broadcasting industry by selling its stations and systems.

In 1984, Dun & Bradstreet underlined its focus on business services and information by acquiring through merger (a $1.08 billion stock transaction), A. C. Nielsen Co., the nation's leading consumer research concern.

Dun & Bradstreet's recent evolutionary history reflects strategic information systems vision. Its management has executed strategic moves supported or shaped by information systems, moves that serve to support or shape the company's long-term objective of concentrating its efforts and resources in the business services and information industry.

In 1979, Robert Weissman (NCSS's president when it was acquired by Dun & Bradstreet and now Dun & Bradstreet's president and chief operating officer) proclaimed: 'NCSS and Dun & Bradstreet are the best fit in the information industry – data from Dun & Bradstreet operating companies plus NCSS leadership in computer services. We're going to rewrite the book on combining information and technology to develop new products for our customers.'

The battle cry voiced by Weissman is reflected in the following moves made during the 1979–1984 time period.

ACQUISITION OF NCSS

This major diversification move enabled Dun & Bradstreet to enter the time-sharing business, a new market pioneered by NCSS, and to exploit NCSS's information system resources (its hardware, software and highly skilled work force) synergistically.

Within a few months after the acquisition, 12 joint projects were initiated, among them Duns Vue, a new credit product, and Moody's Municipal Credit Report Service, both designed for electronic delivery over the NCSS network.

But the NCSS time-sharing business has been a disappointment. As demand declined over the past five years, primarily because of the rapid spread of microcomputer processing, Dun & Bradstreet has had to find new uses for its valuable NCSS resources.

ACQUISITION OF MCCORMACK & DODGE

Like the NCSS purchase, this alliance illustrates a major diversification move with a dual purpose. Dun & Bradstreet expects to exploit M&D's software, systems know-how and 3,000-member customer base synergistically across its various product lines. And it expects M&D, an established leader in its market niche, to continue its impressive growth.

Already, joint projects are emerging between M&D and Dun & Bradstreet's other units. M&D's PC-Link allows users of IBM's Personal Computer to retrieve and transfer mainframe data. This product ties directly to Dunsplus, which is the result of efforts by an NCSS division (now called Dun & Bradstreet Computing Services) and a strategic information systems alliance struck between Dun & Bradstreet and IBM.

ACQUISITION OF NIELSEN

In the case of the NCSS and M&D acquisitions, Dun & Bradstreet exploited the information systems assets of others. With the Nielsen merger, on the other hand, Dun & Bradstreet saw opportunities to exploit its own information system assets. Here, there are both economy-of-scale (possible consolidation of information system services) and economy-of-scope opportunities, which have yet to unfold.

DEVELOPMENT OF OFFICIAL AIRLINES GUIDE/ ELECTRONIC EDITION

Dun & Bradstreet's Official Airline Guides provide information on North American, Worldwide and Air Cargo flights. In 1983, Dun & Bradstreet announced an electronic version of these guides. The Official Airline Guide/Electronic Edition can be accessed by computer terminals. It lists the information contained in the print editions, as well as fares. Users can query the flight data base for comparative fare information within specified arrival or departure periods and for lowest fares between two points.

The Official Airline Guide/Electronic Edition, however, does not handle reservations. Dun & Bradstreet distributes its product directly or through such information networks as Compuserve. Inc., Dialcom, Inc., Dow Jones News/ Retrieval, Bell Canada and Viewdata.

The Official Airline Guide/Electronic Edition is an example of an innovative strategic maneuver targeted at customers who wish to reduce their travel costs – the third fastest rising corporate expense. In the past, travellers generally relied on agents for such information and, depending on the reservation system used by the agent, received flight alternatives, giving priority to the airline providing the system. Now, with the Official Airline Guide/Electronic Edition, travellers can get objective data, favoring only the airlines with the lowest prices. The system will also include international fares, as well as hotel and car rental rates.

CREATION OF DUNSPLUS

By forming strategic information systems alliances with IBM, Lotus Development Corp. and Softword Systems, Dun & Bradstreet created a unique product complementing its other offerings, as well as providing a stand-alone, integrated professional workstation. Dunsplus consists of an IBM Personal Computer (Dun & Bradstreet forged an agreement with IBM to act as a value-added remarketer), spreadsheet (1–2–3) and word processing (Multimate International Corp.'s Multimate) programs and specifically developed Dun & Bradstreet software (from NCSS), outfitting end users with electronic mail, file maintenance, data integration and other capabilities.

As incentives to purchase Dunsplus, Dun & Bradstreet includes as standard features one year's sign-up charges for Western Union's electronic mail service and its own Official Airline Guide/Electronic Edition. Access to Dun & Bradstreet's extensive collection of electronic data bases, and others as well, is a relatively straightforward procedure with Dunsplus.

Built into the offering is PC-Link, M&D's micro-to-mainframe utility program, which allows Personal Computer users to transmit and receive data from corporate data bases. Within the first six months after its introduction in January 1984, Dunsplus attracted more than 50 major corporate customers.

DEVELOPMENT OF DUNSNET

This recent Dun & Bradstreet offering is a packet-switched telecommunications network, similar in function to GTE's Telenet and Tymshare, Inc.'s Tymnet. With Dunsnet, Dun & Bradstreet offers its customers value-added networking services and distributed processing through the use of such microcomputer systems as Dunsplus. NCSS and other Dun & Bradstreet units can also make use of the network.

Dunsnet enables all Dun & Bradstreet users to access its data bases using one standard procedure. It reduces Dun & Bradstreet-generated revenues for Telenet and Tymnet. Dunsnet represents a strategic growth move for Dun & Bradstreet, a kind of forward integration that takes the company a step further toward its goal of being a full-service provider of information services and data to its clients.

FORWARD LOOK

From this short selection of strategic actions taken over a five-year period, it seems evident that Dun & Bradstreet possesses strategic information systems vision. If it didn't, how else can one account for such efforts to use information systems to support strategy. The reader may object that, because Dun & Bradstreet is an information services company, each of the moves cited is natural and has nothing to do with strategic information systems vision.

But this objection is not persuasive. Dun & Bradstreet had choices. It wasn't forced to acquire M&D or Nielsen. It wasn't bullied into forming an alliance with IBM to market the Personal Computer and build a product around it. Dunsnet was not inevitable. Different data-rich firms have made different strategic thrusts, some emphasizing information systems, others not. Dun & Bradstreet itself didn't have such a clear vision of its future in 1979, as indicated by its broadcasting acquisitions. After acquiring NCSS, however, the die seems to have been cast, with Weissman probably sounding the clarion call.

The current evolution of Dun & Bradstreet, inspired by strategic information systems vision, is far from complete. By the end of this decade, in all likelihood, it should emerge as one of the leading information services firms in the world, providing a full line of products supported or shaped by information systems.

MCKESSON CORP

Another example of a firm that has developed a powerful strategic information systems vision is the McKesson Corp., formerly Foremost-McKesson and originally, McKesson-Robbins. In 1984, it was the nation's largest independent distributor of ethical and proprietary drugs, toiletries, fragrances and sundries; wine and spirits; and industrial and speciality chemicals.

Restructured in the late 1920s, McKesson diversified over the next 50 years into such businesses as alcoholic beverage distribution, dairy products (through a merger with Foremost Dairies) and pasta and dehydrated vegetable manufacture (through the acquisition of C.F. Mueller Co.). In 1984, the new McKesson announced that it was leaving the food business (having sold Foremost and Mueller in 1983) to concentrate its resources on the value-added distribution of a variety of products.

What is shaping McKesson's new strategic direction is what is shaping Dun & Bradstreet's: strategic information systems vision. Top management believes that the name 'McKesson Corporation' now 'reflects our history, the present structure of our business and the path we are travelling.'

Thomas Drohan, McKesson's former president, said in the 1983 annual report: 'Perhaps the single greatest advantage that the McKesson distribution companies enjoy, has been – and will continue to be – in computer technology, where our size and diversity have enabled us to achieve the necessary critical mass. Our data processing resources now involve 550 people and an annual budget of more than $65 million. We intend to continue the proliferation of this technology among our current distribution businesses and to seek out opportunities to apply it to other distribution-related businesses. This shift in emphasis – making value-added distribution our primary thrust with a secondary thrust in certain proprietary product areas – reflects the facts as they are today.'

McKesson sees a direct connection between its ability to gain competitive advantage and its use of information systems to support and shape strategies aimed at this objective. Over the past 10 years, the company has introduced computer-based goods and services to help it gain an edge with both its suppliers and its customers, an edge that translates into a distinct advantage over other distributors. These strategic moves run the gamut from those designed to exploit scale and scope economies, to growth and alliance maneuvers to expand into new markets. Among the alliances implemented by McKesson, the following are noteworthy.

COSMCK/ECONOSCAN

CosMcK, a computer-based merchandising program, created in 1981 for druggists, supermarkets and mass merchandisers, helps retailers stock, price-label, rotate and display merchandise according to the marketing reports it generates. Covering 20 departments in 1982, it now extends to 28 categories, such as over-the-counter drugs, pet care and school supplies.

Econoscan, a computerized order-entry system, enables a retailer holding an Econoscan scanning device to record data from shelf labels and then transmit the captured data in the form of an order over telephone lines to a McKesson distribution center, at the rate of 600 items per minute. McKesson fills the order overnight and delivers it the next day in tote boxes arranged to correspond to the various shelf divisions of the retailer's store.

MCKESSON CHEMICAL

This division, the nation's leading full-line distributor of industrial chemicals, implemented a computer-based service for its customers that saves them costly inspection time and enhances McKesson's image as a high-quality, reliable distributor. At selected chemical distribution centers, McKesson installed highly sensitive instruments to analyze the chemical composition of substances. This ensures, for example, that chemical solvents meet stringent customer standards. The instruments are tied via telephone lines to a McKesson computer at its research center in Dublin, Calif., so that the data can be interpreted and checked for compliance.

This is another of the many differentiation-based strategic thrusts supported by McKesson's information systems. McKesson Chemical, like the drug and alcoholic beverage division, also offers its customers an on-line order-entry system designed to streamline ordering, inventory control, purchasing, accounts receivable, delivery and invoicing procedures. For the chemical division, it provides instantaneous information on inventory, customer needs and the safe handling of the more than 1,000 chemical products it sells. Most likely, economies of scope based on order-entry systems know-how are at work here.

PHARMACEUTICAL CARD SYSTEM

PCS, a prescription drug claims processing system, led McKesson to spin off a special business unit to exploit its potential. Introduced a few years ago, PCS now processes more than 27 million claims from 2.3 million cardholders covering 6.5 million people. Employers issue PCS cards as an employee benefit.

More than 45,000 pharmacies, representing more than 80% of the nation's retail druggists, fill prescriptions for PCS cardholders. Coverage is offered by 155 insurance companies in the U.S. and Canada. Data from pharmacists is transmitted to a central McKesson computer for processing. Claims are completed automatically, and tapes are forwarded to third-party reimbursers.

In itself, PCS represents a strategic diversification maneuver. Perhaps even more interesting is the continued expansion of McKesson's PCS operation, symbolizing the power of the company's strategic information systems vision. As claim data is collected by PCS, a special unit, Pharmaceutical Data Services (PDS), uses its software to analyze the data and produce a series of marketing reports targeted at major drug manufacturers, financial institutions and government agencies. The reports include analyses of prescription drug use by hospital, nursing care facility and so on. It is capable of analyzing the flow of pharmaceutical products through the health care system.

In 1983, PCS acquired Dresden/Davis Organization, a medical research company that collects data on drugs prescribed by physicians. This, of course, will become part of PCS's growing data base and move the unit closer to its goal.

ACQUISITION OF SKU

In 1983, McKesson joined Action Industries, Inc., a Pittsburgh maker of household and hardware items, in a 50–50 venture in which they acquired SKU, Inc., a microcomputer software distributor. The leader in the embryonic micro software industry at the time was Softsel Computer Products, followed by Micro D and SKU. The market for personal computer software, then at $2.1 billion, was projected to reach $11.7 billion by 1988, with 25% handled by independent distributors.

Whatever Action's motives, McKesson's aim was clear: to expand the scope of its distribution business and transform the cottage industry of software distribution (with after-tax margins of 4% at most) into a larger, more profitable game. McKesson planned to use previously developed information systems as the synergistic fuel for its entry vehicle. The computerized order-entry systems and other proprietary products it provides to more than 14,000 mass merchandisers, supermarkets and other outlets, would be tailored to this new marketplace. These information systems would not be used merely as aids to improve efficiency but as weapons to shape competitive strategy.

'The name of the game,' McKesson's chief executive officer said at the time, 'has become adding value to distribution. Our primary goal is to set ourselves apart from the competition in dramatic enough ways, that we become the first distributor a supplier thinks of. At the other end, by tying your customers to you as tightly as possible, you get more and more of their business as they grow.'

With the past as prologue to the future, current and new participant in the software distribution industry could expect McKesson to use its information systems to gain competitive advantage by:

- Establishing on-line links with software suppliers and retailers.
- Providing information to suppliers and retailers to help them better manage inventories, collect and analyze market data and plan sales campaigns.
- Providing retailers with shelf management plans, price labels, inventory systems and so on.
- Conducting computer-related technical seminars for suppliers and retailers.
- Joining with software suppliers to develop new products.
- Marketing associated services through its network.

Unfortunately for McKesson and Action, however, this strategic alliance failed. In August 1984, the partners announced they were writing off their combined investment of $8 million and discontinuing the operations of SKU.

A spokesman for McKesson said that 'the market for computer software hasn't developed as we had anticipated.' The parties were unable to stem accelerating losses at SKU.

CONSIDERABLE RISKS

I include this example of a failed strategic thrust to emphasize the point that strategic moves entail considerable risks, and neither information systems support nor shaping nor anything else can guarantee success. What looked like a promising move failed because market demand was misread.

While this ventured failed, another seemed heading for success. In 1983, McKesson purchases 3 P.M., a software developer and marketer of packages for pharmacies and florists. In 1984, McKesson negotiated a pack with the Florists' Transworld Delivery Association.

Under the terms of the agreement, McKesson will deliver, install and maintain personal computers and systems intended to handle a florist's business management functions, such as payroll and accounts receivable and payable. It expects sales from this new venture to total about $75 million over the next five-year period.

BANC ONE

The final example of a successfully developed strategic information systems vision involves one of the most innovative and entrepreneurial firms in the financial services industry, Banc One of Columbus, Ohio. John G. McCoy, the chief executive officer of this multibank-holding company, formed in 1967, retired in 1984 at age 71 after 25 years in that position. When he took the reins at City National Bank (Banc One's forerunner) from his father in 1959, the bank had less than $150 million in assets and primarily business customers.

With assets of more than $7 billion and customers drawn primarily from the consumer sector, Banc One ranked in 1984 in the top 10 among the 100 largest banks in the U.S. on three commonly acknowledged measures of superior performance.

Through an ongoing series of mergers, it now controls 22 affiliate banks in Ohio. For the 16th consecutive year, net income and earnings per share increased. In the 1980–1983 period, net income skyrocketed from $32.8 million to $83.3 million, employees from 3,145 to 6,939 and branch offices from 127 to 314.

These figures represent an extraordinary record of profitability and growth. How can it be explained? Why has Banc One, a relatively small, local bank in 1967, been able to succeed in the increasingly competitive financial services industry, where the competition consists not only of banking colossuses like Citibank, Chase Manhattan and Chemical Bank but also of retail giants like Sears Roebuck & Co. and financial supermarkets like American Express?

While a number of explanations – running from luck to charisma – have been suggested, the most convincing account of Banc One's success can be given in terms of its powerful strategic information system vision – a vision embodied, to be sure, in McCoy, but a vision nevertheless of the integral role to be played by information systems in the bank's strategic evolution.

McCoy, like some of his colleagues, long believed that banks competed at a disadvantage vis-a-vis such omnibus rivals as Sears or American Express. While the latter were free to develop an almost unlimited product portfolio or expand without geographical limit, banks were handcuffed in these two strategic areas by federal and state regulations. Unless banks could find ways around the regulations or get them changed in their favor, they faced the growing prospect of erosion in some of their major business lines.

McCoy's strategic response to these threats was twofold. First, to overcome the geographical expansion constraint, he formed the Banc One Holding Company, which permitted the acquisition of other banks but not across state lines.

Second, to overcome the product development restriction, he encouraged his managers to search for new products that would yield new sources of income and would protect the bank's cash flow stream from exposure to interest-rate fluctuations.

Thus, expansion through acquisition and product innovation were two strategic thrusts that Banc One would follow in its strategic journey. Both, it turned out, were precisely the kinds of movements that could be supported or shaped by information systems.

McCoy developed his strategic information systems vision early. When he assumed the presidency, one of his first moves was to seek board approval for an annual research and development budget, not to exceed 3% of annual profits. He won approval and every year, Banc One has been able to experiment, primarily in the area of information systems.

In 1966, for example, it introduced the first Bank Americard credit card service outside California. In 1967, it initiated a major online credit card processing network that today spans more than 30 states. In 1971, it joined with IBM in making the first significant test of point-of-sale systems using magnetically encoded cards. In 1980, with others, it conducted the first test of inhome banking through the use of customer televisions and the telephone system.

From the 1960s, McCoy realized the importance of information systems in the financial services industry. In a recent annual report, he explained why Banc One was so eager to become the first Bank of America licensee and what made him think it was such a good idea: 'Well, there was some luck involved, but you have to remember that was the time when the computer was first beginning to produce important changes in banking. We thought the credit card was an idea whose time had come because of the new computer capability.

'The first on-line computer systems in banking were designed for credit card authorization. We had one of the first ones here in Columbus. We committed major efforts to computer development in those early years, and we still do today, I might add. By 1970, to tell you how this innovation happens, we began to install the first automatic teller machine equipment in our Upper Arlington branch because we saw it as a way to link the customer, with a plastic card, directly to the computer.'

PROCESSING SERVICES

As Banc One's reputation for information system innovation grew, other firms approached it for processing services. In the late 1970s, Merrill Lynch contracted with Banc One for data processing and Visa debit card issuance services associated with its new cash managements accounts (CMA) service. As a result of this alliance, now also negotiated with other brokerage houses, Banc One is one of the nation's three largest Visa processors.

The primary vehicle to expand Banc One's processing services – related chiefly to credit and debit card processing outside Ohio banking markets and producing more than 30% of the corporation's net income – is the Financial Card Services Division. This spin-off has had an impressive growth record.

In 1983, the cardholder account base processed by Financial Card Services grew by 41.3% to more than 3.9 million. Of these accounts, '14% are Banc One affiliate banks' customers and 7% are Banc One customers originating from outside our market area, while 79% are derived from third-party processing for other banks, thrifts, credit unions, finance companies and brokers. Financial Card Services revenue grew 26% in 1983.'

Late in 1983, a new four-year contract was negotiated with Merrill Lynch related to Banc One's processing of its CMA brokerage accounts. This is the third contract Banc One has had with Merrill Lynch since 1977, when Banc One was selected to be the processor for this revolutionary financial product.

While credit and debit card processing is important to Banc One's overall strategic scheme, it is the centralization of the bank's processing activities that has enabled the company to make its acquisition program work.

A small bank sees in the Bank One affiliation (read: acquisition) proposition an opportunity to cope with the accelerating changes in financial services that would otherwise engulf it – new regulations, the prospect of interstate banking, interstate deregulation and perhaps most critical, new technology demands induced by the convergence of information processing and telecommunications.

For Banc One, its acquisition program – called the 'Uncommon Partnership' because it allows the acquired bank a reasonable degree of independence – enables it to reap large economies of scale. Listen to McCoy on this partnership, taken from the 1983 annual report: 'More recently, the Uncommon Partnership represents our chosen way of managing the holding company even though we could merge everything into a single bank. Instead, each bank is run by bankers from that area, each trying to be sensitive to community needs. As a result, a lot of our management strength and, certainly, the growth and earnings potential, lies with our affiliates. We have limited the concentration of management to those areas that are most sensitive to economies of scale, such as data processing or the handling of investments. I expect this philosophy will remain for some time into the future.'

Thus, Banc One uses the strategic cost thrust to shape its competitive strategy of growth via acquisition. In the case of a recent affiliation, according to another officer at Banc One, 'We were able to save almost a million dollars a year in combined operating expenses by converting the affiliates' data processing systems into our single system. There are some real economies of scale at work here.'

STRATEGIC ALLIANCE

Banc One also forged an innovative strategic alliance with Comp-U-Card, a computerized shopping and below-retail buying service. The two partners created Super Visa, a credit card issued by Banc One, that Comp-U-Card offered as bait to lure new customers.

This strategic information systems alliance serves Comp-U-Card's purpose of enhancing its offering to customers and foregoing the risk and expense associated with starting its own credit card system.

For Banc One, the alliance has already increased the bank's credit card account base by 100%. This has proved to be particularly profitable, because Comp-U-Card's customers have tended to let their accounts roll over to a greater extent than Banc One's other cardholders.

CREATIVE FORCE

For Dun & Bradstreet, McKesson, and Banc One, strategic information systems vision functions as a creative force transforming the organization through strategic moves supported or shaped by information systems. Other organizations, such as Citibank, Federal Express, McDonnell Douglas Corp., American Hospital Supply Corp. and General Electric Co., also possess strategic vision. Each comprehends, in its fashion, the strategic importance of information systems.

Strategic information systems vision is an abiliy that can be developed, and hence possessed, in varying degrees. Its most important prerequisite is the adoption of the strategic perspective on information systems. Without this perspective, the systematic search and exploitation of strategic information systems opportunities would be doomed.

The conventional perspective countenances the existence of only two information systems varieties: MIS and management support systems. Companies holding this conventional perspective lack the vision to see the cornucopia of strategic information systems opportunities falling forever beyond their line of sight.

But by adopting the strategic perspective on information systems, by donning a new pair of conceptual glasses, the world of strategic information systems opportunities appears.

CHAPTER IV

THE INFORMATION SYSTEM AS A STRATEGIC WEAPON

INTRODUCTION

The Information System as A Strategic Weapon

Elisabeth K. Somogyi

It is only recently that information systems have been recognised as tools of competitive strategy. The traditional role of information systems was in the areas of improving efficiency and effectiveness of company operations, especially at unit or departmental level. Although, in an indirect way, systems used in this capacity can have a positive effect on the enterprise, the newly discovered strategic use puts systems, the first time, into the 'firing line'.

Since the late 1970s, systems have been moving out of the back-room support role and started to affect the competitive positions of businesses. Although this capacity of changing the competitive potential of the enterprise is a most prominent characteristic of information systems, the strategic advantage to be gained through systems is only possible because of information technology. The first paper of this chapter, explains how and why information technology became strategic.

The most prominent strategic results achieved by information systems so far have been at the customer interface points of businesses. The characteristic of these systems is that they interconnect directly a company with its clients. A special name was given to these systems to differentiate them from those which are used internally by organisations. The name is: interorganisational systems. The second paper in this chapter gives a full exposure to these systems, with a famous example highlighting their competitive potential. The third paper expands on the competitive potential of information systems and explains how information systems could be used as weapons of competition.

It is clear that these systems – whilst technically not much different from other modern information systems – need a management approach quite distinctly different from the management of internal, administrative-type information systems. Systems which maintain the liaison between a company and its customers, or systems which help a company to start a new product or a new line of business, need – beyond technical excellence – careful attention at management level. The last paper articulates both the need and the methods for segmenting the total systems portfolio of a company and gives guidelines for managing the different parts of the portfolio.

1. STRATEGIC INFORMATION TECHNOLOGY*

Gregory L. Parsons

The significant advances in the related technologies of computers, telecommunications, data access and storage devices, graphics equipment and software, have created a wide spectrum of new opportunities for the business manager of today and tomorrow. The speed, cost, size and capabilities of the new information technology (IT) continue to improve at a rapid pace; there appear to be unlimited applications waiting to be 'computer enhanced.' In spite of the new wealth of technological resources available to businesses, however, the ability of most business organizations to assimilate and apply IT to the best uses, lags far behind available opportunities. Few senior executives feel that their businesses get the maximum benefit from IT; fewer still are able to articulate what impact IT has or should be having on their businesses.

Three senior executives who were not IT managers, responded very differently when asked about the impact of IT on their businesses.

A divisional president of a large industrial corporation stated:

'I think information technology contributes at least three percent of our bottom line profit margins. Operationally, we couldn't get through the week without the system support, and in the marketplace, I don't think we could hold our market share without the technology. But this is mainly a gut feeling. I can't back up these estimates with numbers or specific reasons.'

The chief strategist for a major U.S. bank said:

'The technology is our top strategic concern, not because it outweighs everything else, but because we are unsure what to do with it. Although we have a strategy for the marketplace, the technology issues seem to be eluding us. On the one hand, it's important, everybody agrees on that, but then we end up doing projects based on a series of piecemeal, technical decisions. We can't seem to grasp the bigger picture.'

The chief financial officer of a large consumer goods manufacturing company commented on his view of IT:

'We've really cleaned up our data processing act since the mid-1970s. The systems run well and now we're mainly fine-tuning. I expect we'll be doing primarily maintenance programming in the foreseeable future. I feel that we've gotten most of the benefits from the technology currently available. As the cost comes down, more projects will be financially justified and then we'll do them.'

Two issues emerge from these comments, as well as from many other senior

* Class discussion paper – Harvard Business School

The word 'nation' in this paper refers to the United States of America (Ed)

G. L. Parsons is assistant professor, Graduate School of Business Administration, Harvard University, USA.

executives questioned about IT. The first issue is that IT's importance to the business varies widely from firm to firm. In some firms, IT is a top-level strategic concern; in others, an administrative convenience.

The second issue is that there is no commonly accepted guideline or framework for measuring the importance of IT to business. These executives have a *feeling* about the importance but few could say why. Even fewer could say how important IT would or should be for the future.

The fact is that IT is having a significant impact and is becoming a significant management concern for many firms. More than $1 trillion is expected to be spent on IT investments. The technical improvements in telecommunications, personal computers, computer-assisted manufacturing and computer-aided design are but a few of the relatively recent developments that have made IT an increasingly important component of many firms' products/services and operations.

IT may have a strategic impact on a firm in three ways or at three levels (see *Figure A*). Senior management must know whether IT will represent a major constraint or opportunity as the firm plans for its future. If IT is an important issue for the firm, it must be consciously managed so that the appropriate actions are taken to defend against threats or pursue opportunities to the business that result from technological developments.

To identify when, where, and how IT becomes important to business strategy, an analysis must be performed at three levels (industry, firm, and strategy). This analysis identifies the impact of IT on the competitive domain of the firm, as it changes the competitive environment in which a firm operates and the opportunities for the firm's competitive direction.

INDUSTRY-LEVEL IMPACT OF IT

At the highest level, IT changes the fundamental nature of the industry within which the firm competes. When IT changes an industry, it may affect one or all of the following: (a) the nature of the industry's products/services, (b) the markets of the industry, (c) or the industry's economics of production. In some industries, IT will alter the very nature of the industry's products/services; the geographic distribution possibilities for the products/services will be expanded; and the speed of distribution will be substantially increased. The publishing industry is undergoing a revolution in its products/service area. As the industry's product becomes electronically based, rather than paper based, the time and space constraints defining previous industry competition will change completely. Authors and news sources are writing electronic manuscripts and text, sending it to the publisher as a floppy disk or directly computer-to-computer. Electronic manuscripts are edited with IT, typeset with IT, graphics are IT-generated, promotional materials are distributed with IT, and readers can go to the publisher's electronic database to buy the product. The time lag between idea and mass distribution could be virtually eliminated.

Other industries will have their markets substantially changed by IT. Financial companies will face a market of highly computerized consumers and businesses who

Figure A: Three Levels of Strategic IT Impact

Industry Level:

1. Product/Service
   - Nature of product/services
   - Product life cycle
   - Speed of distribution

2. Markets
   - Overall demand
   - Degree of segmentation
   - Geographic distribution possibilities

3. Economics of Production
   - Relevant range for economies of scale
   - Flexibility-standardization tradeoff
   - Value added stream

Firm Level:

1. Buyers
   - Switching costs
   - Buyer selection

2. Suppliers
   - Avoid switching costs
   - Backwards integration

3. New Entrants
   - Entry barriers
   - Entry deterrents

4. Substitution
   - Relative price-performance
   - Product features

5. Rivalry
   - New basis of competition
   - Shared IT

Strategy Level:

1. Overall Low-Cost Producer
   - Reduces overall costs directly
   - Enhances the ability to reduce overall cost through other functions

2. Overall Differentiation
   - Adds unique features to product/service directly
   - Enhances the ability to differentiate product/service through other functions

3. Focusing on Niche
   - Identify and create markets niches directly
   - Enhances the ability to create market niches through other functions

will demand electronically-based products and services. IT has already created a whole new product line called cash management systems, which are offered by large banks. Financial services companies must now compete in a global market, as IT has erased geographic market limitations. Overall, demand will increase as more products and services are possible. However, the financial product life cycle will shorten substantially as improved IT-based products and delivery systems will create new dimensions of product differentiation that will fuel competition. Already, the life cycle of many insurance products has been halved both by competition and the IT-based ability to develop and support much more sophisticated products.

Still other industries will have the basic economics of production changed by IT developments. IT is cleaving the distribution industry into two types of businesses: the *haves* (have computerized warehousing and inventory) and the *have nots* (do things manually). The *haves* are breaking the industry pattern of regional distribution by developing the ability to serve a national market. This has given the national distributor other advantages, such as economies of scale in marketing, software, hardware, and so forth. The *have nots* are unable to go national and are constrained by IT, not by choice, to local markets. IT will also change the basic economics of production in some industries by substantially changing the industries' historically required tradeoff for standardization versus flexibility. Already, some Japanese equipment manufacturing plants have used IT to achieve unit costs that remain the same whether producing one unit or one million units. This potential will effectively remove many of the traditional competitive advantages in these industries. As well as reducing historical scale economies in some areas, IT will extend scale economies in other areas. The monitoring, controlling and coordinating potential of IT will allow 'bigger' efficient facilities to be built that will capture new scale economies potential in specialists, space, energy, and machinery.

The competing firm will find that traditional rules of competition will change, new economies of scale will appear, entry barriers will be eroded in one area and spring up in other areas, new products/services will appear, distribution channels will be changed, different levels of demand and elasticity will be experienced, product life cycles will be shortened, new competitors will enter the scene, the value-added stream of the industry will be redistributed, and so on.

Before a firm can begin to plan its own longrun direction for the technology, it must understand what the effect of IT will be in the industry. This is entirely consistent with most views of corporate strategy, that start from understanding the external environment of the firm. The impact of IT at the industry level ranges from major (in the banking industry IT is significantly altering the products/services, the markets, and the economies of production), to minor (in the aluminum industry IT is not noticeably affecting any of the industry-level measures). The key to effectively linking IT to the competitive needs of the firm, is to anticipate the impact of IT at the industry level before it occurs, so that plans and policies can be developed to place the firm appropriately in the new industry setting. For example, although video conferencing has not yet substantially changed the airline industry's business travel market, at the current rate of development in telecommunications technology and office technology, it will be a major substitute for some air travel in less than 10 years. The CEO and strategist must ask and get answers to the question of 'What changes will IT bring to our industry over the next five to ten years in terms of products/services, markets and economies of production?' The firm must have one or more projections of how IT is currently or might in the future influence the industry, before the analysis can effectively be carried to the firm level.

In many industries, the analysis will show that in five to ten years, IT, given the rate of technological development, could have a substantial effect. Firms that can identify the emergence of the technology as a major change agent in the future of the industry can gain significant advantages by leading the industry. The development of the reservation system by American Airlines and other airlines in the late 1960s exemplified how IT development contributed to significant industry change (the emergence of the travel agency industry, the demise of Braniff, and so forth).

The danger of failing to understand the potential of IT at the industry level cannot be minimized. As firms devote increasing percentages of resources to their computer and information resources, there is a significant danger of going very rapidly in the wrong direction. Consider the publishing firm that, failing to realize technological developments in the industry, commits its resources to becoming a more efficient paper processor. An efficient paper processing strategy may push the firm into increasingly smaller and less profitable portions of the total industry's market. The firm will tend to ignore new products/services and marketing techniques in the electronic segment of the business and could find itself battling with other dinosaurs in the high-cost, low-margin end of the business. Although this prediction may sound a bit dramatic, consider the situation of another industry, at another time, with another technology – the railroads. The railroads, once the pre-eminent means of transportation, did not understand the nature of the industry and the changes underway when trucks, barges, pipelines and automobiles emerged as alternative technologies for transportation. Railroads developed strategies to become better railroads, with the result that they rapidly became uncompetitive in the broader transportation industry.

FIRM-LEVEL IMPACT OF IT

At the firm level, the impact of IT is determined by the specific competitive forces facing the firm.[1] There are five competitive forces that form the industry structure and the competitive arena for each firm in the industry. These are: the buyers, the suppliers, the substitutes, the new entrants and the rivals of a particular industry. The manifestation of each of these five forces in a specific industry will influence the ability of a firm to earn profits and will shape the potentially successful strategies for the firm. A strong competitive force will be able to extract potential profits from an industry. For example, strong suppliers will be able to raise prices (it's to their advantage to do so) to an industry, resulting in reduced profits. Some industries, because of the cumulative strength of their competitive forces, provide low returns for all the industry's participants. In effect, strong competitive forces take a great deal, and

[1] The concepts of industry structure and analysis are taken from *Competitive Strategy: Techniques for Analyzing Industries and Competitors*, by Michael Porter (Glenwood, IL: Free Press, 1980).

sometimes all, of the industries' potential returns. The U.S. steel industry, for example, has provided very low average profitability over the past decade, because of strong competitive forces, developed to produce an unfavorable industry structure. The suppliers are strong and have been able to hold up prices, the buyers (auto industry) are strong and have been able to resist price increases, other metals are substituting, and new entrants (foreign steel) are flooding the market. The few domestic steel firms that have achieved good returns, have been able to create a position in the industry that is defendable against the competitive forces that have ravaged other competitors. In contrast to the structure of the steel industry, the tobacco industry has had fairly stable and weak competitive forces for many years. This has resulted in an attractive industry structure for the U.S. tobacco companies, and has provided high average profitability within the industry. The competitive forces of an industry are not static, however, but change, due to many external factors, such as regulation or deregulation, general economic events, such as prolonged severe inflation, evolution of an industry to maturity and also technology.

IT changes an industry structure through the competitive forces that shape that industry. As IT affects products/services or operations of a business, it may change the relationship between an industry and its suppliers. It will also change the mix of suppliers. As noted above, publishers are facing the prospect of a totally electronically based source of publishable materials within the next 10 years. As IT penetrates more industries in more functions, the IT suppliers themselves will become an important new industry force. As industries become more technically based, the mix of the labor force will change, requiring more technical employees. This raises job retraining issues.

IT will also change the mix and sophistication of suppliers to these industries. Suppliers of funds to financial institutions are increasingly more sophisticated (and consequently more powerful), because IT allows them to monitor and redeploy their investments with astonishing ease. Competitively, firms in industries where IT is affecting the supplier relationship, must be concerned with how this change will affect the power that the supplier will, or will threaten to, exercise in dealing with the industry.

Buyer relationships of industries will also be affected, as new products/services and new distribution channels evolve based on IT. Buyer groups of the banking industry now have a variety of channels to choose from in receiving their products/services. Automatic teller machines (ATMs), point-of-sale terminals (POSs) and electronic home banking, all provide fundamental changes in the buyer/industry relationship. IT has also altered the product mix ability of industries, as firms package information around a basic service. A large distribution company, for example, has approached the retailers it supplies, with computer-generated inventory management reports as a fee-based service, enhancing its actual distribution service.

IT also influences the rate of substitution in some industries. Electronic mail may substantially substitute for paper communications. Computer-aided design and manufacturing (CAD/CAM) will improve the rate of relative price performance of many products such as new audio and video components. As a result, they will become a substitution threat much sooner because of IT. On the whole, IT will speed up the life cycle of many products.

IT affects the rate of new entry into industries by negating existing or creating new entry barriers and deterrents. (Entry barriers and deterrents will be described in the following section.) In the banking industry, for example, the traditional entry barriers of many branch locations have been seriously eroded by alternative IT-based access to banking products/services. In the distribution industry, IT has created new entry barriers by requiring investment in extensive computer and telecommunication networks to control large-scale distribution facility costs. In effect, IT has created a new scale economy barrier that the new entrant must overcome to be able to price competitively and still be profitable.

Finally, IT changes industry structure by influencing the bases of rivalry among intra-industry competitors. By injecting a new competitive weapon into various settings, IT sparks outbreaks of warfare. Recently, airlines have been accused of using their reservation systems to competitive advantage, listing their own flights ahead of competitors. Certain securities brokerage firms have exploited IT to introduce a radical form of cost competition into the securities industry. In the banking industry, market-share-leading banks see competitors joining forces on shared ATM networks. IT will certainly make a significant contribution to rivalry in many industries in a multitude of, as yet unimaginable, ways.

If there is a significant impact on a firm through the competitive forces of buyers, suppliers, substitution, new entrants and rivalry, IT must be managed as a vital element in the firm's strategy. IT has entered the firm's competitive domain.

In the same way that IT represents a challenge or threat to a firm's established method of doing business, however, IT also represents opportunities for gaining new competitive advantages. Each of the competitive forces can be manipulated to some degree and in some industries, IT provides an effective implement for that purpose.

USING IT TO CREATE COMPETITIVE ADVANTAGES

BUYER POWER

An industry's buyer groups represent a force that, if strong, can reduce the profitability of that industry. For example, strong buyer power exists where customer groups are highly concentrated or purchase large volumes relative to the selling industry's total sales. When a handful of buyers represent an industry's entire market, then the importance of each buyer to each selling competitor is so great, that buyer concessions are a way of life for the industry and potential profits are reduced. Buyer power also increases where there are few or very minor costs associated with changing suppliers or changing to a substitute product. These costs are called switching costs; the lack of them between an industry and its buyers can reduce profitability. IT represents a competitive weapon for reducing buyer power in two ways. By introducing switching costs, IT makes it more costly for a buyer to change suppliers. IT has greatly increased a number of firms' ability to raise switching costs to their buyers. A large medical supply company has installed on-line order entry terminals to its customers and has also supplied them with inventory management software. As the firm's systems are integrated into its customers', the customers lose the easy ability to order from a competitor. After the customers' personnel are trained, procedures are established, confidence is gained, changing suppliers incurs the switching costs of retraining, testing and developing new procedures as well as the implementation costs. The more sophisticated systems increase switching costs and lessen the likelihood of buyers indiscriminately switching to a competitor.

Another way in which IT represents a competitive advantage when dealing with buyers, is by using information systems to segregate attractive buyer groups from unattractive buyer groups. All industries have certain customer groups that are particularly costly to service and represent few long-term advantages. In addition, firms within industries are usually well suited to service some customer groups and not others. The attractiveness of a buyer group to a particular firm is determined by four criteria: (a) the requirements of the buyer versus the capabilities of the selling firm; (b) the growth potential of the buyer; (c) the buying power and willingness to use the power on the part of the buyer; (d) the cost of servicing the customer group. The insurance industry, because of its tradition of providing full services to all business customers, has not, in the past, identified good customer groups for its capabilities. Consequently, the insurance industry, although data rich, is information poor when it comes to questions such as, 'How much does it cost to service a particular market segment?' or 'How should our firm's particular capabilities match potential buyer requirements?' A large insurance firm is building an extensive claims database to go beyond actuarial calculations in beginning to determine which potential markets will be most profitable. As the overall cost of servicing insurance customers increases significantly due in part to deregulation and competition, buyer selection is a strategic issue to which the intelligent use of IT resources provides the key.

SUPPLIER POWER

Suppliers are strong when they are very concentrated – there are few alternative substitutes – or when the buyers face high costs to 'go shopping'. When suppliers are strong, they will extract some of an industry's potential profits. The supplier groups include raw materials, machinery, capital and the labor force.

IT provides a potential resource to mitigate the factors driving suppliers' power, thus improving the firm's competitive position. An example of this, is using IT as an alternative for high-priced labor. The recent developments in robotics and computer-aided manufacturing not only reduce cost of labor outright, but also reduce labor's power in demanding industry profits. Another use of IT is to avoid high switching costs. One of the major problems facing the banking industry, is the inability to manage their largest single cost – the cost of money corporatewide. A bank's money comes from customer deposits, the money markets, certificates of deposit and other sources. The interaction of various rates of prices for these sources of money form a complex problem for bank management, especially under times of extreme volatility in the rates. The lack of comprehensive information systems to monitor and evaluate the overall current and future money position represents a severe disadvantage in dealing with its major supplier, the financial markets. IT is a critical tool to reduce the awkwardness of the banking industry in responding to fluctuations in these markets. Currently, the lack of strategic IT effectively means, banks have no ability to gather information, shop around, or optimally, change suppliers of funds. Banks that can develop their information resources, will be able to price more effectively, gaining larger market shares and profits.

Certain industries, because of historical and economic conditions, are subject to intense supplier power, some of it uncontrollable. For those industries where there is a substantial amount of supplier power that is susceptible to influence, however, IT represents a potential opportunity. This is especially true in the service industries and in high-cost, labor-intensive industries subject to union power.

SUBSTITUTION

The existence of cost-effective alternatives for a product, such as margarine for butter, acts to limit potential profitability in an industry. In other instances, a substitute product can virtually eliminate an industry, such as the silicon chip-based calculator substituting for the electromechanical adding machine. Defensively, an industry must address existing and potential substitutes as affecting both the overall demand for products and the profitability that will result from serving the remaining demand. This reduced profitability results from price competition with substitutes, advertising against substitutes, and product innovation directed at substitutes.

Offensively, substitution represents an opportunity for an industry or a firm within an industry, to increase its own market by offering its products as substitutes to another industry's buyers.

IT should become a factor in business planning when substitution influences the buyer's decision to substitute or not. This will be caused by (a) altering the relative price performance comparison with the substitute by either lowering the cost or by improving the perceived performance; (b) increasing or decreasing the range of functions performed by a product.

As an example of substitution based on IT, the banking industry has been subjected to severe competitive pressure from the money management industry's money market products. Money market funds have been superior substitutes for many of the banks' traditional products. With deregulation removing the limit on interest rates, banks now have the pricing freedom of the money markets. However, the bank's products must now act as substitutes for the money market funds, and must battle switching costs and other barriers to getting customers' deposits back. The banking industry's key competitive advantage is IT, specifically providing customers with the ability to access money and transfer it through ATMs and even home terminals. The banks must add features with IT to increase the range of perceived functions of their product.

NEW ENTRANTS

For existing competitors, new entrants present a concern because the entrants will extract some of the industry's profits. Unless industry demand grows faster than the supply of new entrants, average profitability will decline. New entrants are especially devastating when they do not have the same objectives or constraints as the industry participants. Increased competition as seen in the U.S. automobile industry can be touched off by new entrants (the Japanese), using price-cutting tactics to gain market penetration.

The major structural components of an industry that exclude or slow new entrants, are called *entry barriers*. Entry barriers come in many forms, sizes, and shapes, but they all have the common effect of creating a better situation for an existing industry participant than for the potential entrant. This better situation may be based on costs, reputation, service, technology or some other characteristic that is important to success in the industry. Whereas entry barriers are structural components of an industry, *entry deterrents* are tactics or processes that an industry or a firm can invoke to make a potential entrant reconsider entry. Actions, such as deep price-cutting during a new entrant's test marketing, can act as a deterrent by emphasizing the industry incumbents' relative cost advantages to the potential entrant, as well as confusing the test market results.

Defensively, entry barriers and deterrents are key aspects of an industry's continued success. Without continual maintenance of the barriers, new entrants will sneak into the industry, usually at the most profitable segments of the market. Individually, a firm's competitive strategy must also take into account entry barriers, because often an entrant will aim directly at a vulnerable competitor as the target. Industry leaders are particularly responsible for maintaining entry barriers and creating deterrents. Offensively, the firm that considers entering a new industry, must consider the entry barriers it must overcome and the potential retaliatory action that the violated industry may take. Several options exist for penetrating a new industry: joint ventures and acquisitions – focusing on a nonthreatening industry niche – or developing new technology that circumvents the historical barriers.

IT becomes an important weapon to deal with entrants, both offensively and defensively. A major insurance company has continually led the industry in building and maintaining a large on-line telecommunications network to its agents. This network is and will become a greater entry barrier, as insurance products are rapidly introduced and become increasingly sophisticated as investment products. Agents require much more on-line support, training and promotional backup. This network provides that support; an entrant without it will not be an effective competitor. Another example is a large financial service company that has built a reputation of quality service, with the greatest geographical coverage of any competition. The quality of service and ability to service a worldwide customer base is built upon IT capabilities. The firm's IT represents a capital barrier and also supports a reputation barrier.

IT will also be used, as industrial firms try to achieve new manufacturing economies of scale relative to competitors, entrants and substitutes. The ability of these firms to gain scale economies with IT will depend upon the ability to go beyond the stand-alone applications that have been the predominant industrial use of IT. To develop new scale economies, IT must be viewed as an organizing concept with which to redesign the manufacturing process. From procurement to plant design, from robotics to plant office automation, new economies of scale will be achieved only by identifying the strategic impact of IT and deploying the resources to achieve the desired competitive effect.

RIVALRY

Industries range in their rivalry from intense *guerilla warfare* to relaxed *country club*. Intense rivalry depletes the industry of some potential profits, because actions detrimental to the entire industry occur, as competitors struggle to the death for an advantage. A good example is the airline industry which, because of intense rivalry, is price-cutting far below cost. Although one competitor may eventually win, the entire industry is losing.

Dealing with one's rivals strategically does not always mean destroying them. To operate effectively over time, most industries require a group of good competitors. Having the proper competitors allows a firm to earn more profits, develop new markets, and erect better entry barriers than it could alone. The key to coping strategically with the competitive force of rivalry, is to identify when to compete, and when and how to cooperate.

IT presents major opportunities for firms to facilitate the degree to which, and methods with which, one deals with rivals. By having access to IT-supported data, IT distribution channels and potential IT links within the industry, firms can better both their position and the entire industry. In the banking industry, for example, IT represents a tremendous strategic opportunity for individual firms to deal with increasingly intense rivalry. The first evidence has been the shared ATM network, where rival banks share a common group of ATMs against a market share leader. In the airline industry, shared reservation systems become a way to improve overall service in the industry. In the railroad industry, standardized data and communications networks between firms offer a way to improve the railroad transportation service. Computer-to-computer connections, joint IT ventures and shared software are all examples of cooperative use of IT toward rivals.

Since IT presents a virtually unlimited opportunity to structure the relationship between a firm and its competitors within an industry, any strategy for rivals should include IT as a vital component. The key, of course, is knowing which IT relationships with rivals should be cooperative and which should be competitive.

PLOTTING THE FIRM'S STRATEGIC IT MAP

One of the major hurdles management must overcome before strategically managing IT, is the ability to identify and weigh long-term competitive implications against today's dollars and cents. Traditionally, IT has been viewed as a cost reduction or cost avoidance tool with some intangible benefits. Decisions about various IT projects have normally been made based on a return on investment or a payback criterion. Many of the types of projects identified by analyzing the competitive potential of IT will not have a large quantifiable ROI based on dollars saved. A company was evaluating the prospect of installing in some of its larger customers' stores terminals for submitting orders directly. But the project was turned down, because as the corporate controller said, 'The dollar savings were just not there. We migh be able to cut paper processing a bit and even help us manage inventory a bit better, but nothing like the $200,000 cost of the system.' Clearly, the competitive advantage of tying up the firm's major buyers exclusively to its system was not identified by their current management methods. To help firms identify and weigh competitive advantages of IT, a strategic IT matrix is a useful tool.

Figure B shows a matrix that has been drawn to show the 1982 situation for a firm that distributes periodical literature throughout the United States. Along its horizontal axis, the matrix shows that new entrants and supplier power are the two most significant forces for the company to deal with in its competitive strategy. Some of the buyers are small and fragmented, but the firm also sells to some large chains. Rivalry has not been intense in the past because most competitors are small local operators. Substitution (retailers doing it themselves) is not a problem. Along its vertical axis, the matrix shows the current impact of IT on these forces. It has significant effect on the buyers through a computerized order scheduling and logistics system that results in better and additional services, differentiating the firm from its rivals and introducing switching costs. It has had modest effect on supplier power or substitution. The numbers associated with each competitive force labeled in a circle on the matrix are cross-referenced to the table beside the matrix, which shows the specific areas in which IT has offset or changed a competitive force. This matrix provides a snapshot of IT competitive forces for the distribution company in 1982, but can also be used to develop strategic IT for the future, by identifying potential changes in the competitive forces and opportunities for IT. *Figure C* shows a projected matrix for competitive forces and the impact of IT, as the distribution firm begins to plan its future strategies for 1990.

The firm expects many significant changes to occur in its competitive environment by 1990. Major new entrants are expected to come into the industry through forward integration of one or more of the publisher/wholesalers. This is expected to increase the rivalry pressure and also raise the entry barriers to the small firms. Thus, new entrants are not expected to be a significant issue by 1990. An industry-level analysis of the distribution industry to assess the effect of IT on the industry identified three developments. IT is being forecast to have significantly more impact on (a) substitution, as electronic publishing becomes more available; (b) suppliers, as the firm expects publishers to form direct IT links to the retailers for ordering; and (c) rivalry, as IT is expected to become one of the key cooperative/competitive mechanisms within the industry.

The firm, on the whole, expects all the competitive forces to intensify as shown by the leftward movement of the 'importance of competitive force' bisector, between 1982 and 1990. This effectively enlarges the area in which the competitive forces are important to the firm's strategy. The firm also expects the opportunities for IT to increase significantly. Note that the 'high' impact of IT on competitive forces area on the 1990 map is much larger. In 1990, all the competitive forces of the industry are expected to be significantly affected by IT. This change is expected to occur through economies of scale, learning curve advantage, supplier relationships and rival

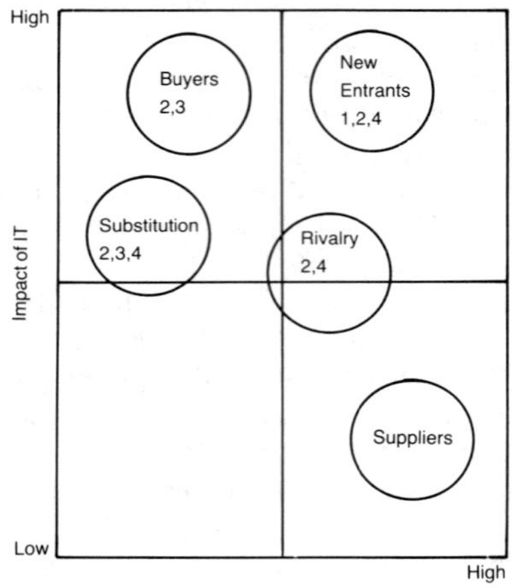

IT Supports

1. Entry barriers
2. Product/service differentiation
3. Switching costs
4. Cost advantages

Figure B. Impact of Competitive Forces on Strategy, 1982

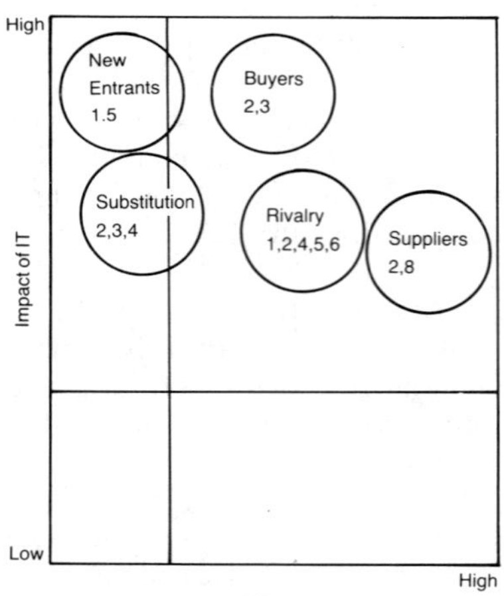

IT Supports

1 to 4 from 1982

5. Economies of scale
6. Learning curve advantages
7. Supplier relationships
8. Rival relationships

Figure C. Impact of Competitive Forces on Strategy, 1990

relationships, all supported by IT. (These are shown as 5–8 in the cross-reference table.)

By developing the matrices of *Figures B* and *C*, this distribution company knows its current strategic IT position, which areas have to be emphasized to maintain its position, and what is to be expected for the future. With the map in hand, the firm can begin to develop supporting plans and tactics to achieve the best strategic use of IT.

The five forces of buyer power, supplier power, substitution, new entrants and rivalry shape the competitive environment for each firm in the industry. These forces vary in the manner and degree to which they will influence each firm in the industry. Each firm, as part of its analysis, must identify the specific competitive forces and underlying economics that it faces. It becomes clear that the competitive forces and the economic factors that drive those forces can be influenced by IT. Sometimes this happens by accident, but knowing where the opportunities exist should improve the firm's luck.

As rapid technological progress continues, the degree and scope of IT's impact increases. Industries using IT in the competitive domain will continue to experience even more strategic consequences of IT, new industries will begin to see IT emerge as a competitive issue and the foresighted as a competitive weapon.

IT'S IMPACT ON PRODUCT DIFFERENTIATION AND COST LEADERSHIP STRATEGIES

The five competitive forces – buyers, suppliers, substitution, new entrants and rivalry – define the industry within which each firm competes. The industry setting not only determines the average profitability that will be available to the participants, but also forms the competitive environment within which a firm's strategy must operate. That is, for a firm to earn above-average returns within an industry, it must have a strategy that allows it to gain a superior position relative to the competitive forces. As noted by Professor Porter, a firm's strategy is its general framework for dealing with competition and may be explicitly considered by management or may evolve incrementally and erratically without a unifying purpose. By explicitly considering a competitive strategy, however, a firm is able to distinguish important issues from incidental issues, to coordinate a broad set of resources, and to time a particular action. Strategies that are not explicitly considered may at times (a) attack the wrong issues or be based on symptoms rather than causes; (b) bring only a narrow subset of the firm's resources to bear on an issue resulting in a minimal impact; or (c) bring about ill-timed actions, either too late to be effective or too early to have the necessary supporting structure to be implemented.

Firms that have proven successful in their industries have been able to position themselves relative to industry forces, by following one of three generic strategies:

- Overall cost leadership on an industrywide basis;
- Differentiation of products/services on an industrywide basis; or
- Focus on a particular market/product niche.

Each of these generic strategies provides a general framework, within which a firm sets functional policies and procedures, and performs activities executing that strategy. The achievement of one of these three strategies gives the firm an advantageous position relative to the industry forces and brings higher than average returns.

IT can enhance the ability of firms to execute a particular generic strategy. For example, a large financial service company owes its cost leadership position in the industry to the sophisticated use of IT to substantially reduce the costs of transmitting and processing transactions. In another example, a brokerage company created a unique and differentiated product, by using IT to combine features of several different financial products into a new package. The product and the company have been extremely successful and have a host of imitators.

Since the execution of a generic strategy requires the broad support of all functional areas of a firm to become effective, IT may contribute in various ways. This is a unqiue characteristic of IT, as opposed to other technologies that may affect a manufacturing process or some product characteristics, but not the other functional areas of the firm. IT is found in the research labs for experimentation support; in the engineering departments for computer-aided design; on the factory floor as production control; in the marketing department for market analysis and distribution support; out in the field with the sales force, as a promotional tool; in the back office for recordkeeping; and in the executive office for planning. In the long run, nearly all functions of all firms will be computer enhanced to some degree. The important issue is, how they are computer enhanced. Knowledgeable IT applications will contribute to the firm's execution of its competitive strategy.

For the firm pursuing an overall cost leadership position, IT should be used to either (a) directly reduce overall cost or (b) contribute to overall cost reduction through the functional areas. For the firm that must maintain an overall differentiated product/service to be competitive, IT should be used to either (a) directly add unique features to the product/service or (b) contribute to quality, service, image and so forth, through the functional areas. Although in some instances, a firm may benefit by an IT application, regardless of whether it contributes to a competitive strategy, much greater benefits will be realized, if the IT applications are consistent and support the firm's competitive needs. In short, the specific IT applications that contribute to cost leadership are very different from the applications that contribute to a differentiation goal. 'Cost leadership requires aggressive construction of efficient-scale facilities, vigorous pursuit of cost reduction from experience, tight cost and overhead control, avoidance of marginal customer accounts and cost minimization in areas like R&D, service, scales force, advertising, and so on.'

IT, used for maintaining a cost leadership strategy, must create or support opportunities in these same areas. IT has been shown to allow substantial cost reduction in the functional areas of engineering, design and manufacturing. In addition, IT can be used to substantially reduce waste, improve productivity and identify marginal customers. The firm vigorously pursuing a cost leadership strategy should identify and pursue those IT projects that further that strategy.

Conversely, the achievement of a differentiated position in the industry has a far different set of requirements. Differentiation requires a perceived uniqueness in design, brand image, technology, product features, customer service, dealer networks, or in other categories. Usually, the most successful differentiated firms have done so in several of these categories. The distribution company from the previous example differentiated itself both in service reliability, responsiveness to customer needs and product features. It is, and is perceived as, the most sophisticated, best quality nationwide periodical distributor.

Just as differentiation requires quite different behavior from its functional areas, it also presents a quite different set of opportunities for IT. Here, IT must contribute superior customer servicing by use of historical customer profiles, availability of spare parts through a dealer inventory system, superior quality through quality control systems and computer-aided manufacturing for flexibility and responsiveness. In addition, IT can create better designs, satisfying the marketplace and the manufacturing requirements. In some situations, IT can also provide access to markets that otherwise are too remote to service.

Figure D illustrates how the IT applications must be specifically chosen to support the generic strategy of the firm. Applications supporting low-cost producers are designed to take advantage of existing and emerging IT to achieve the lowest cost position in the industry. Note that although the list is by no means exhaustive, it is substantially different from the list of potential applications under the differentiation strategy. *Figure D* shows that the strategic success of IT projects within a firm will be dependent upon how well they support the firm's competitive strategy. In one instance, a firm following a low-cost strategy gained few business benefits from an IT system that allowed many options and flexibility to the user, but was costly to operate. Over time, the cost leadership plan of the firm continued to narrow the product line and streamline operations, requiring the functional areas to standardize and limit options. The large, expensive, multioption system, which was still in development, ran counter to the business needs. As a result, the system is only partially used, and parts of it will never be implemented. The users in operations correctly feel that using the system makes it difficult for them to meet their functional objectives, as dictated by the business goal of cost leadership. They now want to scrap the system and buy their own package, which runs on a minicomputer.

In other firms, where IT developments were linked to the specific business strategy, users were enthusiastic about implementing the systems. They saw the systems' value to them as helping to carry out their assignments, as determined within the business plan. In addition, system designers must realize that the maximum benefits of many of these systems will only be achieved by a commitment and acceptance by multiple functions and levels within the organization. This is because effective strategies require a multifunction integration, coordinating departments, implementing support systems, personnel, compensations and other managerial issues, that will need to be considered and resolved before an IT system will contribute significantly to a business strategy. For example, the development of highly sophisticated, IT-enhanced tools for selling insurance will not be effective if sales personnel are not hired, trained and motivated to use the systems.

Although it may seem obvious that IT applications should be consistent with the business strategy, in too many firms there is a monumental lack of attention given to understanding how IT will influence the firm's competitive position in the industry, or

Figure D Potential IT Application Areas

	Generic Strategies	
	Low Cost	Differentiation
Product Design and Development	• Product engineering systems • Project control systems	• R&D databases • Professional work stations • Electronic mail • CAD • Custom engineering systems • Integrated systems to manufacturing
Operations	• Process engineering systems • Process control systems • Labor control systems • Inventory management systems • Procurement systems	• CAM for flexibility • Quality assurance systems • Systems to suppliers • Quality monitoring systems for suppliers
Marketing	• Streamlined distribution systems • Centralized control systems • Econometric modeling systems	• Sophisticated marketing system • Market databases • IT display and promotion • Telemarketing • Competition analysis systems • Modeling capabilities • High service level distribution system
Sales	• Sales control systems • Advertising monitoring systems • Systems to consolidate sales function • Strict incentive-monitoring systems	• Differential pricing systems • Office-field communication • Customer-sales support • Dealer support systems • Systems to customers
Administration	• Cost control systems • Quantitative planning and budgeting systems • Office automation for staff reduction	• Office automation for integration of functions • Environment scanning and nonquantitative planning systems • Teleconferencing

how IT might support a business strategy. As if to illustrate the seriousness of the situation, several major U.S. banks have removed their top information systems executives. Although the explanations given for the management changes varied, the underlying reason was that IT was not being managed in a manner consistent with the competitive needs of the banks.

The fact that these executives could not develop IT that was consistent with the bank's strategy, was not the problem; the persisting problem is that, neither the bank executives nor the information systems executives understand how IT affects their business. Neither group can articulate how computer hardware and software should support or extend the bank's ability to make money.

CONCLUSION

This note has presented a conceptual framework to guide the senior executive in answering the critical question: 'Is IT a competitive weapon in my business?'

For years, technical experts have expressed concern that a firm's computer systems meet the needs of the business. Unfortunately, these experts never bothered to understand the needs of a business from a competitive standpoint: IT was not perceived in the competitive domain of a business. In spite of the general lack of explicit strategic direction, many firms in many industries are using IT to their competitive advantage. As the technology itself continues to evolve rapidly and becomes a major factor in more industries, firms must begin to strategically manage information technology. The broad framework presented here has shown the first steps for linking IT to a firm's competitive environment and strategy, by analysis of the industry, firm and strategy levels of IT impact.

Based on a sound understanding of when, where and how IT will affect a firm, explicit IT plans and policies can be developed that make the necessary tradeoffs and bring resources to bear on the identified opportunities and threats. Without this understanding, developing an IT strategy is just an organizational security blanket and firms will continue to ride a speeding technological roller coaster, spending more money, acquiring new hardware, but fundamentally not knowing why. These firms will have their technological high points and low points, but competitively, they end up where they started, if they are lucky.

2. INTERORGANIZATIONAL SYSTEMS: AN INFORMATION SOCIETY OPPORTUNITY OR THREAT?*

James I. Cash, Jr.

ABSTRACT: Numerous environmental forces exist today that contribute to changing industry and market segments. The least studied of these is the impact of information systems which transcend traditional company boundaries. One of the subtle impacts of contemporary developments in information systems technology is the redefinition of traditional organizational and industrial boundaries. Examples of these interorganizational systems (referred to as IOS), reviewed by the author, imply that a wide range of organizations may have an opportunity to use these systems to improve their operations, services to their customers and their competitive position.

Some of these systems raise public policy issues that are *not* well understood, nor are they being addressed in a comprehensive manner. This article is designed to provide a conceptual framework for thinking about these systems.

INTRODUCTION

An examination of the strategic use of information systems technology by business organizations (McFarlan, 1984) shows that the most dramatic and influential contemporary uses involve systems that transcend company boundaries. These systems, in some cases, dramatically change the balance of power in buyer–supplier relationships, provide entry and exit barriers in some industry segments, and shift the competitive position of intra-industry rivals in most instances. Most examples of these systems indicate that a wide range of organizations may be able to influence key competitive forces that dictate the forms of competition in their industry segment. Further research has indicated that some of these interorganizational systems (hereafter referred to as IOSs) have major social and public policy implications.

Unfortunately, many decisions to participate (or not participate) in these systems

The Information Society, Volume 3, Number 3

* The expression 'Information Systems Technology', used in the text is synonymous with 'Information Technology', a term used elsewhere in this volume. (Ed.)

James I. Cash, Jr. is with the Graduate School of Business Administration, Harvard University, Boston, Massachusetts.

are being made regularly without an appreciation of the broader implications of these decisions. In several cases I found that, the decision to set up computer-to-computer communications capability, across company boundaries, was made at the production clerk level in the given organization. In this paper, I will first attempt to define these systems. Next is a list of the key trends that are contributing to the dramatic increase in these systems. Third, I offer a brief discussion of a sample IOS and its impact. Finally, I will describe two analytical frameworks for assessing the impact of these systems.

IOS FUNCTIONAL DEFINITIONS

An *IOS* is an automated information system used by two or more separate companies. It consists of computer and communications infrastructure that permits the participants to share in the execution of an application (Barrett and Konsynski, 1982).

An *IOS participant* is an organization that develops, operates, or uses an IOS for the purpose of exchanging information that supports a primary business process. Participants can be competitors, organizations in the buyer–supplier chain, or a combination of these.

An *IOS facilitator* is an organization that aids in the development, operation, or utilization of an IOS for participant interchange. The supporting products or services are a part of the primary business of the IOS facilitator.

The most frequent response to an initial description of IOS is 'What's unique about it? Isn't it a special form of distributed data processing (DDP)?' There appear to be four key characteristics that distinguish IOSs:

1. Whereas DDP is generally under the control of a single firm, IOS crosses company boundaries. This introduces very different challenges for a company's internal control, planning and resource allocation systems. These management control systems are generally revised to address the requisite coordination across organizational boundaries.
2. As a result of the information exchange across the boundaries of separate organizations and hence, separate legal entities, the question of government regulation arises. Among the numerous potential issues are questions of legal liability. For example, in an IOS, when does the electronic message passing over communication lines (historically called an order) actually become an order? When an IOS involves competitors, as illustrated by airline reservation systems in a commercial airline industry, what constitutes unfair business practice? When an IOS involves participants engaged in interstate commerce, are ICC regulations sufficiently current to protect consumer interests?
3. The *IOS facilitator* is a unique element in some of these systems. Intermediaries are not new in most industry segments. The role of these organizations, as implemented in an IOS environment, is new. An example of an IOS facilitator is the CIRRUS nationwide* network of automated teller machines (ATMs). CIRRUS, which is not a bank, permits subscribing banks to give their customers 24-hour, coast-to-coast access to their ATM systems. The home banking system

* The word 'nation' and its derivatives refer to the United States of America. (Ed.)

network offered by COMPUSERV is another example of an IOS facilitator.
4. IOSs generally have a broader and more significant potential competitive impact than the traditional internal uses of information systems (IS) technology. Listed below are two examples.

A major bank has developed an application, referred to as the Treasury Decision Support System (TDSS). TDSS is a microcomputer-based system which the bank will give to its largest customers for use by the treasurer. The system communicates with the bank's host computer and will accept input from a range of other systems. TDSS tracks, reports, analyzes and permits simple manipulation of data (on the company's funds in the bank), frequently used by a treasurer. Data for TDSS can be transferred from several sources, including the company's computer, or computers owned by competitive banks. It is conceivable that the company may ask other banks or repositories to transfer, in machine-readable form, data on company funds under their control to TDSS. Currently, the bank that developed TDSS is the only organization, in addition to the (customer) company, that can examine all the data in the micro. This examination would yield a complete profile of the company's fund management. This provides an excellent basis for developing a new (and tailored) product offering for the client.

A major automotive manufacturer, in letters dated June 1984, required its primary suppliers to adhere to the Automotive Industry Action Group (AIAG) electronic data communication standards by June 1, 1985, if they planned to continue their relationship. Once this system is implemented, and the natural evolution of increasing the amount of data in automated systems occurs that would lead to price data on the system, it would be a trivial step to implement a 'shopping' capability. The automotive manufacturer would add instructions to scan the computers of its primary suppliers and place an order with the company's computer that contained the lowest bid or price for the desired product (assuming other things such as product quality are equal). This would permit the automotive manufacturer to encourage competition among its vendors, enhancing its bargaining power with the suppliers.

The last example illustrates a rapidly growing form of IOS that has major implications for a large number of people in our work force. As companies attempt to reduce the time and costs associated with their order-entry and materials purchasing systems, computer-to-computer links seem very attractive. But, what will be the impact on the portion of the work force currently involved in sales activity? A framework for anticipating and proactively managing these impacts will be presented later in the paper.

TRENDS CONTRIBUTING TO IOS IMPLEMENTATION

Some of the key trends that contribute to the implementation of IOS are listed below.

The increasing need for fast, reliable, information interchange (in response to dramatically shifting market and industry forces) between suppliers and buyers of rapidly changing products and services. This trend is primarily based on significant shifts in three areas: the world economic order (redistribution of wealth), increasing international competition (shrinking geographic separation) and increasing commitment to greater deregulation and open competition by regulatory bodies.

The shift in world economics is illustrated by examining the world gross national product (GNP). Shortly after World War II, the U.S. GNP was approximately 50 percent of the world GNP. By 1983, U.S. GNP was approximately 25 percent of world GNP. This shift has dramatically contributed to increased international competition. The injection of new international competitors, with very different cost structures (e.g. labor component of total costs), manufacturing and production processes, etc., has, in many industries, changed fundamental characteristics of products (e.g., cars), reduced the time frame of product life cycles and added significantly new productive capacity (which generally limits prices and margins, and/or increases costs of incumbents). Finally, the impact of increased receptivity to deregulation, observable in industries that range from trucking to petroleum to airlines and financial services, has combined with the shifts mentioned earlier to foster redefinition of products, relationships between buyers and suppliers in a product/service delivery chain, ancilliary services to end consumers, etc. It is interesting to note that some industry segments that are still heavily regulated, such as the insurance industry, are nonetheless affected by this trend.

The evolution of guidelines, standards and protocols in industry segments. One of the responses to pressures from the first trend mentioned above, has been increased interest in developing standard definitions, product encoding, etc., to facilitate faster and more reliable information exchange. Historically, government regulation was the primary impetus for establishing standards. Increasingly, nonregulatory standards are being introduced. Two visible examples are the universal product code (UPC) in the grocery industry and magnetic ink character (MICR) sets and credit card or automatic teller machine card magnetic strips in retail banking. These standards, by forcing consistency of message content, product form, etc., facilitate adoption by multiple organizations.

The significant penetration of information system (IS) technology into a wide range of itnernal business processes. As illustrated in Figure 1, the combination of decreasing costs and increasing capability has resulted in a broader range of internal applications. This penetration has been primarily based on the desire of many managers to exploit decreasing technology cost to offset increasing input of materials and labor costs (Figure 2). A natural extension of having information in machine-readable form, is to transmit these data wherever needed, to try to avoid redundant conversion and regeneration of data. This data and resource sharing is easily justified on both an economic and time-saved basis. The combination of rapidly increasing amounts of internal company data in machine-readable form, standards (mentioned above) for information interchange between companies and clear economic justification, makes it very attractive to participate in interorganizational systems.

The increasing technical quality and capability of IS technology. IS technology has become increasingly reliable. This permits companies to exploit technology in business-sensitive areas, such as the customer-company interface, that would be inappropriate for a less reliable or less stable technology. In addition, the maturation of internal computer and communications systems departments and the associated

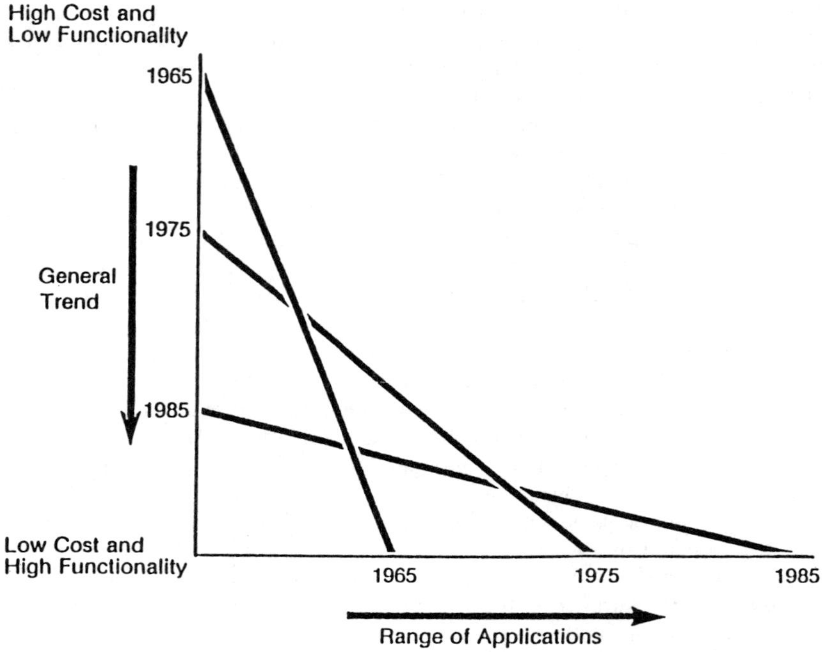

Figure 1. The combination of decreasing costs and increasing capability has resulted in a wide range of internal applications. [*Source*: Cash et al., 1983.].

quality of their support, permitted the examination of potential external uses of these technologies (Cash et al., 1983).

Increasing efforts to add value via information systems technology to exploit product and company differentiation opportunities. Many companies are looking to information systems technology to provide ancillary services which will differentiate their product or company from their compeititors. The importance of differentiation increases, the more 'commodity-like' the product is. The TDSS banking system, described earlier, is an example of adding value via information systems to differentiate a product and the firm.

AN IOS EXAMPLE: AIRLINE RESERVATION SYSTEMS

The most dramatic, and best documented, contemporary example of the potential impact of IOSs is contained in the report and addendum to Congress on airline reservation systems (ARSs), prepared by the Civil Aeronautics Board in consultation with the Department of Justice (Report to Congress). ARSs illustrate a class of IOS that is shared by intra-industry rivals (competitors), as well as organizations that have a

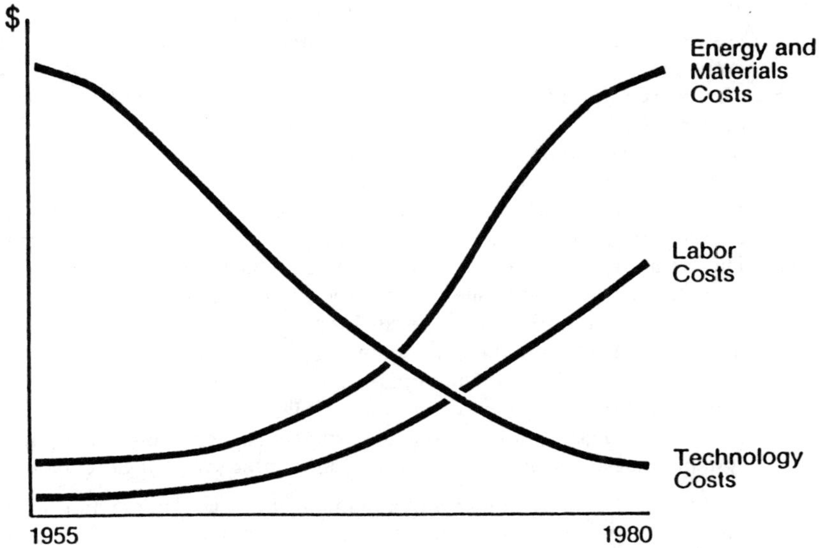

Figure 2. Decreasing technology costs are exploited to offset increasing input costs, such as labor, energy, and materials.

buyer-supplier relationship. In the report, Frontier, a small regional airline, described its view of the unfair competitive advantage enjoyed by United, a major carrier and developer/owner of a widely used reservation system. It alleges that United, via its ARS, unfairly influences travel agents and monitors loading factors of competitive airlines; and, when appropriate, takes competitive action via pricing, or broadcasting special messages to travel agents over the system. Since two carriers own reservation systems that provide the primary market access for approximately two-thirds of the travelers who make reservations using travel agents, this issue came to significant public notice last year.* Appendix A contains a copy of Frontier's testimony, which provides the details of their allegations.

Listed below are observations and questions on specific items contained in the Frontier testimony that distinguish the potential impact of IOSs from internal information systems. These comments are indexed by the section numbers contained in Appendix A.

1. The dominance an early, major investor of IOS technology can achieve, and the associated value of lower-level participants (75 percent of travel agents representing 82 percent of total revenues), can represent a near monopolistic environment.

3(a). Control over 'access' decisions. In a system that is thought to provide unbiased data about a wide range of vendors, a single participant on facilitation could decide who does (and does not) participate in the IOS.

* 1982. (Ed)

3(a) Who defines the appropriate level of integrity that should exist in these systems, and performs formal audit, compliance-checking, and regulating activities?

3(b). How are cost/pricing decisions made and how should they relate to the level of participation? The net-ticketing agreement was projected to cost Frontier $350,000 in 1983. Since most companies totally control the cost line for internal systems, this concern is unique to IOSs.

3(c). How do you avoid display bias when the system is being shared by competitors? This, typically, is not a problem in internal applications.

3(d). Dissemination of sensitive market research data to all affected companies on a timely and fair basis requires specific commitment. When an IOS involves competitors or adversarial suppliers and buyers, one would not normally expect an immediate commitment to equal accessibility.

3(g). Who should or how should organizations control special broadcasting ability enjoyed by owners of dominant IOSs?

3(i). How (or should) charges/costs to participants be monitored for use of systems that are primarily owned and influenced by a single competitor.

Given the rapid diffusion of computer and communications technology into most of our organizations, the potential for similar IOS evolution and impact in a broad range of industries is growing dramatically. The ARS inquiry has specifically documented how an IOS, that grows without effective participant scrutiny, can significantly redefine industry boundaries, shift the power balance along a buyer – supplier chain, and facilitate potentially unfair competitive leverage among intra-industry rivals. Further, it illustrates a dramatic need for social, regulatory and strategic business perspectives to be applied to IOSs.

FRAMEWORK FOR ANALYZING EXTERNAL IMPACT

The variety of existing IOSs is as broad and complex, as are the industries within which they have evolved. To facilitate planning, analyzing and deciding whether to participate in (or develop) an IOS, general managers, legislators and regulators, etc., need a comprehensive framework. The framework must view use of computer and communications technology from a strategic, rather than a tactical perspective. Michael Porter's industry and competitive analysis (ICA) (Porter, 1979, 1980) framework, augmented with potential technology uses, has proven very effective in this respect. Porter's work was directed at strategic business planners and general managers. He argued that many of the contemporary strategic planning frameworks viewed competition too narrowly and pessimistically, because they were primarily based on projections of market share and market growth. He asserted, that the economic and competitive forces in an industry segment were the result of a broader range of factors than the established combatants in a particular industry. According to him, the state of competition in an industry depends on five basic forces: (a) bargaining power of suppliers; (b) bargaining power of buyers; (c) threat of new

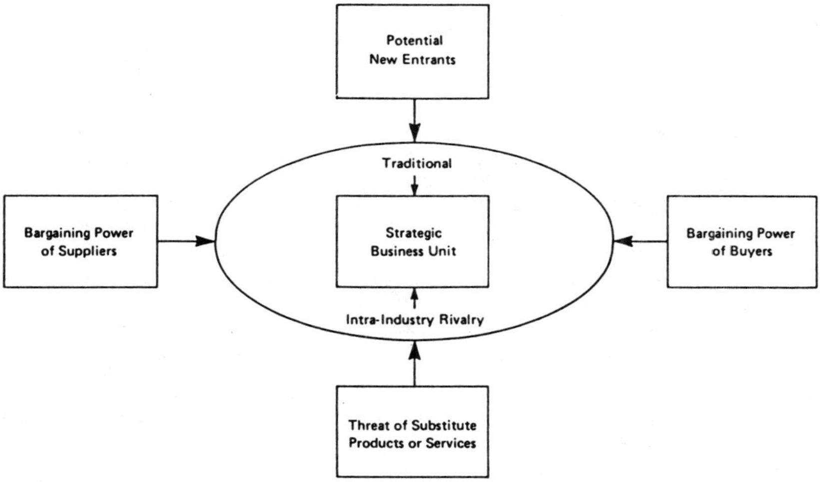

Figure 3. Competitive forces.

entrants into the industry segment; (d) threat of substitute products or services; and (e) positioning of traditional intra-industry rivals. Figure 3 lists the five competitive forces and illustrates the ICA framework.

Although Porter's work did not include information systems as part of the company's resource pool for ICA, it has proven very useful in considering business and industry impact of IOSs. Table 1 contains my extrapolation from the basic ICA model to a description of industry context and potential technology impact.

The left-hand column lists the key competitive forces that dictate the basis of competition in a given industry segment. Note that in a specific industry, not all forces are of equal importance. Some industries are dominated by suppliers (for example, the impact of OPEC exhibited on the petroleum industry), while other industries are preoccupied with the threat of new entrants and/or substitute products (for example, the banking and insurance industries).

The middle column of Table 1 lists key implications of the given competitive force. For example, when new entrants move into an established industry segment, they generally introduce significant additional capacity. They frequently have allocated substantial resources to establish a beachhead in the new industry. The result of new entrants is typically reduced product prices or increased costs for incumbents.

The right-hand column lists uses of IOS to combat the implications of the given competitive force. For example, the establishment of entry barriers can be implemented with an IOS that generates significant economies of scale, or builds switching costs that reduce the ability of suppliers and buyers to move to new entrants, to differentiate product or company, or to limit access to key markets or distribution channels. The Frontier description of United's Apollo ARS in Appendix A illustrates each of these uses, specifically, (1) prohibitive investment required to develop an ARS, (2) the 95 percent rule for transactions processed, (3) the scope of

Table 1 Impact on Competitive Forces

Force	Implication	Potential Technology Impact
New entrants	New capacity Substantial resources Reduced prices or incumbents' costs inflated	Provide entry barriers • Economics of scale • Switching costs • Product differentiation • Access to distribution channels
Buyers	Force prices down High quality More services Encourage competition	Buyer selection Switching costs Differentiation Entry barriers
Suppliers	Raise prices Reduce quality & services (Labor)	Selection Threat of backward integration
Substitute products	Limits potential returns Ceiling on prices	Improve price/performance Redefine products and services
Traditional rivals	Competition • Price • Product • Distribution & service	Cost effectiveness Market access Differentiation • Product • Services • Firm

services and access to 'scare seating,' and (4) 75 percent penetration of agencies (in combination with the 95 percent transaction rule) are examples of the potential impact.

Since two systems, Apollo and SABRE, account for approximately 70 percent of all automated reservation system usage, the potential impact of these systems extends beyond the specific industry and requires a broader perspective than business competitive analysis. Porter's model, augmented with the proposed extensions, is ideal for describing and assessing the potential impact of IOSs. Most organizations will design and implement these systems to combat the key competitive forces that dictate the basis of competition in their given industry segment. The natural extension of this analysis is that the IOS is the enabling vehicle for implementing competitive business strategy. Using IOS to operationalize strategy, is outside the scope of this paper, but is an interesting research area that contains numerous examples (McFarlan, 1984).

INFLUENCE ON INDUSTRY STRUCTURE

In instances of significantly changed bases for competition, restructuring can be observed. Significant shifts in buyer, supplier and intra-industry rival relationships occur, together with the introduction of new or substitute products. In some instances, an IOS was one lever by which organizations facilitated restructure of an industry environment. The best current examples of this can be found in the financial services industry, where, for example, IOS systems have permitted small savings and loan companies to provide brokerage services, etc. In another setting, we observed heavy-equipment manufacturing firms that required their major suppliers to link directly into their computer-aided design/computer-aided manufacturing (CAD/CAM) systems, while also providing ancillary services to its customers via an IOS. In both cases, the IOS sets the stage for redefinition of organizational boundaries and competition patterns in their industry segments.

Organizations may unite under a common set of standards and protocols to provide homogeneity among participants. This can result in the establishment of entry or exit (mobility) barriers. In some instances, the IOS facilitated the introduction of new entrants (e.g., brokerage systems that facilitated the dramatic increase in discount brokerage options). In each case, the objective was to influence the action of competitors: either to establish limited access to a key relationship (supplier, buyer, etc.), or to force entry and participation in the IOS, thereby forcing adoption of standards that were significantly influenced by the initiating organization or consortium.

Similarly, an IOS may be initiated for protection or amplification of a market status quo. Numerous consortiums have been established to introduce nationwide networks of ATMS. Some industry observers believe that decisions to participate in this IOS was justified, in part, by some banks, as a defensive maneuver to protect retail banking markets from potential new entrants (e.g., Sears) which have in-place computer and communication infrastructures to offer interstate banking services.

Clearly, changes can be expected in the rivalry patterns within industries. Further, we can expect industry boundaries to adjust and reshape themselves, as new strategic relationships emerge, and traditional organizational boundaries become blurred.

ORGANIZATIONAL IMPACT

Existing IOSs appeared to have a range of internal organizational impacts on participants. However, the order of effects was clearly observable. The 7-S framework*, popularized in a contemporary book (Athos and Pascale, 1982), has proven useful to categorize observations. Table 2 briefly describes each S. Figure 4 is a schematic of the Ss, and emphasizes the need for appropriate balance between them. The term 'fit' is frequently used to describe the objective of choosing appropriate alternatives for each S which addresses their interdependence.

Initial changes that occur in an organization participating in an IOS, occur in the *systems* category. The specific business process (order entry, production, etc.) impacted by the IOS, is frequently altered to compromise different approaches to things, like quality or internal control procedures, report formats and associated time frame, planning systems, and communication patterns inside a given participant organization. This shift in the underlying business process and communication pattern frequently precipitates changes in the *skills* that are needed by associated employees

* Guidelines on planning and management. (Ed)

Table 2 The Seven Ss

Strategy	Plan or course of action leading to the allocation of a firm's scarce resources, over time, to reach identified goals
Structure	Characterization of the organization chart (i.e., functional, decentralized, etc.)
Systems	Proceduralized reports and routinized processes, such as meeting formats
Staff	'Demographic' description of important personnel categories within the firm (i.e., engineers, entrepreneurs, MBAs, etc.). 'Staff' is *not* meant in line-staff terms
Style	Characterization of how key managers behave in achieving the organization's goals; also the cultural style of the organization
Skills	Distinctive capabilities of key personnel or the firm as a whole
Superordinate goals	The significant meanings or guiding concepts that an organization imbues in its members

Source: Athos and Pascale, 1982.

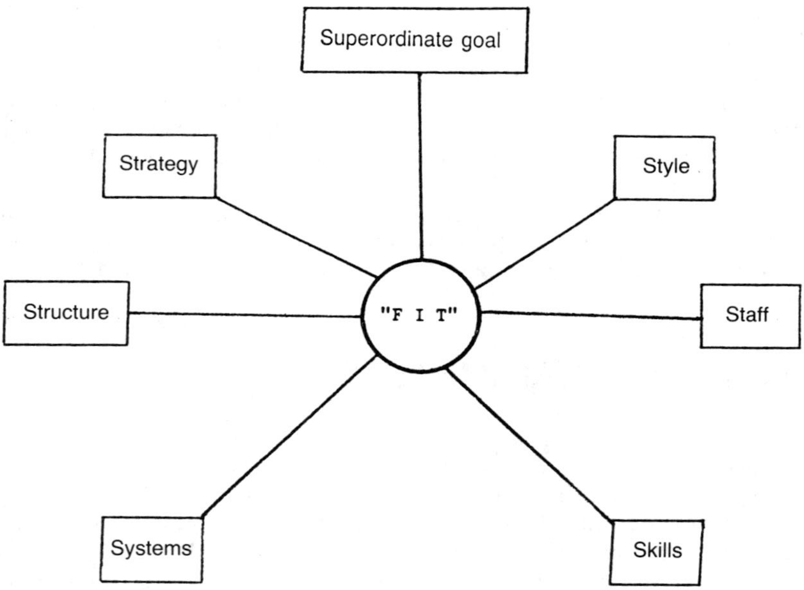

Figure 4. A schematic of the Ss, emphasizing the need for appropriate balance ('fit') between them.

and, in some cases, the emergence of a new *staff* category. Third order effects include the development of new or changed *style, structure* and *strategy*. The key concern related to these changes is the impact on the balance or 'fit' between the Ss. Shifts in *systems*, *skills*, etc., without compensating shifts in the other elements, generate unplanned conflict, contention and, in some cases, dysfunctional behavior.

The order of change among the elements appears to vary, based on whether the organization is reacting, in a participant role, to an IOS implemented by another organization; or is the proactive initiator/implementor of the IOS. In the first case, if a participant is engaged in the IOS in an ad hoc manner, there is usually no general management participation and thus no explicit planning or broad thinking about implications of the system. In these circumstances, the evolution described above seems an appropriate template (if the IOS is strategic):

First-order impact – *systems*
Second-order impact – *skills*, *staff*
Third- and higher-order impacts – *style*, *structure*, *strategy*.

However, in the second case of an organization implementing a strategic IOS, the order changes. This occurs, because explicit planning of desired impact and requisite resources precedes implementation of the IOS:

First-order impact – *strategy*, *structure*,
Second-order impact – *staff*, *skills*
Third- and higher-order impact – *systems*.

Although the IOS was the enabling vehicle for changes in *structure* and *strategy*, *the actual changes in the systems* category occurred last, because of the explicit planning for the introduction. In the cases examined to this point, I have not observed changes in *superordinate goals* which could be attributed to an IOS.

The degree of change in *style*, *structure* and *strategy* appears to be directly related to the significance of competitive forces that the IOS impacts. In some instances, it is clear that the generic pattern of behavior among key managers in the organization had to change because of competitive pressure. In such cases, it is very difficult to isolate the changes as directly related to an IOS, although the IOS addressed key competitive forces. However, it was clear that the IOS was a critical part of the infrastructure that was frequently evaluated to make key decisions on *structure* and *strategy*.

McKenney (1984) is studying this problem of defining internal organizational impact. His work will provide a much better framework for analyzing and describing internal impact upon completion.

SUMMARY

The potential productivity improvements of continuing exploitation of information systems technology are enormous, and mostly positive. Recently, the role and impact of this technology have become much more significant. Specifically, instances in which two or more companies share computer and communication resources to perform a joint business function, constitute a very different category of IS technology exploitation, when compared with exclusively internal uses. These IOSs have unique characteristics that are illustrated in Appendix A, and require broader frameworks than currently available. As managers, legislators, regulators, public policy-makers, etc., view IOSs, they must specifically consider the internal, industry and social impact aspects.

The internal issues focus on the readiness of the organization to deal with the business process, personnel and structural changes that the organization may face in IOS participation, as well as the ability of the organization to evolve under the external pressures that are associated with IOSs. The 7-S framework has proven effective for analyzing and managing this dimension of IOS impact.

The industry issues concern the position of the organization in its market, and its strategy for impacting key competitive forces. Use of an augmented Porter framework to assess potential impact of an IOS in a given industry setting, provides a broad perspective for this analysis.

The social impact and public policy issues are critical. The interorganizational and interindustrial aspects of large, dominant IOSs have clear societal implications. Currently, however, there are more questions than straightforward answers. For example, at what point is the consumer paying an inappropriate price because of biases built into dominant IOSs, as we have observed in the airline industry? What is the appropriate timing of the introduction of regulatory guidelines to avoid unfair business practices via IOSs, without penalizing creativity, innovation and risk-taking by initiators of IOSs that become dominant market access mechanisms or distribution channels? This question is particularly difficult. For example, in the domestic airline industry, United and American have invested substantial resources (more than $200 million each, management and staff time, etc.) and accepted significant business risks, to gain their current competitive advantage. The Appendix to this paper, one perspective of this IOS environment. was used to illustrate potential impact and issues that should be addressed. (The other perspective is contained in a collection of articles and testimony by American Airlines that can be found in a Harvard Business School case study entitled 'United Airlines' [Vitale, 1984].) Premature, formal regulation could discourage risk-taking and cause firms to reduce their commitment to new creative/innovative ways to use information systems technology.

This paper was designed to identify one part of the tremendous change based on diffusion of IS technology and to suggest two frameworks for analyzing potential impacts.

APPENDIX A. COMMENTS OF FRONTIER AIRLINES, INC., BEFORE THE CIVIL AERONAUTICS BOARD, WASHINGTON, D.C.

REPORT TO CONGRESS ON COMPUTER
RESERVATIONS SYSTEMS — Docket 41207

At the present time about 80% of the nation's travel agencies have automated reservations systems.[1] Computerized agencies tend to be the high volume operators, with mostly the smaller (often rural) agencies remaining unautomated. In 1981,

[1] This is Frontier's current best estimate. According to *Travel Weekly*'s Louis Harris Study (May 1982, p. 46), 68% of the travel agencies were automated in 1981, and Frontier knows the growth has continued since then.

computerized agencies accounted for $24.5 *billion* of airline ticket sales! (*supra*). Sales through travel agencies are critically important to Frontier's business since they account for 65% of our total sales volume.

While American Airlines' SABRE system and United Airlines' Apollo system are the largest in use throughout the nation, Frontier's comments focus primarily on United's Apollo system because of its impact upon Frontier and the Denver hub. Frontier is United's chief competitor at Denver, with United enplaning 3.6 million passengers versus 2.5 million by Frontier in 1982. United and Frontier now compete head to head on 31 routes out of Denver, versus only 8 when the Deregulation Act of 1978 was implemented. United's January 1983 Denver departures are 141 a day, up 40% from one year ago.

The combined effect of United's leverage through the Apollo system and its other extraordinary measures at Denver have had a serious impact on the competitive airline picture at this important hub:[2]

- United enplaned 1,013,975 passengers at Denver in the fourth quarter of 1982, a 40.2% increase over the fourth quarter of 1981. This translates into a 36.9% share of Denver enplanements for United at the end of 1982 versus 26.8% for the fourth quarter of 1981.
- The growth of United's domination at Denver is more clearly reflected by comparing quarterly increases during 1982 with one year earlier. United's percentage share of enplaned Denver passengers increased 1.5%, 4.6%, 17.6% and 28.1% during each of the four quarters of 1982 over the same periods in 1981, while Frontier's quarterly share of enplaned Denver passengers *decreased* 9.2%, 6.5%, 8.3% and 9.8% versus the same periods last years.

The ability of United to significantly affect the Denver hub through its Apollo system is shown by the following section.

1. United Dominates the Computerized Reservations System Market at the Denver Hub.

At Denver, the dominance of United's Apollo system among agencies is particularly strong;

- 148 out of 198 (75%) automated travel agencies in the Denver area subscribe to Apollo.
- Apollo has automated four times more travel agencies in the Denver area than its next largest competitor.
- Apollo travel agencies in the Denver area account for about $250 million in airline revenues, or about 82% of total airline revenues generated by Denver's automated agencies.[3]

[2] Based on preliminary fourth quarter 1982 data.

[3] As of March 1982: Apollo 148; SABRE 37; PARS 12; EA 1. Denver metro area includes Boulder, Longmont, Loveland and several other front-range communities. Estimated annual revenues of $1.8 million per agency, which was the average annual revenue figure of 47 Denver Apollo travel agencies as of June 1981.

Frontier believes that United has used its control over one market, i.e., the Denver travel agents' automated reservations systems, as an unfair and anticompetitive means to further United's goals in another market, i.e., that sale of air transportation, where it competes with Frontier and other carriers.

2. Normal Market Forces Have Not Disciplined the Travel Agency Computer Reservation Systems Market.

Normally, competition between United's Apollo system, American's SABRE system, TWA's PARS system and other lesser competitors for placement of computer reservation systems at travel agencies would discipline this market. However, this has not been the case as demonstrated by abuses which have occurred. Set forth below are examples of past practices, as well as future prospects, of the anticompetitive impact of United's control of the Apollo system.

3. United Uses Apollo in an Unfair and Uncompetitive Manner.

(a) *United has disciminatorily excluded carriers from Apollo.* For over two years, United refused to allow Frontier to become an Apollo co-host for 'competitive' reasons. Although Frontier was finally allowed to become a co-host in July of 1982, our prior efforts to join Apollo were stalled by United's claim that its Apollo system did not have the capacity to handle Frontier. However, during the same time period, at least three other major carriers were granted co-host status. After repeated inquiries, Frontier was finally told in August of 1981 by a United Vice President that it was to be excluded for 'competitive' reasons. Further entreaties by Frontier were similarly rebuffed, until soon after the Department of Justice and the CAB* began their investigative efforts into anticompetitive aspects of automated reservation systems.

Frontier also understands that Midway Airlines' complete schedules – direct and connecting – were expunged from Apollo for a period of time. (During the period Frontier was denied co-host status, its direct flights remained in the Apollo system.) United therefore has the power to completely eliminate smaller carriers' schedules from Apollo, unless a fee is paid, regardless of the impact on the carrier, the public or travel agents. Air California now pays such a fee for inclusion of its direct flights, and had Frontier not become a co-host, United threatened complete expulsion of all our flights from Apollo unless a fee were paid.

(b) *'Tying' arrangements under Apollo.* In order to become a co-host under United's Apollo system, Frontier was forced to also agree on a 'net ticketing arrangement' with United. Under the 'net ticketing arrangement.' Frontier pays United a dollar amount for tickets written by United on Frontier, and United pays Frontier a dollar amount for tickets written by Frontier on United. However, Frontier did not want this agreement, since United writes more tickets on Frontier, and we asked that separate

* CAB: The Civil Aeronautics Board. (Ed)

negotiations be held on this subject. United refused, saying it was a package deal. Frontier estimates that the ticketing 'tying' arrangement will cost the company about $350,000 in 1983. Thus, United used its power in the 'tying' product – co-host status in the Apollo system – to impose its will with respect to a separate agreement – net ticketing. Interestingly, in Frontier's negotiations with TWA, a similar package deal was presented to Frontier, i.e., membership in PARS coupled with net ticketing, but TWA agreed to sever the two products and negotiate each separately.

(c) *Bias problems continue even after achieving co-host status.* Even after Frontier achieved co-host status under Apollo, and during Frontier's long-standing co-host status under SABRE, bias problems continue to exist which give host carriers, such as United and American, an unfair competitive advantage.

Host carriers continue to maintain a super-bias which displays their schedules in a superior manner to that afforded co-host carriers. For example, when a travel agent requests flight information from Apollo, the system will display schedules of co-hosts from the desired time *forward*, while United alone will display backwards in time (about two hours), in addition to displaying schedules after the desired time. More comprehensive and complicated rules are employed to display connecting schedules – always designed to give United a leg up on its co-hosts.

In addition to the super-bias enjoyed by United as a host carrier, some co-hosts are more equal than other co-hosts in the tradition of Orwell's *Animal Farm*. Thus, Delta is accorded a special display on Apollo. Host carriers also retain the right to create new categories of co-hosts, such as that United has accorded to Delta, and thereby create new echelons of bias among co-hosts, for which differentiated (and higher) rates can be charged.

To date, host carriers have concentrated on biasing schedule displays in their travel agent systems, but Frontier expects that bias will play a greater role in reservation systems' *fare* displays in the future. Even now, the fare categorization/classification program employed by the United in the Apollo system can result in a competitively inferior display for a carrier desiring to improvise with new fares. A host carrier, such as United, also enjoys a competitive advantage in institution of a new fare, since United can plan and control the display of its new fares in Apollo, whereas Frontier and other co-hosts must hope that the display accorded the new fare in Apollo is a good one (or a co-host must conform his new fare within existing fare display formats, which is not always possible or desirable). If such a new and innovative fare by a co-host does not receive a favorable Apollo display, its acceptance by travel agents can be drastically affected.

(d) *Host carriers have an unfair advantage by their computerized access to confidential information of the competitors.* United and American have *exclusive* and *immediate* access on their respective Apollo and SABRE systems to highly sensitive sales data, which they can use to their competitive advantage. United, for example, generates reports for each Apollo travel agency, identifying by market the total number of passengers carried in the period, and the amount and percentage of traffic carried by each competitive carrier in the market. This information is not available to co-hosts, such as Frontier. The only information United will give Frontier, is the total number of passengers carried by Frontier, and currently even this limited information (which does not indicate Frontier's share of the total market, or other carriers' shares) is available about one month in arrears.

Access to this information gives United/American a tremendous and unfair competitive advantage. United sales representatives have immediate knowledge whether United and its competitors are losing/gaining market share, and United can promptly take measures (e.g., bonus incentives, lower fares, more schedules) to rectify the developing situation. The *immediate* access of United sales representatives to this data allows United sales representatives to contact travel agents long before Frontier knows of market changes. At several travel agencies where Frontier has made inroads into United market shares, the agents have mentioned 'pressure' from United sales representatives to increase United market shares, as reflected in a recent article appearing in *Travel Agent*:

> Agents are also becoming accustomed to receiving printouts of their reservation histories with little comments, sometimes nasty at that, asking why some other carrier was used instead of them. (October 11, 1982, p. 19.)

(e) *United coerces agents into exclusive use of Apollo.* While Frontier has finally attained co-host status in Apollo, United still maintains its schedule bias over Frontier in the system, and Frontier's schedules enjoy a superior display vis-à-vis United in American's SABRE system. Therefore United's efforts to maintain exclusivity with travel agents using Apollo – particularly in the crucial Denver market – harms Frontier (not to mention travel agencies and the public). United uses several means to preclude competition by SABRE and other automated system.

The 95% Rule. Over the last year, United has added a clause to its Apollo contract, requiring the travel agent to '...process 95% of its tickets containing at least one United segment through the Apollo equipment.' To assure compliance, United has the right to audit the agency's books and records without notice. The admitted purpose of this provision, according to United's Senior Vice President in charge of marketing (John Zeeman), is to prevent agencies from maintaining two systems:

> He agreed that this section would have the effect of forcing agents to make a choice between two or more systems, but he said the written document is only a manifestation of a continuing policy of pushing agents to make such choices...It is clear that any agency with two airline systems could not possibly satisfy the 95% rule, but Zeeman said United would not let such an agency have the option of signing the contract anyway. The agency would be asked to choose between Apollo and the second system. (*Travel Weekly*, November 15, 1982.)

The December issue of *Frequent Flyer* speaks of the same subject:

> But to American and United, second, automated res* systems are pure anathema. Reportedly, both carriers have threatened to pull their computer terminals out of agencies that install a competitor's hardware.
>
> United admits that it discourages Apollo users from using another system, particularly SABRE: 'We feel that it is not an effective way to do business,' says

* reservation. (Ed)

Zeeman. ('New Reservations about Airlines Computers,' pp. 45 and 49.)

Other Coercive Efforts. The September 13, 1982 issue of the *Aviation Daily* contains another example of United pressure to preclude a Colorado Springs travel agency from using two systems:

> Myers originally wanted two systems, in order to get boarding passes and last-seat availability for both carriers. He said, a succession of meetings between Ambassador Travel and each airline made it clear that United prefers an exclusive arrangement, so that it can look at any agency's business and determine if it is delivering to United a share of business that reflects the carrier's market share in the area.

(f) *The pending* 'Boarding Pass' *enhancement to Apollo.* United is currently seeking to add a new feature to Apollo which would allow travel agencies to automatically issue boarding passes to United passengers. This feature, we understand, will not be allowed for Frontier passengers, nor will United permit SABRE users to issue United boarding passes, whether manually or otherwise. This seems to be yet another means to be used by United to enhance its airline market position, by way of its control over the Apollo system.

(g) *Host carriers can also control the content of data reaching travel agents.* Host carriers have the ability to control the content of information reaching travel agencies. This control has adverse competitive implications to Frontier and other outsiders. For example, Frontier recently instituted a $99 one-way fare in many markets on its system. While United did insert the Frontier fare information into Apollo, United used the same system to undermine Frontier in the eyes of the travel agents using Apollo. Thus, United inserted a 'sales message' to agents, informing them that it was matching Frontier fares, but gratuitously added that 'Because these fares are *nongenerative*, we have planned a 3/3/83 travel expiration date *to try to minimize dilution of your commission*.' (Wednesday, 1/12/83 message to Apollo users.)

The clear message by United to the travel agents, was that Frontier's new fares would not produce any new passengers, and that all they would do, was reduce travel agents' commission. Standing alone, this may not seem earth-shaking, but how many other messages have been sent which Frontier has not seen?

Other examples of potential anticompetitive effects of hosts' control of information in their automated systems include:

- The Host carrier alone knows the intricate details of the bias system program. The Host also controls when changes are made, as well as variations to bias, that are implemented from time to time in 'special' markets, where a Host may perceive a lower usage of its service or an opportunity to improve market penetration. Despite continuous efforts, Frontier has not been able to effectively monitor its schedules in the Apollo and SABRE systems.
- At times, Frontier schedules are 'dropped' from Apollo/SABRE, or fares are delayed in their entry. Frontier's monitoring catches some of these problems, but not all of them. The host always explains these problems as attributable to a computer mistake or other rational vagary of the system, and Frontier is in no position to contest these explanations. However, with a prime competitor

controlling the system, a co-host's doubts are never really satisfied.

- From time to time, Frontier receives reports from travel agents that Apollo/SABRE sets reflect Frontier flights as being fully booked, whereas, in fact, seats remain to be sold. Again, these occurrences may be unintentional breakdowns, but a co-host never really knows.

(h) *Other means host carriers use to maintain exclusivity or to proselytize travel agents.*

- *According to the October 1982 Michigan Travel Bulletin*, a tour wholesaler in the Detroit area was told by United that its Winter Hawaii Program was in jeopardy, ostensibly because of unavailability of aircraft. In an open letter to United, the publication asked:

  'Why no airplanes? They don't happen to use Apollo computers. We're told that you [United] advised this wholesaler, in so many words, switch to Apollo or else.'

  'Has it really come to this?'
- United discriminates against non-Apollo agencies by with-holding information. For example, we understand, United has informed travel agents that only Apollo users will be able to sell special 'last-minute' fares, based on seat availability, and that these fares will be denied to SABRE travel agencies. In a similar vein, United has threatened to steer commercial accounts to/from travel agencies, depending upon their usage of the Apollo system.
- Large bonuses paid to travel agencies to switch automated systems, e.g.,:

  The July 29, 1982 issue of *The Travel Agent* refers to an allegation that 'one Midwestern travel agent was offered $100,000 to switch reservation systems.'
- Another periodical claims that '. . . United has agreed to provide Apollo free of charge if they drop SABRE. . .
- United has even gone a step further, offering not only cash payments to some agencies of as much as $500,000 to make such a switch, but also to override commissions. . . and installation givebacks.' ('New Reservations about Airline Computers,' *Frequent Flyer*, December 1982, pp. 45, 46.)
- *Business Week* of August 23, 1982 confirms these practices:

To compete, United this spring began offering what one agent calls 'convenience money' as well as bonuses on increases in United sales, contract buyouts, and free installation to tempt agencies – and not just SABRE users – to take Apollo.' (p. 68)

Some agents resent United's pressure tactics, says one: 'Using power and money to buy market share may be a wise move for United from an airline point of view. But its insistence on getting rid of other airline systems, and *the only thinly veiled threat that it will give us rotten service if we don't*, has dire implications for an agent's independence.' (supra, p. 69)

(i) *Concerns about charges.* Exclusion from either Apollo or SABRE can have devastating results because of the number of agencies they serve, and this is particularly true with respect to hub and spoke carriers who rely heavily on a favorable display of connecting flights. In the context, a host carrier can charge just about all it pleases. Since Frontier initially negotiated to become an Apollo co-host, segment charges imposed by United have increased 5 to 10 times the originally quoted rates. Frontier is very concerned that United's leverage on the Apollo system will enable it to extract excessive fees in the future.

CONCLUSION

Frontier and the other smaller airlines are not the only ones hurt by the giant host carriers' control over this distribution system. The travel agent industry and the public at large are also illserved by the current situation.

The American Society of Travel Agents (ASTA) has passed a resolution warning carriers that ''any attempt, either subtle or blatant, to pervert or undermine the impartiality of travel agent system subscribers, will henceforth be resisted whenever possible,' and that the 'deliberate suppression' of computerized information on competing carriers' schedules is 'not in the best interest' of either the public or the agency community' (Vol. XIII, No. 158, *Travel Management Daily*, August 18, 1982). An official of the Travel Agents' Computer Society has likewise stated:

> Most agents see themselves as professionals – able to present unbiased information to clients. They resent a 'dealership' relationship. They feel, it would jeopardize their integrity. ('Bias, Dealerships' Top Concerns,' *The Travel Agent*, October 11, 1982, p. 94.)

So also the members of Associated Travel Nationwide (ATN) issued a press release on August 2, 1982 proclaiming:

> As responsible travel agents, ATN members recognize their primary obligations to the consumer, and in order to meet their needs, full and complete unprejudiced information about air transportation must be available at all times.

The initial adverse effect of giant carriers' control of this distribution system upon their smaller competitors, upon travel agencies, and upon the public, has already been felt. The future impact augurs to be even more pervasive. Smaller carriers, such as Frontier, even with the help of the travel agencies, have not been able to avoid the consequences of the current situation. Frontier strongly believes that legislative relief is necessary, as suggested below.

Frontier's Proposed Remedy

Frontier recommends that the CAB and the DOJ* recommende to Congress that legislation be enacted to remedy the anticompetitive evils resulting from host airlines controlling these automated reservations systems. The law should require nondiscriminatory treatment of all airlines, including hosts and co-hosts, and schedules, fares

* DOJ: Department of Justice. (Ed)

and other information should be displayed on the basis of objective standards. There should be no host or co-host levels, and all airlines should have access to the systems on an impartial basis and for a fee, graduated according to their relative inputs into the system. Each airline owner of a computer display system should also be required to form a separate subsidiary which would operate the computerized display and reservation systems independently of the airline parent.

Respectfully submitted,

FRONTIER AIRLINES, INC.

BY /s/DAVID N. BRICTSON

David N. Brictson
Vice President-General Counsel

REFERENCES

Athos, A., and R. J. Pascale. 1982. *The Art of Japanese Management*. New York: Warner Books.

Barrett, S., and B. Konsynski. 1982. 'Inter-Organizational Information Sharing Systems.' *MIS Quarterly*, Special issue.

Cash, J., F. W. McFarlan, and J. L. McKenney. 1983. *Corporate Information Systems Management*. Richard D. Irwin.

Cash, J., M. McLaughlin, and R. Howe, 1983. 'Changing Competitive Ground-rules – The Impact of Computers and Communications Technology in the 1980s. *Harvard Business School Course Development and Research Profiles – 1983*.

Kaufman, F. 1966. 'Data Systems That Cross Company Boundaries.' *Harvard Business Review*, January – February.

McFarlan, F. W. 1984. 'Information Systems Change the Way You Compete.' *Harvard Business Review*, May – June.

McKenney, J. L. 1984. 'Organizational Impact of Terminal Oriented Communications.' HBS Working Paper.

Porter, M. 1980. *Competitive Strategy*. New York: Free Press.

Porter, M. 1979. 'How Competitive Forces Shape Strategy.' *Harvard Business Review*, March – April.

'Report to Congress on Airlines Computer Reservation Systems' and 'Addendum.' Prepared by Civil Aeronautics Board in consultation with the Department of Justice.

Vitale, Michael. 1984. 'United Airlines.' Harvard Business School Case Study #9-184-83.

3. THE INFORMATION SYSTEM AS A COMPETITIVE WEAPON*

Blake Ives and Gerard P. Learmonth

ABSTRACT: With the help of information system technology, a company can become competitive in all phases of its customer relationships. The customer resource life cycle model makes it possible for such companies to determine not only when opportunities exist for strategic applications, but also what specific applications should be developed.

Information systems have traditionally been considered primarily in terms of their effects on individual organizations. Researchers have concentrated their efforts on delineating the nature of information system function: operational support versus decision support [24], the impact of information systems on end users [44, 45], or the importance of information systems to the organization as a whole [35]. More recently, however, the external use of information systems as competitive weapons has come under consideration. This can be atttibuted to several factors, including a decline in the cost of supporting information technologies; structural changes in the economy, caused by global competition; and, perhaps most importantly, the deregulation of many industries, particularly transportation and financial services. Companies, that were once constrained by regulatory practices, have moved quickly in the wake of deregulation, to replace limited, well-understood and well-regulated product lines with varied, ever-changing selections of new products and services.

Recent studies demonstrate that information systems offer a unique opportunity for competitive advantages in the new business climate. These studies present descriptive models for classifying successful strategic applications and for evaluating the potential of proposed applications. These models are not generally useful, however, for identifying these applications. A more detailed model is necessary: one that can help to find new opportunities for the successful application of information system technologies (IST).

Such an application is strategic, if it changes a firm's product or the way a firm competes in its industry. The model that will be used to explain the use of IST in a competitive strategy is the *customer resource life cycle*. This model considers a firm's relationship with its customers and how this relationship can be changed or enhanced by the strategic application of IST.

* *Reprinted from Communications of the ACM, 27, No 12, December* 1984.

Blake Ives and Gerard P. Learmonth work with the Graduate Program in Computer and Information Science, Dartmouth College, Hanover, U.S.A.

STRATEGIC INFORMATION SYSTEMS

THE HARVARD STUDIES

Much of the research on the competitive application of IST originated at the Harvard Business School. The basis for this research was Michael Porter's work on industry analysis and the formulation of competitive strategies [43]. Porter (see Figure 1) identified five major competitive forces (CFs):
CF1 – the threat of new entrants,
CF2 – the intensity of rivalry among existing competitors,
CF3 – pressure from substitute products,
CF4 – the bargaining power of buyers and
CF5 – the bargaining power of suppliers.

Porter maintained that firms wishing to gain a competitive edge should consider building defenses against these forces and formulate specific courses of competitive action that can directly influence these forces. The three generic strategies that a firm may choose to follow in determining its course of competitive action are

- overall cost leadership (being the lowest cost producer),

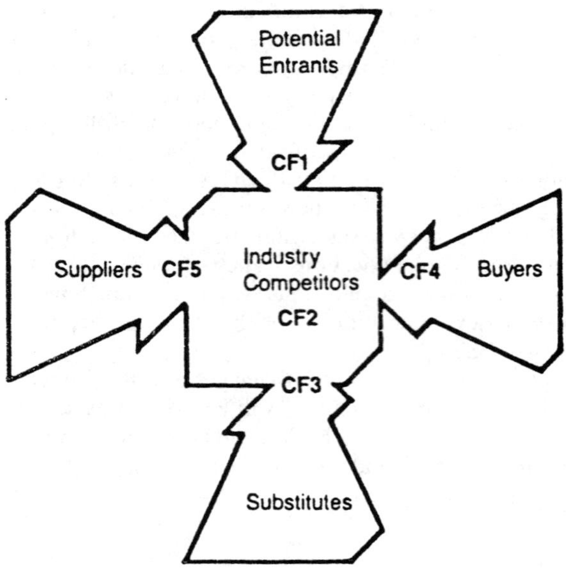

Figure 1. Competitive Forces [43]

- differentiation (of a product or service) and
- focus (i.e., finding a specialized niche in an industry).

Porter's analysis of competitive forces does not specifically address IST, but it does provide a framework for investigating the role that IST can play in a firm's competitive strategy.

McFarlan and McKenney [34] were among the first to formally recognize the new role IST was beginning to play in organizations. Their *strategic grid* (see Figure 2) classifies firms on the basis of the criticality of existing applications and the potential criticality of applications under development.

Recent changes in the banking industry illustrate the use of the strategic grid. Prior to deregulation, banks typically fell into the *factory quadrant* with respect to their usage of IST: Information system support was critical for day-to-day transaction processing, but applications under development were not likely to help a company to achieve a significant competitive advantage. After deregulation, successful banks progressed through the *turnaround quadrant* to *the strategic quadrant*, acting aggressively to get new information-based products to market. This marked a clear shift of IST from a back-office support role to an important instrument of competitive strategy.

In other industries, such as publishing, information systems have not been critical in the past, but may soon move from the *suport quadrant* to the *turnaround quadrant*, as new ISTs begin to offer significant competitive advantages. Eventually, firms in these industries may find themselves in the *strategic quadrant* as IST becomes a critical element of competition.

McFarlan and McKenney use the strategic grid to prescribe an appropriate type of management control system. For example, they argue that it makes more sense to charge for computer resources in the *factory quadrant* than it does in the *turnaround quadrant*. The strategic grid is also useful for evaluating a portfolio of alternative

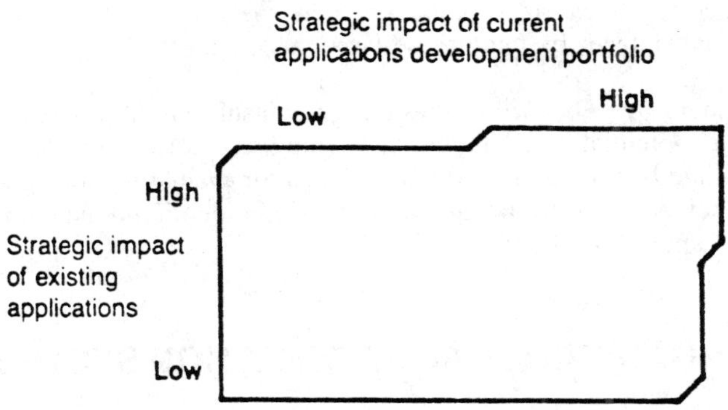

Figure 2. Strategic Grid [34]

information system investments; it offers little assistance, however, to the firm that wants to *identify* new competitive applications of information systems.

Recently, McFarlan [33] mapped the competitive application of IST onto Porter's competitive forces model. He proposed five questions for assessing the strategic impact of IST on a firm. If a particular question is answered in the affirmative, a strategic opportunity exists that deserves 'the highest level thinking.' The five questions, with Porter's competitive forces noted in parentheses, are:

- Can IST be used to build barriers against new entrants (CF1)?
- Can IST change the basis of competition (CF2)?
- Can IST be used to generate new products (CF3)?
- Can IST be used to build in switching costs (CF4)?
- Can IST change the balance of power in supplier relationships (CF5)?

These questions help a firm to determine *when* opportunities exist for strategic applications but, again, provide relatively little assistance in identifying *what* specific applications to develop.

Parsons [40] also builds on Porter's work, taking a broader perspective than McFarlan, by viewing the strategic implications of IST at three levels: the industry level, the firm level, and the strategy level. He suggests that a sound understanding of *when, where* and *how* IST will impact a firm, can lead to the recognition of both opportunities and threats.

At the industry level, Parsons focuses on how IST changes the fundamental nature of the industry [40]. This analysis takes account of real or potential changes in the nature of an industry's products or services, the markets the industry serves and the economics of production in the industry.

At the firm level, Parsons uses Porter's five competitive forces to determine where opportunities exist for IST to directly influence a firm's competitive position. He argues that the traditional criteria for information technology investments (e.g. return on investment) are not always the correct criteria to apply when considering the strategic impact of these investments. It may be difficult, for example, to justify placing terminals in the offices of large customers on the basis of reductions in order-processing costs. Such an installation may nevertheless provide a significant competitive advantage, by tying these large customers to the supplier's order-entry system.

In summary, the Harvard studies have made substantial progress in highlighting the strategic potential of IST, by developing categories for describing existing applications and by providing qualifying criteria for evaluating proposed applications. However, they do not offer adequate assistance in identifying new opportunities for the strategic application of IST.

INTERORGANIZATIONAL INFORMATION SYSTEMS

The strategic importance of information links between customers and suppliers has given rise to an interest in interorganizational information systems. In the airline industry, competing carriers, travel agents and consumers are all interconnected through a network of airline reservation systems.[1] In banking, automated teller machines permit banks to enter new markets with minimal outlays of capital [55]. Distributors like Bergen Brunswig [46], GESCO [46], and American Hospital Supply [4] have set up electronic order-entry links with many of their customers, that provide better customer service, often at lower costs to the distributors. Standards for the interorganizational movement of electronic transactions have been established by trade organizations for the grocery, warehouse, ocean-carrier, railroad and motor-carrier industries, among others [16].

McFarlan recognized the importance of the evolving 'interorganizational electronic link between customer and supplier' [34], but cautions that 'these links offer the opportunity for competitive advantage on the one hand but pose strategic vulnerability on the other.'

Barrett and Konsynski [3] examined the various forms of interorganizational information systems and developed the five-level classification scheme shown in Table 1. At the lowest level is the firm that serves only as a remote input/output node for one or more higher level nodes, and at the highest level is 'a data communication/data processing utility which integrates any number of lower level participants and applications in real time.' Although not rigorously defined, the classification scheme serves as a useful conceptual tool for describing and understanding the multitude of possible interorganizational information systems.

Table 1. Classification Scheme for Interorganizational Information Systems [3]

Level 1	Remote I/O node
Level 2	Application processing node
Level 3	Multiparticipant exchange node
Level 4	Network control node
Level 5	Integrating network node

OTHER MODELS

Several other studies focus on the strategic importance of information systems. These are discussed here.

1. McLaughlin et al. [36] suggest that alternative investments in information systems be judged not simply by cost but also by potential for 'adding value'; that is, the extent to which marginal revenue exceeds the marginal cost of the investment. An airline, for example, might upgrade a passenger reservation system, so it can handle bookkeeping for a 'frequent flyer' program. Management might justify the outlay of a million dollars for IST on the conviction that it can leverage a 20 or 30 million dollar increase in revenues over the following year. McLaughlin et al. [36] note that 'financial services firms currently use about one dollar of computer hardware for every 30 to 40 dollars of value added.'

Value-adding applications[2] of IST may cause improvements in cost-effectiveness,

[1] See The TWA reservation system. Commun ACM 27, 7 (July 1984), 649–665 for an in-depth description of such a system.

[2] McLaughlin et al. use the term 'value-added application'.

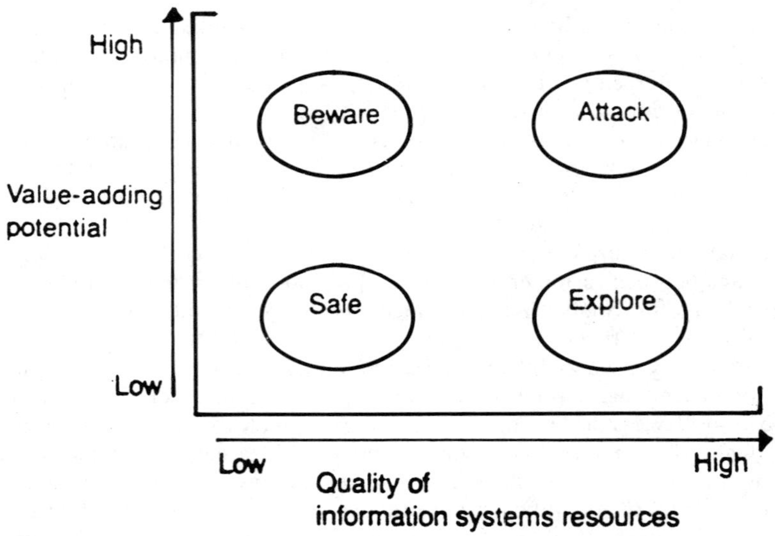

Figure 3. Quality of Information Systems Resources versus Value-Adding Potential of Business [36]

enhanced market access and product differentiation, and also cause structural change in the marketplace. McLaughlin et al. hypothesize, that organizations vary in the extent to which information systems can add value through technology and also in the capabilities of their information systems departments. This relationship is depicted in Figure 3.

An organization with high value-adding potential but weak systems resources, is vulnerable to competitors with better IST resources. On the other hand, if value-adding potential is high and the systems group strong, the organization may be in a position to compensate for the technological weaknesses.

2. Benjamin et al. [5] discussed the strategic opportunities presented by ISTs with 'top executives and technology managers in two dozen companies.' Based on these interviews, they proposed the model illustrated in Figure 4. The model is based on two questions [5]:

- Can IST be used to make a significant change in the way a company does business, so as to gain a competitive advantage?
- Should a company concentrate on using IST to improve its approach to the marketplace, or should it center its efforts around internal improvements?

The internal versus external dimension assumes that the uses of an information system need not be directly related to customers to be strategic. As the Japanese have demonstrated, proper operating decisions can be strategic [6]. In the structural change dimension, the adoption of some IST requires significant modifications to current business practices.

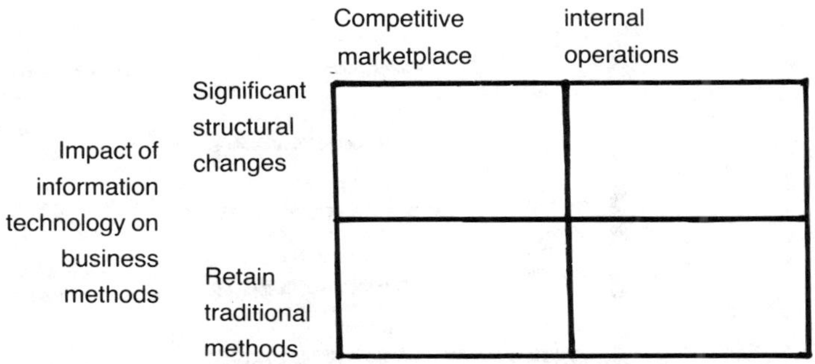

Figure 4. Strategic Opportunities Matrix [5]

3. Notowidigdo [38] also divides strategic information systems into internal systems 'that have direct benefit to the company' and external systems 'that have direct benefits to the company's customers,' but which indirectly benefit the company. He notes that in the past, information systems of benefit to the customer were generally found in the service sector, whereas strategic internal systems were developed primarily in the industrial sector. Figure 5 presents a modified version of his model.

Although Notowidigdo specifies 'Information Intelligence Delivery' as offering a competitive advantage to corporations, we illustrate below that there are many instances where 'Information Intelligence' provided directly to the customer can also result in a significant competitive advantage.

The 'mechanisms' shown in Figure 5 (e.g., service delivery, product delivery) provide a useful starting point for identifying specific strategic applications, but are still too general to be of direct applicability.

USING THE CUSTOMER RESOURCE LIFE CYCLE AS A MODEL FOR ANALYSIS AND INNOVATION

The models discussed so far are generally descriptive in nature. They help managers to recognize the strategic importance of information systems, present a framework for categorizing various types of strategic applications and provide criteria for assigning priorities among alternative investments. We now provide an alternative model that we believe can be used to identify new applications or to map existing applications into new settings. We have incorporated numerous examples of such information system applications to enhance the model's prescriptive capability.

In the context of Porter's work [43], our model focuses on a single relationship,

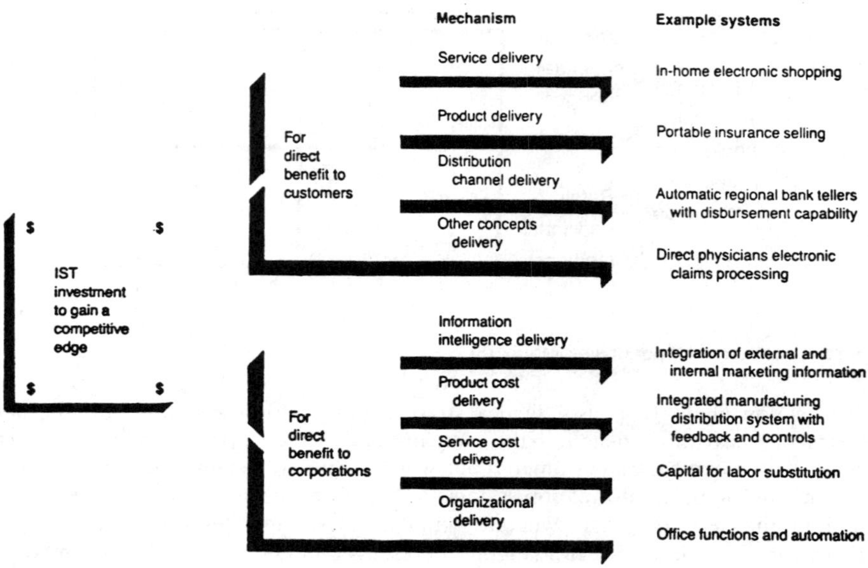

Figure 5. Information Systems as a Weapon to Gain a Competitive Edge [38]

that is, the relationship between the provider of goods or services and the customer. It is here that the primary competitive strategy evolves: Will management elect to *differentiate* the firm from its competitors in the eyes of the customer, try to become the *low-cost producer*, or seek a special *niche* in the market? ISTs can frequently assist in implementing any of these three strategies, but they are particularly useful for differentiating a product on the basis of customer service.

THE PRODUCT/RESOURCE LIFE CYCLE

It is generally accepted that an organization's products or services go through a fairly well-defined life cycle. A typical life cycle model contains stages for

- ascertaining the requirements for the product,
- developing or manufacturing the product,
- managing products in inventory and
- terminating organizational responsibility for the product.

A similar life cycle model can be applied to the supporting resources that an organization uses to achieve its goals. Within IBM's Business Systems Planning process, for instance, four stages are proposed for the life cycle of both products and supporting resources [19]:

- requirements, planning, measurement and control;
- acquisition or implementation;
- stewardship;
- retirement or disposition.

THE CUSTOMER'S RESOURCE LIFE CYCLE

The products that an organization provides to its customers are, from the customer's perspective, supporting resources. To acquire them, the customer goes through a resource life cycle. This frequently requires a considerable investment of time and effort to manage. If the supplier can assist the customer in managing this life cycle, the supplier may be able to differentiate itself from its competitors, usually on the basis of enhanced customer service or, in some cases, by introducing direct cost savings. In the process, the supplier will typically introduce *switching costs* (costs that customers must bear if they wish to switch to another supplier) for its customer base.

A customer's resource life cycle can be supported through the application of IST provided by the supplier. Frequently, transactions with customers are sufficiently homogeneous that the supplier can justify developing support systems which the customer can't afford. Canning [10] has described a Swedish dairy cooperative that developed forecasting models to assist its customers (retail stores) to accurately predict daily requirements for dairy products. Few retail outlets had the resources or expertise to develop such a model, but the large customer base permitted the co-op to do it. By focusing on customers' needs, the coöperative was able to use IST to enhance its customer service.

The IBM 4-stage model is a useful starting point for characterizing a customer's resource life cycle activities, but it is too broadly defined to be directly applicable. Burnstine [7] proposed a more detailed 11-stage resource life cycle. By adding two more stages to his model, we present in Table 2, a 13-stage customer resource life cycle (CRLC) model, which can serve as the focal point for both analyzing and proposing supplier-developed strategic information systems.

APPLYING THE MODEL

The CRLC model is useful for categorizing existing competitive information systems and, more importantly, is a prescriptive tool for generating new applications. The

Table 2. Four-and Thirteen-Stage Resource Life Cycles [7, 19]

IBM stage	Extended model	Description
Requirements	*Establish requirements*	To determine how much of a resource is required.
	Specify	To determine a resource's attributes.
Acquisition	*Select source*	To determine where customers will buy a resource.
	Order	To order a quantity of a resource from the supplier.
	Authorize and pay for[a]	To transfer funds or extend credit.
	Acquire[a]	To take possession of a resource.
	Test and accept	To ensure that a resource meets specifications.
Stewardship	*Integrate*	To add to an existing inventory.
	Monitor	To control access and use of a resource.
	Upgrade	To upgrade a resource if conditions change.
	Maintain	To repair a resource, if necessary.
Retirement	*Transfer or dispose*	To move, return, or dispose of inventory as necessary.
	Account for	To monitor where and how much is spent on a resource.

[a] Not included in Burnstine's [7] original list, but subsumed instead under *Order* and *Test* and *Accept*.

model is described through a series of examples that demonstrate its descriptive power.

The examples are drawn from the recent trade literature and from a survey of information system executives. They are not all successful applications, nor are they all still being used; they are meant to illustrate the model and to promote creative ideas for future competitive information systems.

Although the examples are drawn from a variety of industries, they are often surprisingly similar when viewed in a particular stage of the resource life cycle. In each case, a supplier is using IST to attend to some aspect of a customer's resource life cycle, often by enhancing customer service. In some instances (typically, retail stores), the customer may resell the product to another customer, in which case the supplier may provide IST support to either the immediate customer or to the final customer. In other instances, the supplier may be providing a service of interest to both customers and other suppliers; for example, an airline reservation system provides a service to the air traveller, travel agencies and other air carriers

Some applications bridge two or more CRLC stages: The Swedish dairy cooperative provided retailers with estimated requirements, in the form of pro forma orders; the retailer then had the option of either using these prespecified orders or changing them. The pro forma orders assisted the retailer in the *specification*, as well as the *requirements* stage of the life cycle. We have found applications covering as many as six life cycle stages.

EXAMPLE USES OF IST IN THE CRLC MODEL

Here are the 13 stages of the CRLC, accompanied by examples of suppliers addressing a customer's resource life cycle needs with IST.

1. Establish requirements

In the first stage, requirements are established for the resources to be acquired. This involves estimating future needs for the resource.

- Owens Corning Fiberglass uses data on energy efficiency to help builders evaluate insulation requirements for new building designs. Evaluations are provided free of charge to builders meeting minimum standards of energy efficiency, if they agree to purchase insulation from the vendor [8].
- The Sylvania Commercial Lighting Division of GTE supplies sales personnel with portable computer terminals. The sales representatives then access a system to analyze prospective customers' lighting requirements and can prepare sales proposals on-site [42].
- Several taxi firms have installed terminals in their cabs that display the number of empty cabs cruising in various cab zones; drivers use this information to calculate where requirements are greatest [53].

2. Specify

The customer must specify the attributes of the required resource.

- The Inventory Locator Service allows air carriers to specify the parts they require for repairing airplanes undergoing maintenance. If so requested, the system automatically generates 'request for quotation' letters to potential suppliers [11].
- A greeting-card distributor developed a system for reordering, that frees retailers from involvement in specifying particular cards. When a particular card is sold out, the retailer returns the reorder ticket at the back of the stack; the system determines the type of card (e.g., father's birthday) and resupplies, not with the same card, but with one specified by the system, usually the best-selling card in the particular category.

3. Select a Source

The customer must locate an appropriate source for the required resource. Opportunities for the application of IST are frequently in an intermediary firm that links customers with suppliers. This involves matching clients' resource needs with appropriate suppliers.

- The Official Airline Guide displays potential flights after the user specifies a departure and destination city and the time and date of the flight [27].

- Automated Directory Services provides residents of Washington, D.C., with an on-line alternative to the Yellow Pages; the system gives callers the names of appropriate nearby businesses. Other systems locate alternatives when the desired product is unavailable [26].
- The Phone In-Drive Thru Market of Los Angeles permits customers to order groceries by phone and pick them up at store loading docks. The system suggests alternative products if a requested product is currently out of stock [47].
- The Inventory Locator Service (previously described under *Specify*) also provides a 'parts number cross reference database' to assist users in identifying interchangeable parts provided by alternative vendors.

4. Order

After selecting a source, customers place orders. Reservation systems were among the earliest IST support systems for order taking and have become an effective strategic weapon for some airlines (see, for example, [2]).

- Distributors such as American Hospital Supply, McKesson Pharmaceuticals, General Electric Supply Company and Arrow Electronics have all established sophisticated round-the-clock order-entry systems, that accept a customer-entered order without human intervention [4, 13, 51].
- Bergen Brunswig, a pharmaceutical supply distributor, leases hand-held computers to its customers. Orders can be entered via these devices to one of several warehouses and are shipped the following day [46].
- Comp-U-Card, using an on-line database, lets customers place orders directly with suppliers for products ranging from electronics appliances to chocolates [54].

5. Authorize and Pay for

Before a resource can be acquired, authority for the expenditure must be obtained and payment made (or arranged).

- J. C. Penney has made their on-line retail credit network available to such other retailers as Shell and Gulf. Originally designed to authorize and process credit sales for J. C. Penney, the system is now being offered as a service to organizations requiring credit authorizations. For Shell and Gulf, the network makes credit-card sales competitive with cash sales [32].
- Exxon is pilot testing a debit-card network that immediately debits customer bank accounts for purchases made with Exxon's AutoCard. The retail customer is provided with most of the conveniences of a credit card, but at the same per gallon discount they receive for a cash purchase. The retailer, meanwhile, is spared most of the aggravation of credit-card sales [18].
- Mass Mutual's Magnet information system was designed to calculate large customers' insurance premiums on a daily basis. The company had previously

collected monthly premiums in advance. Customers thus have the use of their money for a longer period of time [8].

6. Acquire

Information technology provides a variety of ways for customers to acquire products directly or to have them delivered more easily.

- Automated teller machines normally deliver money to customers, but also dispense airline and ski lift tickets [18, 30, 36] and store coupons [9].
- New magazines, such as the *I.B. Magazette and Mentor*, published on computer disks, let the reader interact in novel ways with 'articles' and even advertisements [12].
- Dial-up networks, such as The Source, give subscribers access to articles and columns 'user published' by people from their homes and offices [41].
- Telesun Co. permits customers to download purchased software to their personal computers [17]. DRI, a subsidiary of McGraw-Hill, provides a similar capability for econometric data [33].
- INC Telecommunications [50], is also involved in downloading software, but uses satellites and radio to broadcast the product to special receivers.
- Customers at the Phone In-Drive Thru Market of Los Angeles call ahead and then pick up their orders from their cars [47].

7. Test and Accept

The customer or a third party must verify the acceptability of a new resource before putting it to use.

- The First Boston Corporation markets Shelternet, a product that matches people seeking mortgages with mortgage-granting institutions. Shelternet also analyzes buyers' credit ratings and other information, and conditionally approves them. The system is thus providing a conditional test/accept function for its mortgage-granting customers [29].
- Western Union provides a service for matching freight shippers with motor-freight carriers and checking to ensure that responding carriers have appropriate authority and insurance to qualify for the prospective load [14].
- Medicare-Glaser's drug interaction detector tests a prescription against other drugs customers may be taking and flags potential problems [15].
- Emery Worldwide provides certain customers with reports showing transit-time data that permit evaluation of Emery's delivery performance [22].

8. Integrate into and Manage Inventory

Once acquired and accepted for use, a resource must be added to the existing inventory of resources and its usage managed.

- Westvaco, a supplier of paper products to printers, has developed WestTrak. As customer orders are about to be shipped, WestTrak informs customers' computers that an order is in transit and provides essential identifying information about the shipment. When the order arrives, receiving clerks use a wand to transmit an identifying bar code to the printer's computer, which then immediately records the availability of resources placed in inventory [23].
- General Electric Supply Company provides an interesting tool to assist customers in inventory management. Basically, GESCO commits to stock, for a specified time, a prearranged quantity of items that are purchased repetitively. The distributor, in effect keeps inventories for customers [51].

9. Monitor Use and Behavior

Customers must ensure that resources remain acceptable while in inventory.

- ARA Services distributes magazines to a variety of retail establishments. Unsold magazines are returned to ARA for a refund. Returns are machine processed, which permits ARA to monitor sales information, so as to make appropriate decisions about which magazines the customer should stock [39].
- Fidelity Brokerage Services' 'Investors Express' lets users initiate orders to buy and sell stock and to maintain personal portfolio records. It provides a capability for customers to automatically monitor the movements of up to 18 stocks in a portfolio [31].

10. Upgrade if Needed

If requirements change, it may be necessary to upgrade resources.

- The greeting-card distributor system described in *Specify*, automatically selects appropriate greeting cards, in effect upgrading the retailer's inventory on the basis of observed market demand.
- Bergen Brunswig monitors product sales data for druggists and then uses those data to support its 'Space Management' product. For a monthly fee, customers are advised on shelf arrangement and potential upgrades, related to product choice [48].
- PRC Loan Express matches people looking for mortgages with potential mortgage holders. The system provides mortgage holders with the ability to upgrade mortgage offerings as conditions change [49].

11. Maintain

Occasionally, the suppliers need to make repairs to keep resources in good operating condition. This may be a requirement of the transaction or simply good business practice.

- Sears uses information systems to support its maintenance service by sending out annual postcard reminders to people whose maintenance contracts are about to lapse. They also offer special package deals to customers who have made multiple appliance purchases but have yet to purchase maintenance contracts. The program has boosted service revenues and benefited marketing by improving customer goodwill [8].

- Some Chevron retail dealers are now using personal computers to notify customers that they are due for service visits and to support the mechanics who maintain customers' cars. A running record of previous maintenance is also provided. This service encourages customers to consistently rely on Chevron dealers for maintenance needs [56].
- American Express offers a credit-card registry service that provides for lost or stolen cards. A call to American Express initiates appropriate notification to other credit-card providers [1].

12. Transfer or Dispose

Customers will eventually transfer or dispose of resources. As this usually happens after a considerable amount of time, suppliers will not normally be involved. An exception occurs when the resources are rented or must for some other reason be returned to a supplier.

- Avis uses ATM-like machines to shorten the car-return process. Customers enter a few pieces of data, and the machine concludes the rental transaction, returning an itemized receipt [18].
- The Washington Hotel in Tokyo is using an automated registration 'robot' to check guests in with no manual assistance and, on the way out, to 'eat the key and inform you of how much you owe for cold drinks and telephone calls' [20].

13. Account for

Customers must monitor where and how much money is spent for resources.

- AMEXCO has combined traditional credit services with a travel-agency function. Large corporations can obtain travel services from American Express Travel Related Services, pay with a corporate credit card, and receive reports from AMEXCO on how travel funds are being spent [52].
- Many retail drug stores, as a service to their customers, provide a detailed accounting of their customers' drug purchases, for income-tax purposes. Even a small local druggist, with the aid of a personal computer, can offer this competitively attractive service.

CONCLUSION

The strategic application of IST can frequently provide firms with a competitive advantage. IST can help a firm to become the low-cost producer for a given product or service, can help it to define and service a specially defined market niche, or can help it to differentiate its product offering from its competitors'.

The importance of this trend has received attention in the literature – several authors have provided models and frameworks for classifying and categorizing strategic applications of IST. These models, for the most part, are descriptive in nature. They do not help a company to find new or innovative applications.

The CRLC model provides a more detailed descriptive model for identifying and categorizing strategic applications of IST, by focusing on the possible differentiation of a firm's product from competitor's products on the basis of customer service. The application of IST to any of the CRLC stages, serves to build and maintain the loyalty of a firm's customer base. At the same time, however, the model serves as a vehicle for identifying potentially important opportunities for applying IST competitively. As a firm examines its role from the CRLC perspective, it discovers opportunities to enhance its overall strategy.

REFERENCES

1. American Express Card Registry. Advertisement, 1984.
2. H. Banks, 'Fixing tickets', *Forbes* 132, 5 (Aug. 29, 1983), 42–43.
3. S. Barrett and B. Konsynski, 'Inter-organization information sharing systems', *Manage. Inf. Syst. Q.*, special issue (Dec. 1982), 93–104.
4. R. I. Benjamin, 'When companies share, it's virtually a new game', *Inf. Syst. News* (Dec. 26, 1983), 24.
5. R. I. Benjamin, J. F. Rockart, M. S. Scott Morton and J. Wyman, '*Information technology: A strategic opportunity*', Work Paper 108, MIT Center for Information Systems Research, Cambridge, Mass., Dec. 1983.
6. E. S. Buffa, *Meeting the Competitive Challenge*. Dow-Jones, New York, 1984.
7. D. C. Burnstine, *BIAIT: An emerging management engineering discipline*. Work. Paper, BIAIT Int., Inc., Petersburg, N. Y., 1980.
8. *Business Week*. Business is turning data into a potent strategy weapon. *Bus. Week* 2804 (Aug. 22, 1983), 92–98.
9. *Business Week*. A coupon machine at the supermarket. *Bus. Week 2831* (Mar. 5, 1984), 68.
10. R. G. Canning, Developing strategic information systems. *EDP Anal, 22,* 5 (May 1984), 1–8.
11. *ComputerWorld*. Data base keeps aircraft service firms aloft. *ComputerWorld 17,* 35 (Aug. 29, 1983), 34.
12. K. R. Cook, Direct to disk. *PC World 2,* 3 (Mar. 1984), 114–118.
13. E. R. Corey, The role of information/communications technology in industrial distribution. Work. Paper, Harvard Business School, Cambridge, Mass., 1983.
14. *Distribution*. Shipper/carrier electronic dating service? *Distribution 82,* 10 (Oct. 1983), 39, 41.
15. P. A. Englemayer, Safety prompts computer use in drugstores. *Wall St. J. 202,* 49 (Sept. 9, 1983). 31.
16. N. Entwisle, How to get EDI on a party line. *Distribution 83,* 1 (Jan. 1984), 24–26.

17. R. Fixner, The easy way to software shopping. *Link-Up 1*, 6 (Mar. 1984), 34–36.
18. R. M. Garson, easy money. *Datamation 30,* 3 (Mar. 1984), 32.
19. IBM Corp. *Business systems planning: Information systems planning guide.* GE20–0527–3, IBM Corp., Armonk, N.Y., July 1981.
20. M. Inaba, New Tokyo 'desk clerks' eat cash, spit out key, *MIS Week 5,* 18 (May 2, 1984), 26.
21. A. Jenkins, Resorts international. *PC Week 1*, 23 (June 5, 1984), 31–35.
22. B. Johnson, Air freight firm spreads its wings with net. *ComputerWorld 16,* 36 (Sept. 6, 1982), 14.
23. P. Johnston, Hands on management. *Graphic Arts Mon.* (Mar. 1984), 32–34.
24. P.G.W. Keen and M.S. Scott Morton, *Decision Support Systems: An Organization Perspective.* Addison-Wesley, Reading, Mass., 1978.
25. P. Kerr, Deregulation: A puzzle for consumers. *New York Times 132,* 45699 (June 4, 1983), 10.
26. R. Koenig, Call-in firms are taking on Yellow Pages. *Wall St. J. 201,* 41 (Mar. 1, 1983), 37.
27. *Link-Up.* The utility bill: News about information utilities. *Link-Up 1,* 6 (Mar. 1984), 8.
28. *Link-Up.* Travel service reserves trains, planes, and more. *Link-Up 1*, 7 (Apr. 1984), 8.
29. J. Lipman, Home buying process is changing rapidly because of technology. *Wall St. J. 203, 1* (Jan. 25, 1984), 1, 14.
30. R. W. Mahoney, Demand for convenience spurs EFT systems growth. *Computer-World 17,* 35 (Aug. 29, 1983), 29.
31. *MIS Week.* Investor's Express – Dial-up for fast stock quotes. *MIS Week 5*, 13 (Mar. 28, 1984), 30.
32. Martorelli, W. P. Penney commercializes credit net. *Inf. Syst. News* (May 2, 1983), 1, 16
33. F. W. McFarlan, IS and competitive strategy. Note 0–184–055, Harvard Business School, Cambridge, Mass., 1983.
34. F. W. McFarlan and J. L. McKenney, *Corporate Information Systems Management.* D. Irwin Richard, Homewood, III., 1983.
35. F. W. McFarlan, J. L. McKenney and P. Pyburn, The information archipelago – Plotting the course. *Harvard Bus. Rev. 61* (Jan.- Feb. 1982). 145–156.
36. M. McLaughlin, R. Howe and J. Cash, Changing competitive ground rules – The impact of computers and communications in the 1980s. Unpublished Working Paper, 1983.
37. M. Mirowca, Automated self-service machines spread after their success in banks. *Wall St. J. 202, 14* (July 21, 1983), 29.
38. M. H. Notowidigdo, Information systems: Weapons to gain the competitive edge. *Financ. Executive 52, 2* (Feb. 1984), 20–25.
39. G. L. Parsons, ARA Services Inc. – Periodicals distribution group (A). HBS Case Serv. 9–182–157, Harvard Business School, Cambridge, Mass., 1982.
40. G. L. Parsons, Information technology: A new competitive weapon. Note 0–183–121, Harvard Business School, Cambridge, Mass., 1983.
41. *PC Magazine.* The source for magazines. *PC Mag. 3, 1* (Jan. 24, 1984). 525–529.
42. A. Pollack, Automating offices to give managers a competitive edge, *New York Times 131*, 45189 (Jan. 10, 1982), 38.
43. Porter, M. *Competitive Strategy.* The Free Press, New York, 1980.
44. J. A. Quillard, et al. A study of the corporate use of personal computers. Work. Paper 109, MIT Center for Information Systems Research, Cambridge, Mass.,

Dec. 1983.
45. J. Rockart and L. Flannery, The management of end user computing. *Commun. ACM 26, 10* (Oct. 1983), 776–784.
46. *Sales and Marketing Management.* S&MM's special computers in marketing section: Bergen Brunswig. *Sales Mark. Manage. 129, 8* (Dec. 6, 1982), 52–53.
47. *Sales and Marketing Management.* And now, the drive-in supermarket. *Sales Mark. Manage. 131, 4* (Sept. 12, 1983), 20.
48. *Sales and Marketing Management.* Bergen Brunswig writes a winning prescription. Sales Mark. Manage. 130, 1 (Jan. 17, 1983), 38.
49. *Saving Institutions.* Computers flash mortgage data coast to coast. *Savings Inst. 105, 1* (Jan. 1984), 82–84.
50. L. B. Stahr, Special delivery software. *PC World 1, 11* (Oct. 1983), 69–73.
51. T. C. Taylor, GE posts a sentry to give customers better service. *Sales Mark. Manage. 129, 8* (Dec. 6, 1982), 46–48.
52. *Travel Weekly.* Update (interview with Jonathan Linen, President, travel division of American Express Travel Related Services). *Travel Wkly. 43, 58* (July 2, 1984), 1.
53. J. Urquhart, It's 'over and out' for some radios as taxis enter the computer age. *Wall St. J. 200, 16* (July 23, 1982), 19.
54. J. Ware, The online shopping mall. *Link-Up 1, 6* (Mar. 1984), 34–36.
55. W. J. Wheat, Oklahoma, Liberty Bank dispenses gas, as well as cash. *Am. Banking Assoc. Banking J. 75, 5* (May, 1983), 53, 56.
56. S. Whitemore, XT-managed stations fuel Chevron profits, *PC Week 1, 16* (Apr. 17, 1984), 5, 57.

4. STRATEGIC INFORMATION SYSTEMS MANAGEMENT*

John M Ward M.A., F.C.M.A.

INTRODUCTION

Since the 1950's when computers were first used by commercial organisations, the overall objective has been to improve the competitiveness of the enterprise. In the early days, in spite of the cost and risks involved, computers were seen as a means of improving the efficiency of those operations where the primary task was information processing. Many of the early applications merely used the computer as a rapid, reliable calculator, fast printer and data filing system – to standardise and expedite clerical operations. The benefits were essentially derived directly from, and limited by, the capabilities of the available information technology (IT). In time, previously impossibly complex tasks were undertaken using computers – forecasting, optimisation, planning – enabling resources to be deployed more effectively and improving co-ordination of operations. The organisation benefitted from improved information systems (IS), not just technology. In the 1970's, the realisation dawned that the computer had become a repository of a potentially valuable management resource – information. Unfortunately, the information had been stored to maximise efficiency of storage rather than ease of access. Nor were the tools and techniques of systems development suitable for ad-hoc enquiry and analysis – the requirements to support management processes effectively. Only recently has it been possible to overcome the problems generated by evolved, rather than planned, information management. Organisations can now gain advantage from using the information they have used the computer to store for control and co-ordination.

The rapid improvement in IT price/performance; the integration of computing and communications technologies and significant developments in software capability has also opened up new opportunities. Products and services can be directly modified or derived from the use of technology, systems and information. The relationship between an organisation and its environment can be changed directly by using IT based procurement and distribution channels.

As a result, many organisations will become dependent for success on the appropriateness of their information systems. Effective IS and IT investments will only occur if IS/IT consideration is integrated with the corporate strategic planning process as both input and consequence. The relationship required is shown in Figure 1.

* This paper was prevented at a Pergamon Infotech State of the Art seminar on IT Strategy, in April 1986.

J. M. Ward is a lecturer at the Cranfield School of Management.

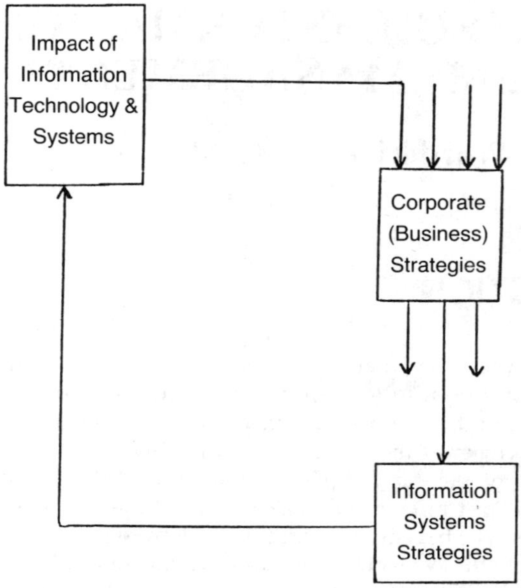

Figure 1. Relationship of Corporate and IT/IS Strategies

Once this has been achieved, resources and technologies must be managed according to their strategic contribution, not the historical perception of their role and value.

BUSINESS OBJECTIVES OF INFORMATION SYSTEMS

Until recently the use of IT has been aimed at achieving internal objectives often localised or accumulated across functions. Those internal objectives would normally have been derived from external/market place objectives. But the view of management generally was that IT/IS had the potential to improve internal performance but not to alter significantly the way business was to be conducted externally. The role and designated title and position of IT/IS units in organisations has often confirmed this perception, and consequently divorced the processes of managing information from the management of the business.

These IS units developed 'strategies' within the constraints of their role, in order to provide required services and applications and manage resources. These 'strategies' were often just summaries of activities and rationalisations of policies, to provide a sense of direction towards goals, perceived by IS management, as supporting the needs of the organisation.

Only rarely were the strategies derived directly from business strategy. Even less often was an IS strategy considered as an integral part of business strategy. Executive management did little to encourage strategic thinking by IS groups – whose importance was often noticed more for the problems they caused than the contribution they might make! Consequently business and IS objectives were at best related on a project by project basis rather than as a coherent approach to general IT/IS exploitation.

Whilst the overall objective of deploying IT is to improve competitiveness, it can be broken down into three particular objectives, with changing emphasis as the use of IT has evolved. The objectives are

– to improve the efficiency of operations (1960s onwards)
– to increase the effectiveness of management (1970s onwards)
– to improve the competitiveness of the business (directly) (1980s onwards).

In the first two, IT may make an important or strategic contribution to business performance, although it is difficult to relate the contribution of IT to any particular change in business fortunes, due to the derived or secondary nature of the IT/IS objectives.

Strassman (Ref 1) has complied the most recent analysis of how IT has or has not achieved the objectives of improving efficiency and management effectiveness. From his work some conclusions can be drawn.

In terms of competitiveness, improved efficiency of information processing may reduce some direct and indirect business costs. The benefits are derived from task by task automation of simple applications. Based on extensive example analysis, it can be shown that cost per output unit in structured, repetitive tasks has been improved by the use of IT. But considering the total cost of the technology and specialist resources deployed in attempting to increase information processing efficiency, the contribution to overall profitability is at best marginal.

The second objective expressed by Strassman as the 'effectiveness approach to productivity' has greater potential if achieved to improve an organisation's long term competitiveness. But measurements are elusive. The Strategic Planning Institute (Ref 2) has recently extended the database of its PIMS (Profit Impact of Marketing Strategies) programme. The study – Management Productivity and Information Technology (MPIT) – attempted to analyse how IT contribution could be measured as part of a 'value added' approach to assessing managerial performance.

The limited results available from the analyses are generally inconclusive – no correlation existing between investment in IT and the ratio of value added/cost of management. The only rather obvious conclusions that can be drawn are, that good managers will employ IT effectively, poor managers will gain little or no benefit from it, and the organisations will benefit or otherwise accordingly.

Strassman considers that the lack of any pattern of performance improvement is probably due to the lack of focus for deploying the technology and the pre-occupation with piecemeal, efficiency-seeking cost reduction. The arrival of micro-computers, office automation and application generators has provided managers with technology they can use to improve effectiveness. But there is little evidence that technology based systems of information management have produced enough benefits to justify all of the investment.

There are other reasons why IT/IS may now be able to contribute more directly to business performance. The MPIT study shows that IT is generally more effectively deployed where a corporation is structured in Strategic Business Units (SBU), rather than primarily functionally organised. The study shows that it is more feasible to develop a coherent IT strategy for an SBU than for any other organisational grouping. This would seem logical – vertical integration of management and focus of business purpose enables a co-ordinated approach to the management of resources – including information. The recent re-orientation of many major corporations to SBU structures has distributed large proportions of service/support functions, re-positioning them within the line management of the units. These functions (accounting, market research, forecasting, planning, etc) are heavily information based. With the restructuring, both line and specialist functional management focus their information requirements on SBU primary activities. This produces more appropriate and integrated systems.

In the last few years, new, more direct opportunities of gaining advantages from IT have arisen as a joint consequence of increasingly fierce, global competition and the performance of the technology. These are usually described as the competitive or strategic used of IT – using IT to change the way an organisation conducts its business externally, not just how it manages or carries out its internal functions and processes.

THE IMPACT OF IT/IS ON COMPETITIVE STRATEGIES

Recently numerous articles have appeared in the influential business journals arguing the strategic advantages to be gained from IT. Rockart et al (Ref 3) and McFarlan (Ref 4) describe examples of how competitive advantage has been obtained and propose a matrix/questionnaire analyses to assist in assessing the competitive implications of IT. Parsons (Ref 5) suggests a structure for analysing the IT impact on the competitive forces governing an industry and a firm's relative business performance and strategy, derived from Porter's (Ref 6) models for competitive strategy. Wyman (Ref 7) used Porter's generic strategies to persuade, by example, how IT can create effective new ways of doing business. All these suggest that 'Information Technology' can be the key to achievement in

- redefining the boundaries of the industry, removing constraints to growth
- developing new products or services
- realigning the balance of power in the supplier-customer relationship
- changing the basis of competition amongst existing rivals
- establishing barriers to deter new entrants.

Most recently, Porter & Millar (Ref 8) explain and exemplify the strategic role of 'Information' in gaining competitive advantage. They consider the information content of products and the information intensity of value chains (as described by Porter in Ref 9) to be critical to the competitive impact of IT. The value chain concept enables both internal productivity from IT to be re-examined, as well as the potential role of IT in the overall industry value system to be evaluated.

By adopting aspects of all these approaches, a process of analysis and assessment can be produced to enable resources to be deployed in proportion to the contributions IT/IS can make to the business.

As suggested earlier, the first step is to define the strategic business units of the company and the industries within which they compete. This SBU approach is fundamental to most processes of corporate strategy formulation and offers the most direct route to managing IS strategically.

Parsons proposes a three level strategic IT impact analysis:

(a) Impact of IT/IS on the industry:
  - How the products/services of the industry, the markets and 'production' economics can be altered by IT/IS.

(b) Impact of IT/IS on the competitive forces within the industry:
  - How the rival firms are able to exploit IT to increase their business leverage over customers of, and suppliers to, the industry and reduce the threat from new entrants or substitute products.

(c) Impact of IT/IS on the 'Strategy' of the Business Unit:
  - How the required generic strategies of low cost, differentiation or niche can be enabled or enhanced by appropriate investments in IT/IS.

The information content of the product will obviously be a prime determinant of IT/IS impact at all three levels. The information intensity of industry value chains will be a key factor in (b) and (c) above, even if the product itself is low in information content.

The basic objective of all these techniques of assessment is, to identify areas of the business where IT/IS investments will be critical to future business success. This enables strategically important developments to be differentiated from the more traditional, if still valuable, applications of IT. The various applications can then be managed according to their business contribution, rather than their technological peculiarities or complexity.

The next stage is to identify strategies for the successful management of the 'portfolio' of systems derived, but also allowing for the capability of the organisation to deliver the required systems.

GENERIC STRATEGIES

The Porter view (Ref. 6) of generic competitive strategies is very useful in identifying overall strategies for success in differing business environments. It provides a model for assessing alternatives, focusing on key factors and developing coherent business behaviour patterns.

A similar analysis by Parsons (Ref. 10) suggests Generic IT Strategies which classify the majority of available strategies under six headings:

- Centrally Planned
- Leading Edge

- Free Market
- Monopoly
- Scarce Resource
- Necessary Evil.

An organisation may be in many industries, each business exists in a different competitive environment, and the company should adopt a generic strategy appropriate for each business unit in its environment. Failure is often the result of either copying a strategy, successful in one environment for one business, into another where it is inappropriate for the business, given its relative competitive position. Failure also occurs where a 'hybrid' strategy evolves which causes conflict of objectives and hence poor decisions.

As with generic business strategies, the generic IT/IS strategies have similar implications. No one strategy may suit the whole organisation and a "hybrid' may lead to inappropriate resource management. Deriving the appropriate relationships of business and IS strategy, and managing the inevitable mixture will be reviewed later. First, it is worth considering the key aspect of each of the generic strategies proposed by Parsons.

1. Centrally Planned

- IT/IS strategy is totally integrated and inter-dependent with corporate strategy through a centralised, senior, dedicated agency.
- This enables understanding of competitive opportunities and requirements, resources to be optimally deployed and large investments to be undertaken.

The strategy is very demanding of senior management time, and can be difficult to make effective in many organisations.

2. Leading Edge

- This implies an intrinsic acceptance that IT/IS will create competitive advantage and hence 'state-of-the-art' technology must be sustained.
- It involves R & D expenditure and often many wasted investments, and requires senior management commitment to the concept, if not heavy involvement.

It can be expensive and requires adept management to convert entrepreneurial ideas to effective applications.

3. Free Market

- This implies that user management knows what is best for the business, including IS/IT.
- Internal services must compete with outside vendors and expect little attention from senior management.

It can cause duplication of investment and differential rates of development across the organisation.

4. Monopoly

- IT/IS is a sole source utility or service within the organisation.
- User satisfaction with services is the main measure of its effectiveness.

It can mean innovation is slow and hence unable to respond to competitive needs, since the users do not perceive IS in that role.

5. Scarce Resource

- A very popular strategy which ensures careful management of IT/IS resources using financial controls.
- Investments must be well justified in hard financial terms.

Given management's view that IS is a cost centre and the objective is controlled, well justified use of IT, it is not conducive to IT being exploited or speculated with as a business weapon.

6. Necessary Evil

- A strategy of only deploying IT/IS to meet legal requirements and for very high return investments.

The strategy has many disadvantages, unless IT/IS is almost entirely irrelevant to the business.

According to Parsons, these strategies are 'the central tendencies which firms use to guide IT/IS within the business'.

Before considering the steps required to determine the appropriate strategies to be adopted, it is worth discussing the default options – what strategies will tend to evolve as a result of generic business strategies. Using Porter's generic competitive strategies – Low Cost Producer, Differentiation, Focus/Niche, the following default strategies can be deduced:

1. Low Cost Producer
   The emphasis is on general cost effectiveness, justifying investments, etc, will tend to *Scarce Resource* (and *even Necessary Evil*) strategies being adopted. Alternatively, if the strategy of low cost is to be achieved by profit centred autonomy of units, a *Free Market* Strategy is likely to fit corporate values best.
2. Differentiation
   The desire for product enhancement means less focus on cost and more on service – maintaining differentials and satisfying customers. This will tend to produce *Monopoly* or *Leading Edge* strategies, or where products or markets overlap significantly, perhaps a *Centrally Planned* Strategy.
3. Focus/Niche strategies are likely to split as above, depending on the secondary strategy adopted – Differentiated Focus or Low Cost Focus.

These defaults may be entirely inappropriate both at corporate and business levels, unless a company is in one industry, and in an industry where IT is having little or no effect. Businesses or products with differentiation strategies will be inadequately served by IT/IS if the dominant strategy is *Scarce Resourcing*, due to a prevailing strategy derived without conscious analysis from *Low Cost* objectives elsewhere – and vice versa.

Equally importantly, *Low Cost* could be best served by a *Leading Edge* strategy and *Free Market* might be the best way of achieving *Differentiation*. There is no best fit to be derived from this analysis alone.

MANAGING THE APPLICATION PORTFOLIO

Information Systems applications are investments and are the products of development. Like investments, they provide more or less of a return, and like products, they have life cycles. Both the range of applications possessed and possible can be considered as a portfolio to be managed. The strategic importance of portfolio constituents can be analysed as a basis for determining the appropriate approach to managing them – choosing which strategy should be adopted.

McFarlan, (Ref 4) proposes a useful matrix for considering the portfolios as a whole – to position the company's information systems. When considering locating a company's overall position in the matrix, two aspects are reflected. The matrix relates both the impact of information technology on the industry and the degree of computerised information systems penetration in the company – both the potential requirements and the stage of development reached.

Whilst it is useful to map the business's dependence on its systems as a whole onto such a matrix, it is more valuable to consider each actual or potential application area and its position in the matrix. For example: although in Banking, IT/IS is strategically important, many of the applications in a bank (e.g. Payroll, Capital asset registers etc) may belong in the support category; systems for processing cheques may be in the factory segment due to the declining proportion of future business dependent on them. Others, such as home banking may, at present, be in the turnaround category – of

STRATEGIC – Applications which are critical for future success	TURNAROUND (OR HIGH POTENTIAL) – Applications which may be of future success	HIGH STRATEGIC IMPACT OF FUTURE IS/IT
FACTORY – Applications which are critical to sustaining existing business	SUPPORT – Applications which improve management and performance but not critical to the business	LOW
HIGH	LOW	
STRATEGIC IMPORTANCE OF EXISTING OPERATIONAL SYSTEMS		

Figure 2. Current and Future Strategic IS Importance Matrix

STRATEGIC	TURNAROUND
CENTRALLY PLANNED Leading Edge	LEADING EDGE FREE MARKET Centrally Planned
MONOPOLY Scarce Resource	SCARE RESOURCE Free Market Necessary Evil
FACTORY	SUPPORT

Figure 3. Viable Generic Strategies related to Strategic importance of SIS

great potential but with uncertainty about how they can produce competitive benefits. This variation on the McFarlan matrix is represented in Figure 2.

Parsons (Ref. 10) has related his generic strategies to the situations identified in the matrix and shows which strategies are likely to succeed best in each segment, as shown in Figure 3. The generic strategies in capital letters are those considered most effective in the segment, and in lower case are those which may work, but with less probability of success.

Hence by assessing the strategic contribution of existing and potential applications, according to the strategic grid and then choosing an appropriate generic strategy, a set of approaches can be adopted to manage the portfolio as a whole.

The obvious resemblance of this matrix to the Boston Consulting Group square will not have passed unnoticed! The matrix can be used as an analysis tool with regard to systems portfolios, as well as product portfolios, although in a more qualitative way.

The correlations of 'Cash Cows' to Factory systems – the current 'profit earners', the importance for the future of 'Stars' and Strategic Systems, the uncertainties involved in managing 'problem children' and Turnaround applications are easy to draw. 'Dogs' and Support applications are less obviously related perhaps (see Figure 4), except that resources should be allocated sparingly.

HIGH RESOURCE USE LOW	STRATEGIC 'Stars'	TURNAROUND 'Problem Children'
	FACTORY 'Cash Cows'	SUPPORT 'Dogs'
	HIGH	LOW
	BENEFIT GENERATION	

Figure 4. Portfolio Matrix Comparisons

Two particular aspects of the analysis are worth comparing directly.

IS Applications, like products, have life cycles – and contribute more or less to the business and drain more or less resources from the business during the evolving phases of their lives. Hence they move around the matrix during that life cycle.

Cash cows and Factory systems generate the funds – benefits of money and corporate experience that can be used to undertake more risky ventures.

In the IS matrix, the importance of experience in developing and sustaining complex and critical systems is as important as generating investables benefits – or the organisation will be incapable of tackling the more problematic, more advanced systems effectively.

Benefit generation equates to cash generation, resource use equates to cash use in the Boston sense. The Strategic and Turnaround applications will demand both substantial and high quality resources to make them successful – these must not, therefore, be being drained in sustaining Factory and Support applications, the latter in particular should be resourced only when absolutely necessary.

In the 1960s 'Payroll' and 'Invoicing' systems were Turnaround applications – consuming vast resources with little certainty of success! They were of strategic importance for a period, as an example of how computer systems could improve efficiency and to demonstrate the modernity of a company and its management. For many years, they were factory systems, sections of the business having become dependent on their smooth operation – but they should, in most large companines, have long since moved into basic support mode, not being critical, but still valuable. Systems, that required ten consecutive hours of uninterrupted computer time, can now be executed in an odd five minutes and printed output produced off-line.

On-line order handling systems, pioneered by airlines, were strategically important and provided a competitive edge to those companies who succeeded in developing them before proprietary online software became generally available. But once everyone in the industry had the systems, they lost their strategic value. However, in most cases, they are still of critical importance (factory), since no other viable method exists for handling the transactions efficiently and feeding product delivery and replenishment systems reliably.

These two examples serve to demonstrate, that over an extended period, most applications will evolve through at least two of the sectors of the matrix. The length of time an application dwells in a particular segment and the route taken round the matrix is partly externally controlled – dependent on the equivalent activities of competitors. But it can be directed to follow a more managed evolution, in order to gain maximum advantage and ensure minimum resource waste. By identifying the correct sector for an application, an appropriate strategy for that application can be selected (See Figure 3).

For example, if for a particular business pursuing a lowest cost strategy, materials management was critically important to ensure that investments in robotics were not left idle and supplies are known to be unpredictable, the systems are strategically important. The choice should be between a centrally planned strategy or using leading edge technology to achieve both optimum cost advantage from automation and maximum supplier leverage to guarantee supplies. Both these strategies can be expensive and appear inconsistent with a low cost posture – a scarce resourcing of IS is generically attractive – but the tail must not wag the dog! The smaller systems investments may need to be indulged to enable the larger capacity investments to produce the cost advantage required.

In reverse, a company that uses information systems to differentiate its products or services (eg. to ensure that service specialists are fully equipped to deal with customer needs urgently), should not indulge all of its systems to that degree. Other applications should be resourced sparingly, eg. internal accounting, since funds and resources saved there can be used more competitively at the sharp end of the business. Excess capacity may be important to sustain the competitively used systems but it would erode the profit component of the premium obtained, if allowed to prevail throughout the portfolio.

Similar analytical assessments can be applied throughout the matrix to identify for each application or group of applications, the sector in which it currently lies and then the strategy which best fits the applications in the sector.

The applications residing in each sector will require different strategies which means different approaches to managing them. When it comes to justifying actual projects and technology investments, the weighting of hard cash benefits to 'intangible' business benefits will differ. In the Support sector, stringent return on investment (ROI) criteria should be applied, whereas ROI should be only a contributing consideration, once the strategic importance has been recognised, otherwise resources are likely to remain allocated to applications whose benefits are of historical, not future, importance.

IMPLICATIONS FOR IS MANAGEMENT

Two key aspects emerge from this approach to managing the IS portfolio and adopting a mix of appropriate strategies.

1. The whole process of application management is different in each sector because the objectives and risks differ.
   This will effect : user – IS relationships
   : planning & control processes
   : methodologies/tools/software/technologies
   : organisations & people & skills
   : management styles, etc.

   For each sector, an appropriate profile of each aspect of IS Management can be identified for the organisation.
2. Converting applications successfully from one segment to another means, a different strategy will probably become more appropriate. If the necessary changes in managing the application are not made then either
   – the application will provide less benefits than it should or
   – the application will consume more resources than it deserves.

   Overall, its business contribution will be less than optimum. 'Transition Management' approaches have to be adopted and each application considered against its business life-cycle, as well as the more traditional system life cycle management

evolution. The business life cycle of applications will differ depending on external factors – industry, competitive and technological – as well as internal management requirements.

These management issues are similar to those involved in managing a product portfolio – different management styles and expertise are required to manage a product at different points in the life cycle. Information systems need similar sensitive handling, since the objectives, risks and practices to be managed will be different as the application evolves through its life:

- The early uncertainties need entrepreneurial management to champion the application through the phases of doubt, or to decide to stop when benefits cannot be realised.
- Strategic systems need more nurturing – adept team and resource development, flexible approaches to problems and opportunities.
- Factory systems need tight control of quality and change to avoid disruption to the business, but an awareness of how the system needs to develop to sustain the business benefit.
- Support systems should only be touched when absolutely necessary and should not be an issue. Consolidation and replacement by less resource demanding alternatives should be the prime objective in managing them.

Thus, for example, the managerial characteristics of an entrepreneur, a developer, a controller and a caretaker will be needed in the different sectors and for an application as it evolves. The wrong style of management will place inappropriate importance, too much or too little, on a system. Converting systems across sector boundaries, in order to manage the portfolio effectively, will be inhibited unless management approaches can be changed.

CONCLUSION

In order to manage information systems strategically, i.e. so that IS/IT can be used to influence industry development, become a competitive weapon and enable business strategies to be implemented and sustained, the first key steps are:

- Identify the impact of IT on the industry and its component forces
- Monitor competitors' use of IS/IT and assess business impact
- Assess the criticality of existing applications
- Identify the areas for possible competitively advantageous use
- Analyse the application portfolio to determine the correct mix of generic IS strategies required
- Manage the evolving portfolio elements in direct proportion to their business importance, not their technical peculiarities.

REFERENCES

1. Paul A Strassman 'Information Payoff', The Free Press (1985)
2. Strategic Planning Institute 'Management Productivity and Information Tech-

nology (MPIT)', Overview Report (1984)

3. R I Benjamin, J F Rockart, M J Scott Morton, J Wyman 'Information Technology: A Strategic Opportunity', Sloan Management Review (Spring 1984)
4. F W McFarlan 'Information Technology changes the way you compete', Harvard Business Review (May-June 1984)
5. G L Parsons 'Information Technology: A New Competitive Weapon', Sloan Management Review (Fall 1983)
6. M E Porter 'Competitive Strategy', The Free Press (1980)
7. J Wyman 'Technological Myopia – the need to think strategically about technology', Sloan Management Review (Summer 1985)
8. M E Porter, V E Millar 'How information gives you competitive advantage', Harvard Business Review, (July-Aug 1985)
9. M E Porter 'Competitive Advantage', The Free Press (1985)
10. G L Parsons 'Fitting Information Systems Technology to the Corporate Needs: the Linking Strategy', Harvard Business School (Teaching Notes) (June 1983)